W9-CCL-459

LIBERATING SCHOOLS

Education in the Inner City

LIBERATING SCHOOLS

Education in the Inner City

edited by David Boaz

CATO INSTITUTE
Washington D.C.

Library of Congress Cataloging-in-Publication Data

Liberating schools : education in the inner city / edited by David Boaz.
    p. cm.
    Most chapters are papers previously presented at a conference
convened by the Cato Institute in Washington in October 1989.
    Includes bibliographical references and index.
    ISBN 0-932790-82-8 — ISBN 0-932790-83-6 (pbk.)
    1. Education, Urban—United States—Congresses. 2. Educational
change—United States—Congresses. 3. School, Choice of—United
States—Congresses. 4. Socially handicapped children—Education—
United States—Congresses. I. Boaz, David, 1953–   . II. Cato
Institute.
LC5131.L53   1991   91–15697
370.19'348'0973—dc20   CIP

Cover Photo: Joseph Rodriguez/Black Star

Printed in the United States of America.

CATO INSTITUTE
224 Second Street, S.E.
Washington, D.C. 20003

Contents

Preface

For the past decade Americans have been intensely concerned with the quality of American education, which is hardly surprising given the importance of education to society and the growing evidence of problems in American education. Nowhere are those problems more severe than in our inner cities, where learning has all but ceased in many schools. It was concern about inner-city children that led the Cato Institute to convene a conference, "Education and the Inner City," in Washington in October 1989. Most of the chapters in this volume were originally presented at that conference.

The editor's introduction provides an overview of the problems of American education and a proposed solution: educational choice. The introduction examines the reasons for the failure of American schools and answers some of the criticisms of educational choice. William A. Niskanen of the Cato Institute lays out the data: rising inputs—the number of teachers and other employees, their salaries, and other expenditures—combined with falling outputs, as measured by test scores, graduation rates, and post-school employment and earnings.

In the next two chapters journalist Bonita Brodt and Ben Peterson, a pseudonymous Los Angeles teacher, give us some insight into life inside big-city schools. Their stories remind us of just how bad inner-city schools are, perhaps lending support to the editor's argument that there is little or no downside risk in trying a sweeping reform such as vouchers. Their articles also illustrate the culture of despair and helplessness that the welfare state has brought to the inner city.

The next several chapters discuss various possibilities for educational reform, focusing for the most part on different aspects of choice. Joan Davis Ratteray of the Institute for Independent Education argues that public schools have failed black students and describes the many minority-run private schools that have sprung up in inner cities. Education scholar Myron Lieberman urges that for-profit companies should get into the education business and that choice plans should include them. John E. Chubb and Terry M. Moe of the Brookings Institution offer a comprehensive series of questions and answers about choice, expanding on the material in their seminal *Politics, Markets, and America's Schools*.

Educators Sy Fliegel and Robert Peterkin describe their experiences with successful public school choice plans in East Harlem and Cambridge, Massachusetts. Legal scholar John Coons of the University of California at Berkeley, a long-time activist on behalf of equal opportunity, argues that public school choice is not enough and that private schools must be included in any successful choice plan.

In the last two chapters economist James D. Gwartney and former Delaware governor Pete du Pont tie together two major themes of the book: the value of choice and the particular needs of poor, minority, and inner-city children. Gwartney proposes a voucher tied to family income, falling in value as income rises, to give greater assistance to low-income families. Du Pont proposes that we declare the worst school districts in America "education enterprise zones" and start a choice plan there—much as has been done recently in Milwaukee under Polly Williams's voucher plan.

As concern about the quality of American education begins to lead Americans toward major structural reforms, the Cato Institute is pleased to present these essays. We believe they make a major contribution to the national debate on educational reform.

1. The Public School Monopoly: America's Berlin Wall

David Boaz

No public policy issue is more important to any nation than education. Education is the process by which a society transmits its accumulated knowledge and values to future generations. Education makes economic growth possible, in the first instance by ensuring that each new adult doesn't have to reinvent the wheel—literally. By passing on what it has already learned, the present generation enables the next generation of philosophers, scientists, engineers, and entrepreneurs to stand on the shoulders of giants and see even farther. And only by educating its young people about its history, its literature, and its values can a society—a nation—be said to have a culture.

It is important to remember the distinction between education and schooling. As Mark Twain is supposed to have said, "I have never let my schooling interfere with my education." Education is a process of learning that goes on at all times of day and in all periods of life. It involves books, newspapers, movies, television, experience, and the advice of friends and family. Schooling, on the other hand, is only a small part of any person's education. Nevertheless, for convention's sake, this paper uses the term "education" even though we are really discussing schooling.

Given the importance of education to society, it is not surprising that Americans today are so concerned about the quality of American schools. Throughout the past decade, we have bemoaned the decline of our schools and debated how to reform them. Yet we have had seven years of reform and the schools seem to be little changed. Perhaps it is time to learn, as the reformers around Soviet president Mikhail Gorbachev came to understand, that bureaucratic monopolies don't work and that reform won't fix them. We have run our schools the way the Soviet Union and its client states

1

ran their entire economies, and the results have been just as disillusioning.

As Albert Shanker, president of the American Federation of Teachers, acknowledged in a recent article:

> It's time to admit that public education operates like a planned economy, a bureaucratic system in which everybody's role is spelled out in advance and there are few incentives for innovation and productivity. It's no surprise that our school system doesn't improve: It more resembles the communist economy than our own market economy.[1]

But if the Berlin Wall can come down, surely we can liberate American students from the public school monopoly.

How Bad Are the Public Schools?

Just as there were Western intellectuals who continued to hail the performance of the Soviet economy until Gorbachev blew the whistle, so there are those Americans who doggedly insist that the government schools are working pretty well. But the facts tell a different story. SAT scores fell from 978 to 890 between 1963 and 1980; they then recovered slightly, rising to 904 by the mid-1980s, but have remained flat since then. It is sometimes claimed by the education establishment that test scores have fallen because more students are taking college admissions tests these days. But the absolute number of students with outstanding scores has fallen dramatically as well; between 1972 and 1988 the number of high school seniors scoring above 600 (out of a possible 800) on the SAT's verbal section fell by about 30 percent. In 1988 only 986 seniors in the entire country scored above 750—fewer than half as many as in 1981 and probably the lowest number ever.[2]

Other tests show similar results. According to the National Assessment of Educational Progress, half of all high school seniors cannot answer the following question: "Which of the following is true about 87% of 10? (a) It is greater than 10, (b) It is less than 10, (c) It is equal to 10, (d) Can't tell." And, NAEP reported, "only 7%

---

[1]Quoted in "Reding, Wrighting & Erithmatic," Wall Street Journal, October 2, 1989.

[2]Lawrence A. Uzzell, "Education Reform Fails the Test," Wall Street Journal, May 10, 1989.

2

of the nation's 17-year-olds have the prerequisite knowledge and skills thought to be needed to perform well in college-level science courses." The International Association for the Evaluation of Education reported that in 1982 the average Japanese student outscored the top 5 percent of American students enrolled in college-preparatory math courses.[3]

A 1989 survey by the National Endowment for the Humanities found that 58 percent of college seniors couldn't identify Plato as the author of *The Republic*, that 54 percent didn't know that the *Federalist Papers* were written to promote ratification of the U.S. Constitution, that 42 percent couldn't identify the half-century in which the Civil War was fought, and that 23 percent thought Karl Marx's phrase "from each according to his ability, to each according to his need" appeared in the U.S. Constitution[4] (although the latter mistake may just reflect the respondents' observation of Congress's actions). Of eight industrialized countries, the United States is the only one in which people over 55 do better than recent high school graduates at locating countries on a world map.[5]

By comparison, consider author Avis Carlson's description of her feeling of achievement in getting her eighth-grade diploma in a small town in Kansas in 1907. To get her diploma she had to define such words as "panegyric," "talisman," "triton," and "misconception"; to find the interest on an 8 percent note for $900 running 2 years, 2 months, and 6 days; to name two countries producing large quantities of wheat, cotton, coal, and tea; to "give a brief account of the colleges, printing, and religion in the colonies prior to the American Revolution"; and to "name the principal political questions which have been advocated since the Civil War and the party which advocated each."[6] Can we imagine applicants to Harvard passing that test today?

[3]Uzzell.

[4]Kenneth H. Bacon, "College Seniors Fail to Make Grade," *Wall Street Journal*, October 9, 1989.

[5]Surveys conducted by the Gallup Organization for the National Geographic Society; cited in Gilbert M. Grosvenor, "Superpowers Not So Super in Geography," *National Geographic*, December 1989, p. 816.

[6]Avis Carlson, *Small World Long Gone: A Family Record of an Era* (Evanston, Ill.: Schori Press, 1975), pp. 83–84. Some things never change, though, except in the details: In Carlson's youth, students were also required to "write 200 words on the evil effects of alcoholic beverages."

3

Instead, today we find colleges and businesses doing the work of the high schools: 25 percent of U.S. college freshmen take remedial math courses, 21 percent take remedial writing courses, and 16 percent take remedial reading courses.[7] Meanwhile, a recent survey of 200 major corporations has found that 22 percent of them teach employees reading, 41 percent teach writing, and 31 percent teach mathematical skills. The American Society for Training and Development projects that 93 percent of the nation's biggest companies will be teaching their workers basic skills within the next three years.[8]

When the poor quality of U.S. education is pointed out, we are frequently told that we need to spend more on the government schools. Otherwise frugal taxpayers sometimes can be coaxed to support tax increases if the goal is to improve education. But the poor-mouthing by the education establishment is a massive scam. As William A. Niskanen points out in chapter 2 of this volume, since World War II, real (inflation-adjusted) spending per student has increased about 40 percent per decade, thereby about doubling every 20 years. In 1989–90, expenditures on elementary and secondary education were $212 billion, a 29 percent real increase since 1980–81. Per-pupil expenditures in government schools were $5,246[9]—or more than $130,000 per classroom of 25 children.

Because SAT scores have been falling while spending has soared, it is obvious even to the casual observer that more spending on schools does not lead to greater educational achievement (see Figure 1–1). Scholarly research and international comparisons confirm this impression. The United States spends significantly more of its GNP on education than do France, Finland, Great Britain, South Korea, and Spain, among other countries—yet students from all those countries outperform Americans on math tests. Our leading economic competitors, Japan and West Germany, also spend less

[7]U.S. Bureau of the Census, *Statistical Abstract of the United States: 1988* (Washington: Government Printing Office), p. 142; cited in Lewis J. Perelman, "The 'Acanemia' Deception," Hudson Institute Briefing Paper no. 120, May 1990, p. 16.

[8]"C Stands for Company, Turned into Classroom," *Wall Street Journal*, March 1, 1990; cited in Perelman.

[9]"1989 Back-to-School Forecast," Department of Education news release, August 24, 1989.

Figure 1-1
SPENDING AND ACHIEVEMENT IN AMERICAN SCHOOLS

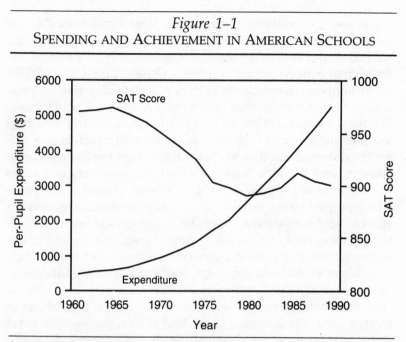

SOURCES: Educational Testing Service; U.S. Department of Education, *Digest of Educational Statistics 1989* (Washington: National Center for Education Statistics, 1989), Table 145; and "1989 Back-to-School Forecast," U.S. Department of Education news release, August 24, 1989.

NOTE: SAT scores for 1961–67 are averages for all students; subsequent scores are averages for college-bound seniors.

than we do and achieve better test results.[10] Education economist Eric A. Hanushek of the University of Rochester reviewed 65 studies of the relationship between educational spending and student performance and reported that only 20 percent found a positive relationship.[11] His conclusion, as reported in the *Journal of Economic Literature*, was, "Expenditures are unrelated to school performance as schools are currently operated."[12] John Chubb and Terry Moe of

[10]John Hood, "Education: Is America Spending Too Much?" Cato Institute Policy Analysis no. 126, January 18, 1990.

[11]Eric A. Hanushek, "Impact of Differential Expenditures on School Performance," *Educational Researcher* 18, no. 4 (May 1989).

[12]Cited in Peter Brimelow, "Are We Spending Too Much on Education?" *Forbes*, December 29, 1986, pp. 72–76.

the Brookings Institution came to the same conclusion: "As for money, the relationship between it and effective schools has been studied to death. The unanimous conclusion is that there is no connection between school funding and school performance."[13]

Furthermore, the productivity of our educational system is abysmal. In how many other industries is the basic structure of production the same as it was 200 years ago? The school day and the school year are still geared to the rhythms of an agricultural society. As for the classroom itself, a teacher still stands in front of a group of students and lectures. Sure, we've added computers and video instruction in many classrooms, but those are basically just expensive toys used by the teacher. We actually have more teachers per student now than we did 20, or 200, years ago—in sharp contrast to the experience of every industry in the competitive sector of our economy, wherein firms are constantly learning to produce more with fewer employees. Now, the traditional teacher-at-the-front-of-the-classroom method may be the most efficient way to educate students—but we have no way of knowing that in the absence of market competition, which is the best system the world has yet discovered for testing and comparing alternative methods of production and distribution. And is it really likely that there are no innovations, no efficiencies possible in such a labor-intensive enterprise? Lewis Perelman of the Hudson Institute calculates that we could get 16 years of education—a high school diploma and a college degree—in 10 minutes at a cost of 5 cents if education had improved its efficiency over the past 40 years at the same pace as the computer industry.[14] That may be an extreme example; few industries have progressed as fast as the computer business recently. But, with soaring investment and declining results, education seems to have a productivity record worse than that of any other industry.

Figures on SAT scores and school spending cannot capture the special tragedy of our inner-city schools, which have become a key element of the vicious circle of poverty. A better indicator is the story of the Washington, D.C., high school valedictorian who was

[13]John Chubb and Terry Moe, "Letting Schools Work," NY: The City Journal, Autumn 1990.

[14]Lewis J. Perelman, "Closing Education's Technology Gap," Hudson Institute Briefing Paper no. 111, November 28, 1989.

refused admission to a local college because he scored only 600 on the SAT. Like so many other urban teenagers, he had been conned into thinking he was getting an education. Virtually every major newspaper in the country has recently—if not regularly—sent reporters into inner-city schools only to discover that such institutions are nightmares of gangs, drugs, and violence, with little if any learning going on.[15] Indeed, physical violence is a constant presence at inner-city schools. A study by the United Federation of Teachers uncovered 3,386 incidents of crime and violence against New York City school employees in 1989–90, a 26 percent increase over 1988–89.[16] Furthermore, a New York–based company, Guardian Group International Corporation, has begun marketing bullet-resistant vests and other protective items for pupils.[17]

Phil Keisling has written that inner-city students are "consigned to lives of failure because their high school diplomas are the educational equivalent of worthless notes from the Weimar Republic."[18] Bonita Brodt, who studied the Chicago schools for the *Chicago Tribune*, writes in this volume that she found

> an institutionalized case of child neglect. . . . I saw how the racial politics of a city, the misplaced priorities of a centralized school bureaucracy, and the vested interests of a powerful teachers union had all somehow taken precedence over the needs of the very children the schools are supposed to serve.

And a Carnegie Foundation for the Advancement of Teaching study concluded, "The failure to educate adequately urban children is a shortcoming of such magnitude that many people have simply written off city schools as little more than human storehouses to keep young people off the streets."[19]

---

[15]For instance, see Athelia Knight, "Pursuing the Legacy: A Year at McKinley High School," *Washington Post*, September 13–16, 1987; *Chicago Schools: 'Worst in America'* (Chicago: Chicago Tribune, 1988).

[16]*Education Week*, November 14, 1990, p. 3.

[17]Ibid., September 19, 1990.

[18]Phil Keisling, "How to Save the Public Schools," *New Republic*, November 1, 1982, p. 27.

[19]Cited in Barbara Vobejda, "Big Cities Missing Out on Education Reform, Study Finds," *Washington Post*, March 16, 1988.

7

It's not that urban schools are underfunded. The Boston schools, for instance, spend $7,300 per enrollee each year, and more than $9,000 per student in average daily attendance.[20] The figure is $5,800 per enrollee in Washington, D.C., and over $7,000 in New York City.[21] Rather, the problem is that costs soar and school bureaucracies expand exponentially while the D.C. school system manages to "lose" 10-year-old Melissa Brantley, leaving her in second grade for three years; the school system can't find any records indicating why.[22] It's no wonder that state Rep. Polly Williams of Milwaukee says that the $6,000 per child per year spent by the Milwaukee public schools "isn't going to the kids. It's going to a system that doesn't educate them and to a bunch of bureaucrats."[23]

University of Chicago economist Kevin Murphy suggests that the poor quality of education provided for black students may account for half the slowdown in black economic progress during the 1980s (as measured by the black/white income gap, which narrowed during the 1970s and remained roughly constant during the 1980s).[24]

Is it any wonder that those who know the urban schools best— the teachers in them—are much more likely to send their own children to nongovernment schools? In Chicago, private schools are attended by 22 percent of all children—but by 46 percent of the children of Chicago's public school teachers.[25] Elsewhere, the proportion of teachers' children in private schools is 29 percent in Los Angeles, 25 percent in Atlanta, 36 percent in Memphis, more than 50 percent in Milwaukee—in every case significantly higher

[20]Boston Municipal Research Bureau, Boston Public Schools Research Department; cited in Warren Brookes, "The Urban Education Deficit," Washington Times, January 18, 1990.

[21]U.S. Bureau of the Census, Statistical Abstract of the United States 1990 (Washington: Government Printing Office, 1990); Gary Putka, "New York Archdiocese Begins Campaign to Save 140 Catholic Schools in City," Wall Street Journal, January 30, 1991, p. A12.

[22]Rene Sanchez, "Slipping through the Safety Net in D.C. Schools," Washington Post, July 5, 1990, p. A1.

[23]"Champion of Choice: Shaking Up Milwaukee's Schools," interview with Polly Williams by John H. Fund, Reason, October 1990.

[24]Kevin Murphy, "The Education Gap Rap," American Enterprise, March/April 1990, pp. 62–63.

[25]Chicago Tribune, May 3, 1984; cited in Herbert J. Walberg et al., We Can Rescue Our Children (Chicago: Heartland Institute, 1988), p. 11.

Figure 1–2
PUBLIC SCHOOL TEACHERS WITH CHILDREN IN
PRIVATE SCHOOLS

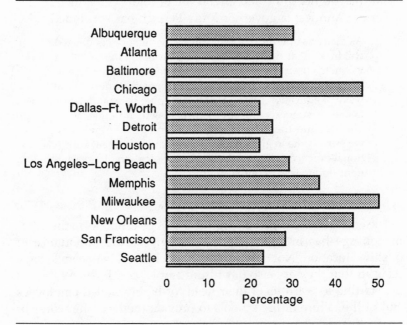

SOURCES: Denis P. Doyle and Terry W. Hartle, "Where Public School Teachers Send Their Children to School: A Preliminary Analysis" (Washington: American Enterprise Institute, unpublished ms., n.d.); *Chicago Tribune*, May 3, 1984, cited in Herbert J. Walberg et al., *We Can Rescue Our Children* (Chicago: Heartland Institute, 1988), p. 11; Clint Bolick, director, Landmark Legal Foundation Center for Civil Rights, remarks before State Bar of Wisconsin, Individual Rights and Responsibilities Section, Milwaukee, January 17, 1991.

NOTE: Figures for Chicago are circa 1984; those for Milwaukee are circa 1990. Figures for all other cities are based on 1980 census data.

than the proportion of all children in the city (see Figure 1–2).[26] In New York City, as of 1988, no member of the Board of Education and no citywide elected official had children in the government

[26]Heritage Foundation Education Update, Fall 1986, p. 7. See also Denis P. Doyle, "Public Teachers, Private Schools," *American Spectator*, November 1984, pp. 32–33; and Denis P. Doyle and Terry W. Hartle, "Where Public School Teachers Send Their Children to School: A Preliminary Analysis" (Washington: American

9

schools.[27] California's superintendent of public instruction, Bill Honig, opposes educational choice, but he moved his son out of the Honig family home in San Francisco to a home in Fremont, California, so his son could attend junior high school there.[28] Former Minnesota governor Rudy Perpich has concluded:

> As many as one-third of the nation's 40 million school-aged children are at risk of either failing, dropping out or falling victim to crime, drugs, teenage pregnancy or chronic unemployment. What is even more troubling is that, despite the wave of education reform that is sweeping the country, the evidence suggests that the gap between the educational "haves" and the "have-nots" is widening. As Americans, we must come to grips with the fact that our present educational practices are contributing to the creation of a permanent underclass in our society.[29]

Why Education Matters

The emergence of a global, high-technology economy in the information age has brought home to Americans the importance of quality education. Not only are these our children, we seem to have realized, but they are also our future employees. Business groups are starting to warn us of their need for highly skilled employees and of the failure of the schools to provide them. In the words of David Kearns, chairman of the Xerox Corporation:

> Public education has put this country at a terrible competitive disadvantage. American business will have to hire a million new workers a year who can't read, write, or count. Teaching them how, and absorbing the lost productivity while they're learning, will cost industry $25 billion a year

Enterprise Institute, unpublished ms., n.d.). For Milwaukee, see Clint Bolick, director, Landmark Legal Foundation Center for Civil Rights, remarks before State Bar of Wisconsin, Individual Rights and Responsibilities Section, Milwaukee, Wisconsin, January 17, 1991.

[27]Samuel G. Freedman, *Small Victories* (New York: Harper & Row, 1990); cited in David J. Garrow, "A Teacher Who Made a Difference," *Washington Post Book World*, May 6, 1990, p. 1.

[28]"California Superintendent Exercises Choice," Heritage Foundation Education Update, Summer 1990.

[29]Quoted in "Educational Choice: A Catalyst for School Reform" (Chicago: City Club of Chicago, August 1989), p. 2.

for as long as it takes. Teaching new workers basic skills is doing the schools' product recall work for them.[30]

A recent National Alliance of Business poll of the 1,200 largest U.S. corporations has found that only 36 percent of them are satisfied with the competence of new employees. Too many such employees lack the reasoning and problem-solving skills employers need and often require on-the-job remedial education in basic reading and math. Moreover, personnel officers said, competence in both reading and math has slipped over the past five years.[31]

John W. Kendrick of George Washington University, one of the nation's leading experts on productivity, has suggested that 70 percent of a country's productivity trends can be explained by "the knowledge factor"—the knowledge and skills of its workers. That would suggest that the decline in U.S. productivity that began in the 1970s can be explained by a falloff in the knowledge factor as those students with declining SAT scores entered the workforce. Cornell University economist John H. Bishop argued in the March 1989 *American Economic Review* that the decline in test scores accounted for 10 percent of the productivity slowdown in the 1970s and 20 percent in the 1980s, and that it might grow to 40 percent by the 1990s.[32]

However, important as our economic competitiveness is, it is not the most important reason to worry about the quality of U.S. education, especially education for poor, minority, and inner-city children. Education used to be a poor child's ticket out of the slums; now it is part of the system that traps people in the underclass. In a modern society a child who never learns to read adequately— much less to add and subtract, to write, to think logically and creatively—will never be able to lead a fully human life. He or she will be left behind by the rest of society. Our huge school systems, controlled by politics and bureaucracies, are increasingly unable

[30]David T. Kearns, speech before the Business Council, Hot Springs, Virginia, October 7, 1988.

[31]William H. Kolberg, president, National Alliance of Business, in congressional testimony cited by William Raspberry, "Better Education, Better Business," *Washington Post*, November 21, 1990.

[32]Kendrick and Bishop cited in Warren Brookes, "Public Education and the Global Failure of Socialism," *Imprimis*, April 1990.

11

to meet the needs of individual children. Too many children leave school uneducated, unprepared, and unnoticed by the bureaucracy.

Why the Schools Don't Work

As John Chubb and Terry Moe have pointed out, "Until the first few decades of the 1900s, there was really nothing that could meaningfully be called a public 'system' of education in the United States. Schooling was a local affair."[33] But then Progressive reformers set about creating a rational, professional, and bureaucratic school system, based on the concept of the "one best system."[34] Control of schools was vested in political and administrative authorities, often far removed from the local neighborhood school.

The one best system grew out of the Progressive Era, when the best-educated Americans believed that experts armed with social science and goodwill—and power—could make decisions about all sorts of social institutions that would be implemented by government to benefit all Americans. The Progressives were not socialists, but the one best system was essentially socialist in nature. Obviously it was intended to be one system for the whole society, centrally directed and bureaucratically managed, with little use for competition or market incentives.

That system has survived to this day, even though the failure of socialism is now recognized around the world. That failure had been recognized long ago in Eastern Europe; when the Soviet Union lost the will to use military force to support its puppets, socialist governments fell like rotten trees. Longtime socialist Robert Heilbroner was forced to concede in 1989, "Less than seventy-five years after it officially began, the contest between capitalism and socialism is over: capitalism has won. The Soviet Union, China, and Eastern Europe have given us the clearest possible proof that capitalism organizes the material affairs of humankind more satisfactorily than

[33]John E. Chubb and Terry M. Moe, *Politics, Markets, and America's Schools* (Washington: Brookings Institution, 1990), p. 3.

[34]Ibid., pp. 3–6. See also David B. Tyack, *The One Best System: A History of American Urban Education* (Cambridge: Harvard University Press, 1974).

socialism."[35] And in October 1990, Soviet president Mikhail Gorbachev's economic reform plan began by asserting: "There is no alternative to the transition to the market. The whole world experience proved the vitality and efficiency of the market economy."[36]

That was no surprise to most people in the United States, where free enterprise has always been an article of faith. Our economy has been perhaps the freest the world has ever seen, with millions of firms competing vigorously to serve hundreds of millions of customers. Yet we have organized a few key elements of our economy along socialist lines—notably the postal service and the public schools.[37] In every school district a centralized bureaucracy runs all the schools, collecting taxes and disbursing funds from the district office. Such a unified, centralized system is a dinosaur in the information age. If this sort of system worked well, Eastern Europe would have the world's most dynamic economies.

We expect to get high quality and low prices in every industry—from housing to clothing, from groceries to televisions—through vigorous competition by many producers. Competition is the only way to guarantee steady progress in any field, whether it is competition of ideas or of goods. Competition forces people to develop better ideas—products that consumers will prefer and better ways of manufacturing and delivering those products—and to adopt the ideas developed by successful competitors. Without such a process, an industry, or an athletic team, or scientific discipline, will stagnate.

Yet somehow we expect to get high quality, although perhaps not low prices, in education through one centralized system. Part

[35]Robert Heilbroner, "The Triumph of Capitalism," New Yorker, January 23, 1989, p. 98.

[36]"Excerpts from Gorbachev's Economic Program," New York Times, October 17, 1990, p. A8.

[37]Many people have trouble grasping the argument that a centralized monopoly school system is run along socialist lines and displays many of the familiar problems of socialism. For instance, Amitai Etzioni, University Professor at George Washington University and one of the nation's most respected social scientists, recently ridiculed the idea, saying that it's absurd to compare the public school system to socialism, the schools don't have tanks and don't shoot people in the public square. (Remarks at the Washington Circle, George Washington University, December 12, 1990.) But socialism had plenty of problems before the Tiananmen Square massacre, and it is those systemic economic problems that are paralleled in the government school system.

13

of the problem is that we're far more skeptical of the suppliers of consumer goods—the businesses that produce and sell them—than we are of the suppliers of education—the teachers, the superintendents, the school boards. When businesses try to use protectionism or other schemes to gain monopoly prices, we quite rightly resist. But when the education establishment wants to centralize control of the schools and then raise taxes, we treat them not as self-interested suppliers but as "experts."

Socialism doesn't work in an entire economy, and it doesn't work in one industry. Compared with competitive capitalism, socialist industries are expensive and stagnant. They don't generate much productivity, innovation, creativity, or efficiency. Without competition—and the incentive to make money by attracting more customers—they see little reason to offer new products, try out new ideas, or cut costs. That's why the postal service and the government school systems display all the energy and creativity of Soviet agriculture.

The problem of the government schools is the problem inherent in all government institutions. In the private sector, firms must attract voluntary customers or they fail; and if they fail, investors lose their money, and managers and employees lose their jobs. The possibility of failure, therefore, is a powerful incentive to find out what customers want and to deliver it efficiently. But in the government sector, failures are not punished, they are rewarded. If a government agency is set up to deal with a problem and the problem gets worse, the agency is rewarded with more money and more staff—because, after all, its task is now bigger. An agency that fails year after year, that does not simply fail to solve the problem but actually makes it worse, will be rewarded with an ever-increasing budget. What kind of incentive system is that?

Not only is our public school system run along socialist lines, it has become increasingly centralized. Through most of the 20th century, school districts have been getting larger, reflecting the century's enthusiasm for consolidation, centralization, and planning. The number of school districts plunged—from 101,382 in 1945–46 to 40,520 in 1959–60 to 15,747 in 1983–84[38]—and the number of parents and students in each district rose dramatically during

[38]U.S. Department of Education, *Digest of Education Statistics 1987* (Washington: National Center for Education Statistics, 1987), p. 70.

14

the same period (see Figure 1–3). State and federal funding—and, naturally enough, state and federal control—grew at the expense of local funding and control. The percentage of school funding provided by local government fell from 60 percent in 1960 to 43.9 percent in 1987.[39]

As school districts became larger and state and federal funding became more significant, local parents and taxpayers had even less control over the way the schools were run. School bureaucracies increased dramatically in size. Between 1960 and 1984 the number of teachers in government schools grew by 57 percent, the number of principals and supervisors in those schools grew by 79 percent, and the number of other staffers grew by 500 percent (see Figure

Figure 1–3
NUMBER OF PUBLIC SCHOOL DISTRICTS, 1945–80

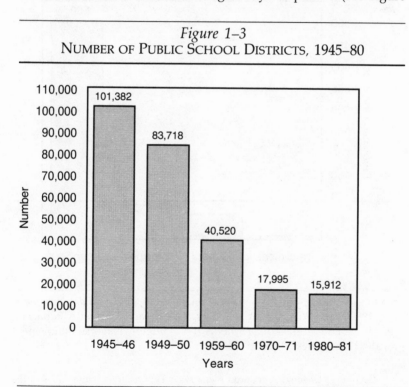

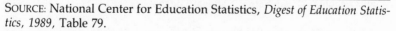

SOURCE: National Center for Education Statistics, *Digest of Education Statistics, 1989*, Table 79.

[39]Brookes, p. 4.

15

1–4).[40] Thus, it's no surprise that the percentage of education dollars paid to teachers fell steadily during the 1970s, from 49.2 percent in 1970–71 to 38.7 percent in 1980–81.[41]

When two Japanese government officials visited Chicago a few years ago, they were taken to the main offices of the Chicago Board of Education. They asked their hosts if the massive bureaucracy

Figure 1–4
INCREASE IN SCHOOL ENROLLMENT AND PERSONNEL,
1960–84

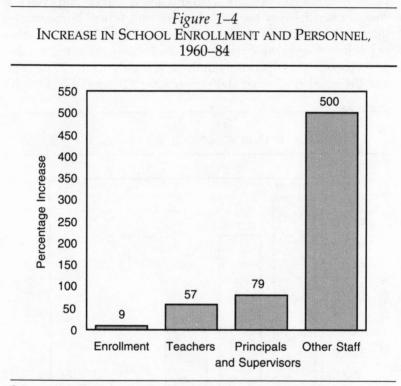

SOURCES: National Center for Education Statistics, *Digest of Education Statistics, 1989*, Table 35; Lynne V. Cheney, "American Memory: A Report on the Humanities in the Public Schools" (Washington: National Endowment for the Humanities, 1987), p. 25.

[40]Lynne V. Cheney, "American Memory: A Report on the Humanities in the Public Schools" (Washington: National Endowment for the Humanities, 1987), p. 25.

[41]National Center for Education Statistics; cited in E. G. West, "Are American Schools Working? Disturbing Cost and Quality Trends," Cato Institute Policy Analysis no. 26, August 9, 1983.

was the U.S. Department of Education and were amazed to be told that what they saw was merely the administrative offices of the schools of one city. They said the offices of the Japanese National Ministry of Education were not as large.[42] In fact, as of 1987, there were 3,300 employees in the central and district offices of the Chicago public school system.[43] By contrast, the schools of the Catholic Archdiocese of Chicago serve 40 percent as many students in a much larger geographical area but make do with with only 36 central office administrators.[44]

The same kind of contrast is found in smaller districts. In California, for example, the Catholic schools in Oakland serve 22,000 students and have 2 central administrators (plus 7 clerical staff), whereas the Berkeley public school system needs 27 administrators for 10,000 students and the Richmond public school system needs 24 administrators for 30,000 students (and these figures for Berkeley and Richmond do not include administrators paid with federal and state funds).[45] In the nation's largest school district, New York, John Chubb found an even more striking contrast: 6,000 administrators in the government schools and only 25 in the Catholic schools, although the Catholic schools served about one-fourth as many students.[46]

Such massive bureaucracies divert scarce resources from real educational activities, deprive principals and teachers of any opportunity for authority and independence, and create an impenetrable bulwark against citizen efforts to change the school system. Like other large bureaucracies, school systems become susceptible to influence only from special-interest groups, notably the teachers' unions and other elements of the education establishment—or maybe we should say the education-industrial complex.

[42]Harold Henderson, "The City File," *Reader* (Chicago), October 9, 1987; cited in Walberg, p. 12.

[43]Casey Banas, "Enrollment's Down, Central Office Workers Up," *Chicago Tribune*, September 29, 1987; cited in Walberg, p. 12.

[44]Archdiocese of Chicago, *Chicago Catholic Schools*, 1987–88 Report; cited in Walberg, p. 12.

[45]Barbara Erickson, "Parochial vs. the Public Schools," *Berkeley Independent & Gazette*, May 18, 1980, p. 1.

[46]"Making Schools Better" (New York: Manhattan Institute, Center for Educational Innovation, 1989), pp. 10–11.

Parents frequently complain that they want more discipline, more teaching of values, and fewer drugs in the schools. The sorts of problems they complain about stem in large measure from the problem of running a government monopoly institution in a democratic society (even if the society is one characterized more by interest-group democracy than by true popular control). A monopoly generally provides the same sort of product or service to all its clients. In a small, homogeneous community, a one-size-fits-all school may not be a serious problem (even though some children might benefit from schools with more emphasis on science, the arts, discipline, and so on). But in a large and diverse community, a monopoly institution is sure to serve many or most of its clients poorly. When the monopoly is the educational system, which touches on our most deeply held values and prejudices, many people are sure to chafe under its strictures. As economist Walter Williams has written:

> A state monopoly in the production of a good or service enhances the potential for conflict, through requiring uniformity; that is, its production requires a *collective* decision on many attributes of the product, and once produced, everybody has to consume the identical product whether he agrees with all the attributes or not. State monopolies in the production of education enhance the potential for conflict by requiring conformity on issues of importance to many people.[47]

What sorts of conflicts can arise? Parents, taxpayers, and other voters can disagree over school prayer, ethnic history, saluting the flag, school uniforms, gay teachers, and drug testing, for instance—not to mention more directly educational issues such as phonics and the new math. For most of these issues, there is no one right answer; different people have different needs, different situations, and different values. In a market system, different preferences and different approaches to production get tested, and customers can choose from a wide variety of options. In a political system, however, one group "wins," and the losers are stuck with products or

[47]Walter E. Williams, "Tuition Tax Credits: Other Benefits," *Policy Review* (Spring 1978): 85.

18

services they don't like. Different preferences become the subject of endless political, legislative, and judicial battles.

Even in basic academic subjects, there is a danger in having only one approach taught in all the schools. Underlying the notion of the one best system, one school system for all students, is the fallacious idea that there is a "correct" understanding of mathematics, history, science, or any academic discipline. A competitive system of education, for instance, would probably not have led to every American school's teaching economics from a Keynesian perspective, complete with the Phillips curve and government pump-priming mysticism, long after that approach had been rejected by most thoughtful people.

There is merit, to be sure, in having the school system inculcate society's values in all students. But our society's principal value is individual freedom, which is difficult to instill through central direction. And the pluralism of a society based on political and economic freedom and built by immigration is not conducive to the calm and apolitical development of a unitary value system for thousands of local schools. Such an ideal may be achievable in Japan, but it is only a pipe dream for the United States.

Occasionally, the government school systems do attempt to serve children's differing needs. Some states have set up centralized high schools for gifted students; a few years ago, New York City established Harvey Milk High School for gay students; in 1990, Milwaukee set up two schools for black boys only, and New York City, Chicago, and Baltimore discussed variations on the same theme; in the suburbs of Washington, D.C., some school systems have set up "alternative" schools that emphasize reading, writing, and arithmetic (strange what passes for an "alternative" approach to education in these modern times). But these attempts to satisfy customers, which happen millions of times a day in the marketplace, are notable in the politicized school systems for their rarity. The usual approach was enunciated by Joe Voboril, chairman of the Portland (Oregon) School Board's legislative committee, in opposition to an education tax credit initiative:

> What is wrong with their thinking is that public education is not like the free market place. In a free market place you change your mix if your product is not selling. Public schools

19

serve everyone. We can't change our mix and that's the big
difference.[48]

Educational Reform in the 1980s: How Long, O Lord, How Long?

In 1983 the National Commission on Excellence in Education
issued its report, *A Nation at Risk*, which declared that "a rising
tide of mediocrity" threatened America's schools.[49] The nation's
political leaders rallied around, with the usual reaction: if the
schools are failing, give them more money. But a few governors
and others also promised educational reform.

More than 250 state task forces were created, and many states
adopted "comprehensive" reform packages. A year after its report,
the commission issued a euphoric progress report, declaring that
"the response to the announcement that American education is in
trouble has been nothing short of extraordinary."

It has now been 8 years since *A Nation at Risk*, not to mention 13
years since the creation of the Department of Education. What have
been the results of all the reform? According to a 1988 survey by
the National Center for Education Information, 87 percent of school
superintendents thought the schools in their communities had
improved in the past five years. But only 25 percent of the public—
the consumers—agreed with them.[50]

Spending on education has soared since 1983, but test scores
have made little progress. According to the NAEP, reading test
scores for students aged 9, 13, and 17 were virtually stagnant—
increasing less than one point on a scale of 500—from 1984 until
1989.[51] As noted above, SAT scores fell about 90 points in the 1960s
and 1970s and gained only 14 points in the 1980s, with even that
progress slowing to a halt by late in the decade.

A 1990 report by the Educational Testing Service, "The Educational Reform Decade," found that there had been a good deal of

[48]Cathy Kiyomura, "Former Reagan Aide Backs Measure 11," *Oregonian*, October 16, 1990.

[49]National Commission on Excellence in Education, *A Nation at Risk: The Imperative for Educational Reform* (Washington: Government Printing Office, 1983.)

[50]C. Emily Feistritzer, "Profile of School Administrators in the United States"
(National Center for Education Information, 1988), p. 32.

[51]Cited in Kenneth J. Cooper, "Test of U.S. Students Shows Little Progress,"
Washington Post, January 10, 1990, p. A1.

"reform" in school *inputs:* stricter attendance rules, minimum grades required for permission to take part in extracurricular activities, stricter conduct rules, longer school days, more competence testing, more homework, higher teacher pay, and a longer school year.

But what about school *outputs?* For the 1980s, ETS found, there were no gains in average reading proficiency; very little improvement in mathematics, and none at all at the more advanced high school levels that might be expected after several years of high school math; no improvement in civics knowledge, and some ground lost among 17-year-olds; and no progress in writing.[52]

Despite this dismal record, school boards and administrators continue to ask for just a little more time to show improvement. But the students who entered high school when test scores began their long fade-out are now 41 years old. The students who entered first grade when the Department of Education was created have graduated from high school. The students who entered school when *A Nation at Risk* was published are now in the ninth grade, and some 20 million students have left high school since then. How many more generations of students will leave school uneducated and unprepared while the education establishment pleads for just a little more time? The establishment's "reform" has been a failure. It is time to take education away from the establishment.

Empowering Parents, Students, and Teachers

The government schools have failed because they are socialist institutions. Like Soviet factories, they are technologically backward, overstaffed, inflexible, unresponsive to consumer demand, and operated for the convenience of top-level bureaucrats. With every passing year, as we move further into the information age and the global economy, they become more inadequate. They are incapable of keeping up with the needs of a dynamic and diverse society.

In the marketplace, competition keeps businesses on their toes. They get constant feedback from satisfied and dissatisfied customers. Consumers don't vote on what sorts of products they would

[52]Educational Testing Service, "The Educational Reform Decade" (Princeton, N.J., 1990); cited in Fred M. Hechinger, "About Education," *New York Times,* November 21, 1990.

21

like every two or four years, nor are they forced to buy a particular package that may not reflect all their preferences. They vote every day, every hour, every time they choose to buy or not to buy. Firms that don't respond to the message they get from customers go out of business.

Like all government institutions, the public schools lack that feedback and those incentives. A successful principal doesn't get a raise; an unsuccessful one doesn't get fired. The public school system poorly serves almost everyone: students are denied access to a high-quality education; parents are treated as nuisances (in how many other businesses are the customers blamed for the failure of the product?); good teachers are loaded down with bureaucratic red tape and paperwork and denied the chance to be creative and to attract customers who like their approach; principals are told to carry out the instructions laid down by a centralized bureaucracy; and the whole country suffers because students leave school uneducated. Winning is limited to the bureaucrats and the interest groups that want to control what is taught in the schools.

In their massive surveys of public and private schools, Chubb and Moe found that autonomy from direct outside control is essential to effective school organization. Furthermore:

> Autonomy turns out to be heavily dependent on the institutional structure of school control. In the private sector, where schools are controlled by markets—indirectly and from the bottom up—autonomy is generally high. In the public sector, where schools are controlled by politics—directly and from the top down—autonomy is generally low.[53]

Both bureaucracy and direct democratic control, said Chubb and Moe, interfere with autonomy and school effectiveness. They found that teachers and principals are much more likely to see each other as partners in private schools than in public schools. The politicized bureaucracy of the government schools makes teachers and principals adversaries; the dynamic, market-directed private schools make them colleagues.

What could change this state of affairs? The time has come to give the competitive market economy—the system that has given

---

[53]Chubb and Moe, *Politics, Markets, and America's Schools*, p. 183.

us two centuries of dramatically increasing living standards, the system on which we rely for everything from food and clothing to VCRs and world travel—a chance to improve our educational system. We need to give parents and students a chance to choose their schools. Parents don't normally attend. We need to give teachers and principals a chance to be more successful by producing successful students, and—what is just as important—a chance to lose their jobs if they fail.

Ideally, the private sector would be totally responsible for education. Government involvement in education necessarily means all the inefficiencies of socialist production or funding, as well as government control over what children learn and how they learn it— a set of circumstances that should concern a free society. Still, some government involvement seems inevitable for the foreseeable future, so—for now—we should look for opportunities to enhance competition, creativity, and quality even in the face of such obstacles.

A key point to keep in mind is that nongovernment schools, which have to offer a better product to stay in business, do a better job of educating children. Defenders of the education establishment have tried to dismiss that success by claiming that the private schools start with a better grade of students—once again, blaming the customers for the enterprise's failure. But that excuse has been exposed time and again. Urban Catholic schools serve a clientele not terribly different from that of the government schools. Marva Collins's school in Chicago received national publicity for its success with poor black children, many of them declared "learning disabled" by the neighborhood government schools. Joan Davis Ratteray of the Institute for Independent Education describes in this volume the success of many minority-run independent schools. Any remaining doubts should have been eliminated in 1982 when James S. Coleman and his colleagues, after a comprehensive investigation of the results of public versus private schools, concluded that "when family backgrounds that predict achievement are controlled, students in . . . private schools are shown to achieve at a higher level than students in public schools."[54]

[54]James Coleman, Thomas Hoffer, and Sally Kilgore, *High School Achievement: Public, Catholic, and Private Schools Compared* (New York: Basic Books, 1982). See also J. Cibulka, T. O'Brien, and D. Zewe, *Inner-City Private Elementary Schools: A Study* (Milwaukee: Marquette University Press, 1982); Andrew Greeley, *Catholic High Schools and Minority Students* (New Brunswick, N.J.: Transaction, 1982); James Cole-

Private schools have always been available to the rich. Today, one is stunned to discover in the research of Ratteray, Coleman, and others how low the incomes are of some parents who manage to send their children to Catholic or other private schools. But it is time to make high-quality, nongovernment schools available to all parents. Parents should not have to pay twice for education—once in taxes and again in tuition for alternative schools. Giving all parents access to independent schools would bring forth a flourishing supply of new schools and would inject a healthy dose of competition into our educational system. We should look forward to a system in which schools are established by all sorts of institutions—by the Catholic church, the Black Muslims, the YMCA, the Urban League, Operation PUSH, Citicorp, Xerox, Sylvan Learning Centers, the Nature Conservancy, the American Association for the Advancement of Science, Phillips Academy, Boston University, and so on—and by visionary teachers and entrepreneurs. Let them all compete to provide the best possible education.

So how do we make independent schools available to all families? We need a program of educational choice. Such a program would ensure that every parent could choose from a variety of schools, both government run and independent. The government would pay or reimburse each child's educational expenses up to a certain level, but students would not be required to attend a government school to receive government funding.

The program of educational choice could be adopted at the federal, state, or local level. It would probably make sense to adopt a choice program at the state level for at least three reasons: (1) state governments increasingly provide the bulk of school funding, (2) a statewide program would offer families more choices than a local district program, and (3) it would be less than ideal in a federal system to implement sweeping educational changes at the national level. A statewide school-choice plan would be an ideal way to respond to political and judicial demands for "educational equalization"; it would help to equalize financial resources available to students throughout the state without further centralizing education in the state capital.

man and Thomas Hoffer, *Public and Private High Schools: The Impact of Communities* (New York: Basic Books, 1987).

The simplest way to create a system of educational choice is a voucher plan. Under such a plan, the state would give the parent or guardian of every child a voucher worth, say, $2,500 per year to be spent on educational services at any public or private school in the state. (Actually, there's no reason to forbid families to spend their vouchers at an out-of-state school, and such an option would give families even more opportunity to choose just the right school for each child.) Government-run schools would accept the voucher as full payment, but independent schools should be free to charge an additional amount if they choose so as to allow more variety in the educational system. If schools could not charge more than the voucher, then elite, expensive schools would probably refuse to accept vouchers at all; that would mean that to send a child to, say, the Harvard School in Chicago, a family would have to come up with the full $4,000, leaving families that could just manage $1,500 shut out of the school and reducing the demographic diversity of elite schools.

Defenders of the government school monopoly usually charge that voucher plans would cost the taxpayers more money because they would now be paying for students who attend private schools. But there would be a net loss to the taxpayers only if very few students switched from government to independent schools. Given that the average school district spends $5,246 per enrolled student per year, the taxpayers would save $2,700 for every student who left a government school and claimed his or her $2,500 voucher. According to one analysis, if as few as 8 percent of students left the government schools, the taxpayers would save money.[55]

One real objection to a voucher plan is that the government might use it to further regulate nongovernment schools. Colleges that receive federal funding and private businesses that sell to the government have certainly found that government money always comes with strings attached. Once an institution becomes dependent on government funding, it becomes very difficult to turn down the government's mandates. Of course, a voucher should not be seen as government funding for schools; the funding is for families, who would choose the schools. A voucher is no more government

[55]See E. G. West, "An Analysis of the District of Columbia Education Tax Credit Initiative," Cato Institute Policy Analysis, October 27, 1981, p. 13. See also E. G. West, "The Real Costs of Tuition Tax Credits," Public Choice 46 (1985): 61–70.

support for a particular school than food stamps are government support for Safeway. But governments always seek to expand their control, and there would certainly be an attempt to use vouchers that way—especially if the private schools were to effectively challenge the monopoly of the public schools. Through the regulatory process, state governments could turn independent schools into perfect copies of the government schools—burdened by paperwork, hamstrung by bureaucracy, top-heavy with administrative personnel and guideline writers. The government would have surreptitiously destroyed the existing alternatives to the public school monopoly.

Some advocates of school choice would try to counter that tendency by increasing the separation between the government funding and the nongovernment school. One way to do that is through a program of education tax credits or tax refunds. Under such a system, the government would not give families a voucher that would be turned over to the school and then submitted to the government for payment. Rather, parents (or guardians, or preferably any individual or business) would pay the school directly for the child's education and then request a tax refund for the amount they spent on education—up to, say, $2,500—on their state income tax form. No government check would ever be written to an independent school, and it would be even more clear that the schools were not receiving government funds.

The tax refund program, too, has problems. First, bureaucrats no doubt would ignore the fact that the schools were receiving their funds directly from parents and would still try to use the program to regulate the schools. Second, many low-income families pay little or no income tax and would not be able to benefit from the program. Many tax refund plans, such as those proposed in the District of Columbia in 1981 and in Oregon in 1990, take that fact into account by allowing individuals and corporations to receive a tax credit for money spent to educate other people's children in independent schools. But that leads to the third problem, which is that such plans are complicated to explain, especially in initiative campaigns (which may well be necessary to get around the entrenched legislative support for the education establishment). These problems may make vouchers the preferred way to break the education monopoly.

In the case of either vouchers or tax credits, those who design the specific plan should try to limit the potential for regulation in the enacting legislation, as was done in the Wisconsin voucher program and the unsuccessful Oregon tax credit initiative. If there must be some sort of regulation, the state or city should seek to regulate outputs, not inputs—that is, they should require participating schools to meet performance standards for their students rather than arbitrary requirements on textbooks, classroom size, teacher education, number of restrooms, and so on.

Public School Choice Is Not Enough

The school choice plan that has gotten the most attention in the past five years is public school choice. In this volume, Sy Fliegel and Robert Peterkin describe public school choice plans in East Harlem (in New York City) and Cambridge, Massachusetts. In 1988, Minnesota introduced a statewide public school choice plan.

Under public school choice plans, a student can go to any public school in the district or state. Because district and state funding is based largely on average daily attendance, funding follows the students. There have been some promising results from such plans, especially in East Harlem (although if one starts out with the worst schools in New York City, any change should offer some improvement).

However, as John E. Coons points out in this volume, public school choice is really a form of market socialism, an idea that was once—in the 1930s—the last best hope of socialists who realized that pure socialism really wouldn't work. The idea is to make government bureaus—or schools—act like private, competing firms. But why do private firms compete? Because if they attract customers, their managers, stockholders, and employees prosper. And if the firms don't attract customers, those people lose their jobs and investments. Why would a government bureau compete, or compete efficiently? Under the original market-socialism concept, such a bureau would face at least the negative incentive of going out of business if it failed to attract customers. However, under the existing public school choice plans, according to Myron Lieberman, not a single principal has lost his or her job because the school couldn't attract customers.

Moreover, negative incentives are really not enough to produce a dynamic, creative, and innovative system. We could, after all, employ the Stalinist incentive system: meet your quota or run the

27

risk of execution. But that system didn't make the Soviet Union a dynamic economy. There are no positive incentives for teachers and principals in a public school choice system, at least not of the kind that we usually use in a capitalist system to make people give us what we want. No principal or teacher will get a raise for attracting more students to his or her school. (In fact, such a prospect would probably be disconcerting and irritating in a bureaucratic system; one would have to do more paperwork, requisition more supplies, rearrange classrooms, and so on.) A successful manager in a private business gets a raise, or gets hired away for a bigger salary. A successful entrepreneur expands his or her store or opens a branch. Can one imagine a public school choice system allowing a successful principal to open another school across town and run both of them? So there is little incentive, either positive or negative, to do a good job in a bureaucratic system, even one with parental choice.

As for parents and students, it's obviously helpful for them to have more options. Some government schools, for a variety of reasons, are better than others, and public school choice does allow families to choose schools they think will be better. (But if everyone agrees that, say, Jefferson High is the best in town, a choice plan has to resort to a lottery or some other form of rationing to keep attendance at the preferred level; a free-enterprise system would encourage Jefferson to expand and its competitors to try to emulate it.) But families still don't get the full benefits of competition—the basic system they count on to deliver automobiles, housing, food, books, movies, banking, and other goods and services.

Magnet schools are one form of public school choice, under which a school district may emphasize specialized programs—science and mathematics, performing arts, computers, or foreign languages— in one or several schools. Frequently, magnet programs are designed to keep white and middle-class students in public school systems. We have come so far from solid basic education in the United States that the Arlington, Virginia, school system in the Washington, D.C., suburbs now has several "alternative" schools that offer a strong emphasis on reading, writing, and arithmetic skills. Magnet programs are often astoundingly expensive and often have little in the way of results to show for the money, as has

28

happened in Kansas City, Missouri.[56] And the *Washington Post* regularly reports on the plight of parents forced to wait in line for hours or days to get their children into preferred magnet schools.[57] In Prince George's County, Maryland, for example, there were almost 4,000 applications for about 1,100 magnet school openings in the 1989–90 school year. In response to the days-long parent campouts, the school superintendent suggested that the system switch from first-come, first-served to a lottery. Can one imagine a private firm responding to increased demand in such a way? The market is shouting, "Make more schools like this," and the suppliers respond by looking for new ways to ration access.

Myron Lieberman has described the likelihood of competition and innovation under public school choice:

> Let us assume that a company owns 90 percent of the grocery stores in a state and controls all the assets of those stores. Company policies, which can be changed at any time, govern the products the stores sell, the days and hours the stores are open, the territories they serve, and a host of other matters. Shoppers can legally patronize the stores owned by other companies, but the cost of doing so is prohibitive, even if those stores are conveniently located and have high-quality merchandise. Moreover, shoppers must pay for the products sold by the dominant company's stores whether they patronize those stores or not.
>
> Let us also assume that the dominant company uses various means of discouraging potential competitors from entering the market. It requires entrants to offer certain products, operate stores of a certain size, locate stores in certain areas, provide their employees with certain benefits, and meet other expensive and time-consuming conditions.[58]

Clearly, we would not call such a situation competition, and we would not expect to get high-quality products, good service, and

[56]Rick Atkinson, "Kansas City's High-Stakes Education Gamble," *Washington Post*, May 13, 1990.

[57]See, for example, Michele L. Norris, "Lottery Urged for Pr. George's Magnet Schools," *Washington Post*, December 1, 1989; Stephen Buckley and Rene Sanchez, "Enrollment Ritual Becomes an All-Nighter," *Washington Post*, April 3, 1990.

[58]Myron Lieberman, "Education Reform as a Conservative Fiasco," *Cato Policy Report*, November/December 1989, p. 7. See also idem, *Beyond Public Education* (Westport, Conn.: Praeger, 1986); idem, *Privatization and Educational Choice* (New York: St. Martin's, 1989); idem, *Public School Choice* (Lancaster, Pa.: Technomic, 1990).

innovation from that dominant grocery company. Add to Lieberman's scenario the layers of bureaucracy and central planning found in large public school systems, the inability to fire unproductive employees, and the difficulty of opening and expanding outlets, and the likelihood of progress becomes infinitesimal. Bureaucracies don't compete very well.

If we want to give low- and middle-income families the same educational opportunities that wealthy families have, we must give them access to nongovernment schools. That means providing a program of vouchers or tax credits that will transform parents from hapless clients of a bureaucratic monopoly to consumers with real clout—the clout that comes from having money to spend on or to withhold from a particular supplier.

Objections to Choice

In response to the growing demand for educational choice, diehard defenders of the education monopoly have thrown up a smoke screen of charges against vouchers and tax credits. Many of the charges are the same complaints that have always been made against competitive capitalism. In fact, if American history had evolved in such a way that education was provided privately with school stamps for the poor, but food was sold in government-run grocery stores with assigned geographical areas and a Central Grocery Authority in every city and a State Department of Public Nourishment laying down the rules, the nourishment establishment would be telling us, "Of course private enterprise can provide education, but food is different; it's vitally important, consumers wouldn't know how to choose proper foods, you could never be sure there was a grocery store in your neighborhood," and so on.

Liberty magazine recently speculated about an alternative world in which telephone service had become the province of government:

> "But Mr. Freeman, how could private industry possibly provide telephone service? . . . With eight million operators, we still can't get decent phone service. The Post Office Phone System will never be privatized." . . .
> Ever since Michael Faraday had invented the telephone in Britain, governments had built giant, showy telephone systems, each trying to outdo the others with the mightiness of their networks. Elaborate palaces of communication

adorned world capitals. Massive cables with millions of wires carried signals across the country to those congressional districts fortunate enough to have one of the giant National Telephone Bases. Border translation stations, staffed with thousands of bilingual specialists, hummed with the commerce of the planet, moving vital data between financial nerve centers in mere hours. It would be hard to imagine private firms running a massive system such as this![59]

The point is that whatever enterprise the government chooses to monopolize will most likely become a massive bureaucratic undertaking, and we will find it difficult to imagine how the enterprise could be privately run. The only way that education is different from other industries is that the government runs it, so that it is expensive, inefficient, and stagnant.

"Choice Is Unconstitutional"

One objection to choice that may be unique to education is the claim that vouchers and tax credits are unconstitutional under the First Amendment because government money would be given to schools run by religious denominations (unless, of course, religious schools were forbidden to participate in a choice plan). In the first place, it should be noted that the G.I. Bill (formally, the Serviceman's Readjustment Act of 1944) was a voucher program for college students. Veterans chose the colleges they wanted to attend, and the federal government paid their tuition. Many veterans attended religious colleges, even seminaries. If the University of Notre Dame can accept students with education vouchers, why can't Potomac Muslim School?

The Supreme Court has long recognized a substantial degree of educational freedom. In a 1925 decision striking down Oregon's attempt to ban private schools, the Court ruled that

> the fundamental theory of liberty upon which all governments in this Union repose excludes any general power of the state to standardize its children by forcing them to accept instruction from public teachers only. The child is not the mere creature of the state; those who nurture him and direct

[59]Keith Lofstrom, "A Place Much Like Our Own," *Liberty*, November 1990, p. 10.

his destiny have the right, coupled with the high duty, to recognize and prepare him for additional obligations.[60]

Half a century later, Justice Lewis Powell observed in *Wolman* v. *Walter* that private schools

> have provided an educational alternative for millions of young Americans; they often afford wholesome competition with our public schools; and in some states they relieve substantially the tax burden incident to the operation of public schools. The State has, moreover, a legitimate interest in facilitating education of the highest quality for all children within its boundaries, whatever school their parents have chosen for them.[61]

In the late 1970s and early 1980s, however, the Court struck down a number of measures designed to assist private schools and their students, holding that because many of the benefits ultimately flowed to religiously sponsored institutions, the "primary effect" of such benefits was inevitably the advancement of religion. But in fact the primary effect of programs designed to ease access to private schools (including religious schools) is to expand educational opportunities. As Clint Bolick of the Landmark Center for Civil Rights has argued:

> Indeed, religiously affiliated schools appear to influence the academic success of students far more than their religiosity. More than half of inner-city parochial school students are Protestants, and fewer than 15 percent of the students in such schools describe themselves as "very religious." Even in parochial schools with mandatory religion classes, students still spend more time in secular academic classes than do public school students.[62]

In 1983, in *Mueller* v. *Allen,* the Supreme Court upheld a Minnesota statute that provided tax deductions for primary and secondary

[60]*Pierce* v. *Society of Sisters,* 268 U.S. 510, 535 (1925).

[61]*Wolman* v. *Walter,* 433 U.S. 229, 262 (1977) (Powell, J., concurring in part, concurring in judgment in part, and dissenting in part).

[62]Clint Bolick, "Solving the Education Crisis: Market Alternatives and Parental Choice," in *Beyond the Status Quo: Policy Proposals for America,* eds. David Boaz and Edward H. Crane (Washington: Cato Institute, 1985), pp. 219–20.

school expenses. Although available for both private and public school parents, most of the benefits were claimed for expenses in religiously affiliated schools. Writing for a five-member majority, Justice William Rehnquist declared that a tax deduction designed "to defray the cost of educational expenses incurred by parents— regardless of the type of schools their children attend . . . plainly serves [the] purpose of ensuring that the state's citizenry is well-educated."[63] He went on to conclude that the First Amendment prohibition against the establishment of religion "simply [does] not encompass the sort of attenuated financial benefit, ultimately controlled by the private choices of individual parents, that eventually flows to parochial schools."[64]

Mueller suggests that vouchers and tax credits may survive constitutional challenge if they are not restricted to religiously affiliated schools and are conferred directly upon parents rather than on the religiously affiliated schools.[65] Changes in the Supreme Court since 1983 make it likely that the Court will be even more sympathetic to educational choice in the 1990s than it was then.

The bottom line is that at present most nongovernment schools— and certainly most of the affordable ones—are to some degree religiously affiliated. If those schools are excluded from a school choice program, many parents will be unable to find a high-quality neighborhood school. And a voucher program that allows parents to purchase education from a Catholic school is no more an establishment of religion than is a social security program that allows recipients to use their check to make a tithe to the Catholic church.

"Choice Won't Help Unaware Parents"

One of the favorite—and most revealing—criticisms of educational choice is that it won't help parents who are uneducated, unambitious, or unaware. There is a great deal of paternalism, if

[63]*Mueller* v. *Allen*, 77 L.Ed.2d 721, 728 (1983).

[64]Ibid. at 731.

[65]For a full explanation of the impact of the *Mueller* decision, see Clint Bolick, "Private Sector Educational Alternatives and the *Mueller* Decision," *Journal of Social, Political, and Economic Studies* 9 (Spring 1984): 79; idem, "A Crack in the Wall: The Supreme Court Paves the Way for Private School Tax Relief," *Cogitations on Law and Government* (Winter 1983): 46; idem, "Choice in Education: Part II: Legal Perils and Legal Opportunities," Heritage Foundation Backgrounder no. 809, February 18, 1991.

not outright racism, in this charge. It's not the parents in Scarsdale and Fairfax County who are said to be unable to choose their children's schools; it's the parents in the ghetto. Now one might respond that random selection would give inner-city children better schools than they have now. And, as economist Thomas Sowell has pointed out, this patronizing attitude means that "black parents who want to make a better future for their children must be stopped and their children held hostage in the public schools until such time as all other people in the ghetto share their outlook."[66]

In any case, there is simply no evidence that most poor black parents cannot do an adequate job of finding good schools—if they have the wherewithal to do so and they know that their involvement in the decision will make a difference. And if even 20 percent of the parents in an inner-city neighborhood—maybe even fewer—took their children out of the local government schools, the pressure on those schools to shape up would be severe. As for inner-city parents being able to choose among many different schools, economists have demonstrated that it really isn't necessary for all or even most consumers to be well informed about market alternatives; a small number of educated consumers will force all suppliers to compete for *their* business, thereby providing reasonable combinations of price and quality for all their customers. For instance, my mother read the grocery ads carefully and compared the price and quality of meats and produce at different groceries. I just dash into the Safeway down the block and buy what's available. But because there are shoppers like my mother, I can be reasonably certain that Safeway and its competitors are attempting to offer the best value for the money possible. Certainly even an ignorant consumer like me is better off than if the government ran all the groceries in town.

"Choice Would Enhance Segregation"

A charge frequently thrown at advocates of educational choice is that choice would lead to more racial segregation in the public schools. In large measure this argument stems from memories of the "segregation academies" set up in some southern cities in

---

[66]Thomas Sowell, "Tuition Tax Credits: A Social Revolution," in Sowell, *Education: Assumptions versus History* (Stanford, Calif.: Hoover Institution Press, 1986), p. 106.

34

response to the busing orders of the 1970s. But it reflects a misunderstanding of the situation in our schools today. In the first place, choice would have the greatest effects in our inner cities, and in most inner cities the public schools are already effectively segregated. In Manhattan, for instance, the public schools are nearly 90 percent black or Hispanic, while the private schools are more than 80 percent white.[67] And James S. Coleman and Thomas Hoffer found that nationally there was a smaller percentage of black students in private schools but less racial segregation within the private sector.[68] By definition, the movement of children from the almost-all-black public schools to the less-black private schools would increase integration.

Today few private schools are segregation academies. As long as a decade ago, Oakland's inner-city Catholic schools were 95 percent black and Hispanic (and 48 percent non-Catholic). Here's what Barbara Erickson of the Berkeley Independent & Gazette found when she studied those schools:

> When Henry Jespersen came to teach at St. Columba School in Oakland after five years in the public schools, he was surprised at what he found there. They were inner-city kids, mostly poor, black and from single-parent families, and they were reading and solving math problems at levels far beyond their counterparts in . . . public schools of the same racial and economic composition.[69]

St. Mary's College High School in nearby Albany, California, was 39 percent black, 51 percent white, and 10 percent Asian and other.

The story is the same around the country: in major cities there is more racial integration in private schools than in public schools. That suggests that white parents don't object to large numbers of black students; they object to the quality of education in inner-city government schools.

Besides, do we really want to make racial integration more important than quality education for black students? In Queens, New

[67]Howard Kurtz, "Racial Quotas and the 'Tipping Point,'" Washington Post, October 19, 1987, p. A1.

[68]James S. Coleman and Thomas Hoffer, Public and Private High Schools: The Impact of Communities (New York: Basic Books, 1987), p. xxiv.

[69]Erickson, p. 1.

York, during the 1980s, more than 1,400 students every year asked to transfer from Andrew Jackson High School, a struggling, all-black high school, to high schools in nearby white neighborhoods— but the New York City Board of Education refused to let any of those nearby high schools admit more than 50 percent black students. The board's noble goal was to encourage integration, but the result was to trap black students in an ineffective high school.[70] Surely black students will be better served by schools they choose than by government schools that offer them no choices.

"Choice Means the Public Schools Won't Be a Melting Pot"

The traditional argument in favor of a unitary, near-monopoly school system—related to the concern about racial segregation—is based on the myth of the American melting pot: everyone goes to the same school and learns to get along with people of different races, different incomes, different cultures. In small towns this myth may still be reality; indeed, it was in the small Kentucky town where I went to school. But most Americans now live in cities or suburbs, and there's much less social interaction in those schools. As noted above, inner-city schools are overwhelmingly poor and black. Suburban schools are heavily middle and upper middle class. And even if they are racially integrated, almost all the students come from families of similar socioeconomic status. Charles Glenn, a long-time equal-opportunity advocate who now serves as executive director of the Office of Educational Equity in the Massachusetts Department of Education, points out that "the student body of the elite boarding school Phillips Academy in Andover, Massachusetts, is more diverse than is that of Andover High School."[71]

Only massive interdistrict busing programs could overcome the effects of largely homogeneous neighborhoods and communities. Busing tends to cause middle-class parents to withdraw from school systems that insist on sending their children to schools that are perceived as being low quality or even dangerous. As state Rep. Polly Williams of Milwaukee has said, busing is

> feel-good politics for [white liberals]. They think their kids are going to have a neat cultural experience by going to

[70]Kurtz.

[71] Charles Glenn, "Parent Choice and American Values," in *Public Schools by Choice*, ed. Joe Nathan (St. Paul: Institute for Learning and Teaching, 1989), p. 47.

school with African-American kids. But they don't want to
really relate to them; they just want to take them out to the
playground . . . so they can point to some black kids. . . .
It reminds me of a zoo. It has nothing to do with education.[72]

The melting pot theme emerged in the late 19th century as a
rather un-American fear of diversity. The Progressive reformers
wanted to force everyone into the same schools so that everyone
would receive the same education designed by those elite reformers. One of the oft-stated goals of the reformers was to use the
schools to "Christianize the immigrants"—most of whom were
Catholic. To do that they tried to discourage attendance at private
and parochial schools, a campaign that was most pronounced in
Oregon's attempt to ban nongovernment schools. What those
reformers did not realize is that the United States thrives on diversity. Our common commitment is to political and economic freedom, not to a particular set of religious and moral values. We are
most likely to produce students with the values of both individualism and respect for others by allowing parents to choose from a
diverse array of schools.

As with the concern about segregation, the real issue is whether
we want our schools to provide education or a social experience. It*
hardly makes sense to sacrifice educational achievement in the
name of a largely mythical melting pot.

"There Aren't Enough Schools"

Perhaps the most absurd criticism of educational choice is that
students can't really benefit because there aren't enough private
schools to absorb all the students who might want to transfer: after
all, there are, say, only X private schools in Cleveland and *they're
all full!* People who make such charges completely misunderstand
the nature of the free market—and have apparently never walked
down the street in a capitalist country.

The whole point of the market is that it is constantly changing,
responding to changes in supply and demand. A few years ago
there were no personal computer stores and no video stores. And
there certainly wasn't enough poultry and seafood in the groceries
a few years ago to satisfy today's demand for lower-fat meats. But

[72] "Champion of Choice" (*Reason* interview).

when demand arose for such products—or when entrepreneurs perceived that there would be demand for those products if the products were made available—stores were established to meet the demand. On every block, old stores are closing and new stores are opening to keep up with changing consumer demand. When every family has the ability to choose a private school, we can count on entrepreneurs—nonprofit and profit-seeking—to respond. After all, we want choice to lead to diversity and dynamism. We should look forward to seeing new schools established, new teaching methods tested, and new technologies employed—all of which will happen when consumer demand is there.

A related objection is that there won't be enough alternative schools in poor neighborhoods. Again, that is certainly true today, when few poor parents can find the money to send their children to independent schools. But when all parents in Harlem have $2,500 per year to spend on each child's education, we can expect schools to spring up in response (although many Harlem parents may well want to send their children to schools on the Upper East Side, in Scarsdale, or in the Catskills). There are, after all, groceries and other stores in ghettos, even though fewer than in more affluent areas because the local people have less money. But a voucher plan will mean that poor parents will have as much money to spend on education as many middle-class families, so there may well be more schools than groceries in poor neighborhoods.

"Choice Isn't Necessary; Monopoly Works in Other Countries"

People sympathetic to the idea of educational choice often point out that centralized monopoly school systems seem to work in other countries; Japan is the example usually cited. There are several problems with this argument. First, to say that one centralized monopoly is more efficient than another is not to prove very much. The U.S. Postal Service may be more efficient than other national postal monopolies, but that doesn't mean a competitive system wouldn't be better. Second, the Japanese educational system in fact has a number of competitive elements that ours lacks. Admission to good high schools is highly competitive, so parents and students work hard in the lower grades to pass that hurdle. Many high school students attend private after-hours schools, called *juku*, at family expense, to improve their chances of college admission. And the Japanese have recently been attempting to make their own schools less centralized and more creative, more like their view of American schools. Third, as Chubb and Moe have demonstrated, much of the problem with American education is not simply centralization but bureaucracy. A less-democratic society than ours, with a social consensus on what should be taught in the schools and little concern for due process in expulsions and so on, would find it easier to maintain traditional high standards. But the United States is not Japan, and we are not going to have a political system that will let the educational authorities set the rules without democratic input.

Which leads to the final point: as James Fallows put it, we should not seek to be more like Japan, we should seek to be "more like us."[73] Consensus, conformity, and order may be Japan's strengths; pluralism, diversity, individualism, and creative *disorder* are ours. Rather than try to emulate an alien system, we should build on our own strengths.

"Choice Means Giving Up on Public Schools"

This is the last-ditch defense of the education establishment: with educational choice, you're giving up on the public schools. Shouldn't we try to make the public schools work instead? The problem is that we've tried government monopoly for years, and it's just getting worse. Costs keep rising and test scores keep falling—despite a decade of high-priced reform. How many more generations of students will leave school unprepared while administrators say, "Give us just a little more time"? Teachers in government schools, who should know the state of those schools best, send their children to private schools at rates far in excess of other parents—yet they don't want to make it easy for other parents to choose alternatives.

Some defenders of the education monopoly boast that they send their children to the public schools: they say such things as, "When our children reached school age, we moved to Palo Alto, or Greenwich, so we could keep our children in the public schools." For those parents, we already have educational choice; it's just that parents have to be able to afford a $500,000 mortgage in an elite

[73]James Fallows, *More Like Us: Making America Great Again* (Boston: Houghton Mifflin, 1989).

suburb to send their children to a good school. It's time to make school choice a little more affordable.

Sometimes the claim is that educational choice would cause a wholesale flight from the government schools. But given the difficulties of finding a new school, quite possibly farther from home than the neighborhood government school, as well as the natural tendency to stick with the familiar, surely such a wholesale flight would indicate that the government schools are truly terrible. If that were the case, why should we want to force students to stay there? At least the mass exodus would give the government schools a strong signal that they need to reform; and if they were unable to do so, society would be far better off if parents were allowed to get their children a good education elsewhere.

As for the notion that a school-choice plan would allow the private schools to "skim the cream" of the students and leave the government schools with "the dregs," such an attitude reflects a bureaucratic mentality that treats students and parents as a caseload rather than as customers. Profit-seeking businesses rarely describe potential customers as dregs. Schools would develop to meet a variety of educational needs, and some of them would likely be able to motivate the students written off by the bureaucratic schools as unmotivated, undisciplined, or uneducable. Indeed, Marva Collins's Westside Prep in Chicago has a long tradition of teaching Shakespeare to elementary students tagged as "learning disabled" by the public schools; those students weren't learning disabled, they were schooling disabled. Under educational choice, all schools would improve to attract the students whose parents are most demanding, and consequently, the schools would be better able to educate the less-motivated students.

No Downside Risk

The fundamental issue is that the government schools are failing. Like bureaucratic monopolies from Moscow to Nairobi to Buenos Aires to the U.S. Postal Service, they have failed to serve their customers, fallen woefully behind in technology and innovation, and demanded higher and higher subsidies. American schools are not teaching the skills that American workers need to compete in a global market. Our current school system is doing the worst job with students who need a good education most—those whose families fail to give them the knowledge and the learning skills they will need to earn a decent living.

Yes, there will probably be bad schools in a competitive education market, just as there are bad restaurants, bad barbershops, and bad automobiles. But anyone who has compared the range of restaurants and automobiles available in the competitive U.S. market with that found in an uncompetitive market such as Poland's will recognize that the odds of finding a good product in a competitive market are enormously higher than in a monopoly system. Indeed—and obviously—even what may be judged to be bad products in a competitive market are almost always an order of magnitude better than the best products available in noncompetitive systems. And the U.S. educational system is in many ways less competitive than, say, the Warsaw grocery market. At least Poles are not assigned to groceries by geographical districts.

For anyone who doesn't trust private education providers, the neighborhood public school will still be available under a school-choice plan. Alternative schools that are not as good as the existing public schools will not likely attract much business. And particularly in our inner cities, the public schools are so bad that a range of alternatives could hardly be worse.

Political Prospects for Choice

Support for radical reform of the education monopoly is growing. A 1990 Gallup poll showed that 62 percent of Americans favored educational choice. Support was slightly higher among parents with children in the public schools and in big cities. It was highest among middle-income people and among nonwhites, 72 percent of whom backed choice. Interestingly, support varied directly with age: 54 percent of people over 50, 63 percent of those aged 30 to 49, and 72 percent of those aged 18 to 29 supported choice.[74] A 1985 poll by the Chicago Panel on Public School Policy and Finance revealed that 69 percent of parents with children in Chicago's public schools would enroll their children in private schools if they could afford it.[75]

[74]Stanley M. Elam, "The 22nd Annual Gallup Poll of the Public's Attitudes toward the Public Schools," *Phi Delta Kappan*, September 1990, pp. 42–55.

[75]Patrick J. Keleher, Jr., "Equity, Economics, and Education Vouchers: Redistributing the Redistribution" (Chicago: TEACH America, 1990).

Public school choice has been in effect in East Harlem for some 15 years, and even this halfway form of educational choice has produced some impressive results, as Sy Fliegel reports in this volume. When East Harlem's public school choice plan began in 1974, District No. 4 ranked last out of New York City's 32 districts in reading scores. Within a decade the district ranked 16th, and it held that ranking through the 1980s. The proportion of students reading at or above grade level rose from 15.9 percent to 62.6 percent. In 1988 Minnesota created a statewide choice plan, allowing students to attend any school in the state (subject to certain bureaucratic restrictions). Although it's too early to judge the success of the Minnesota plan, it's already being emulated; in 1989 alone, 23 states considered some form of educational choice.[76] And four states—Nebraska, Iowa, Arkansas, and Ohio—have now followed Minnesota's lead and implemented statewide choice plans.

Cambridge, Massachusetts, enacted a citywide choice plan in 1981, as described by Robert Peterkin in this volume. Despite strict rules about racial balance, more than 90 percent of Cambridge students get to attend one of their first three choices, and average combined SAT scores of public school students have risen 89 points over the past seven years. And, after a decade of public school choice, both white and black students in Montclair, New Jersey, are scoring well above national averages on standardized tests.[77]

Even the nation's governors—in a sense the chief executive officers of our 50 monopoly education systems—are declaring their own systems bankrupt and in need of fundamental change. At the 1989 presidential summit on education in Charlottesville, Virginia, President Bush and the governors declared their "willingness to dramatically alter our system of education" because "more of the same will not achieve the results we need."[78] Unfortunately, like Mikhail Gorbachev, so far they have been better at identifying the problem than at implementing a solution.

[76]Clint Bolick, "A Primer on Choice in Education: Part I—How Choice Works," Heritage Foundation Backgrounder no. 760, March 21, 1990.

[77]Jaclyn Fierman, "Giving Parents a Choice of Schools," *Fortune*, December 4, 1989.

[78]"The Statement by the President and Governors," *New York Times*, October 1, 1989, sec. IV, p. 22.

Business leaders have long been committed to improving the public schools in the face of overwhelming evidence that monopoly doesn't work. Perhaps the low point of their efforts has been the numerous "Adopt a School" programs around the country, in which a particular business gives money and other contributions to one local school. It would be equally logical to try to solve the problems of the U.S. Postal Service with an "Adopt a Post Office" campaign. In both cases the problems are systemic, structural, and a result of the system's monopoly status—and not simply of a shortage of money. But some business leaders are finally beginning to suggest that the very system that has made U.S. business successful be applied to schools. The California Business Roundtable is backing statewide "school of choice" legislation. The City Club of Chicago and the Illinois Manufacturers Association have joined forces to support educational choice.[79] The Louisiana Association of Business and Industry, forced to rely on the graduates of one of the country's worst statewide school systems, has proposed a choice plan for that state. And the Arizona Business Leadership for Education, a group of leading executives, has issued a report calling for a "market-driven system" of open enrollment on a statewide basis.[80]

Dissatisfied parents and taxpayers have pressured city councils and legislatures to come up with a variety of alternatives to the education monopoly, although few such alternatives really qualify as school-choice plans. As of 1990, each of the 600 government schools in Chicago is governed by an elected parent-majority council with wide authority over the school's educational priorities and budget—and the power to hire and fire the principal. Chelsea, Massachusetts, has turned over the management of its public schools to Boston University for 10 years. Boston University president John Silber also tried to get the city of Boston to make the same arrangement; he promised to cut costs and produce better results. Half a dozen states have authorized themselves to take over the

[79]Heritage Foundation Business/Education Insider no. 1, March 1990.
[80]Peter West, "Arizona Business Leaders Issue School-Reform Plan," *Education Week*, November 14, 1990, p. 22.

management of school districts that fail to produce adequate results; the first place such a threat has been carried out is Jersey City.[81]

In some parts of the United States, teachers, frustrated by the bureaucracy of impersonal school systems, have transformed themselves into entrepreneurs, contracting with schools or school districts to provide specified services. About 50 such teachers have formed the American Association of Educators in Private Practice.[82] Ombudsman Educational Services Ltd. of Libertyville, Illinois, operates what founder Jim Boyle calls "electronic one-room schoolhouses." As a public school teacher, principal, and assistant superintendent, he found it impossible to implement new ideas. So he opened Ombudsman and now has 800 students at 22 schools in Illinois, Minnesota, and Arizona. The schools provide individualized instruction for students about to drop out. Boyle charges less than half what the contracting school districts spend per student and boasts an 85 percent success rate.[83] In Miami Beach, the Dade County school system has contracted with Education Alternatives Inc., a for-profit company from Minneapolis, to run South Pointe Elementary School for five years.[84]

Around the country, more and more parents are giving up on the government schools and the various reform plans and are putting their children into alternative schools. In metropolitan Baltimore, for instance, public school enrollment is down 15 percent in 10 years while private school enrollment is up 50 percent.[85]

Other parents are fed up not only with public schools but also with private schools—which, in today's barely competitive market, often have similarly uncreative styles of teaching and learning. Some of those parents have begun teaching their children at home. It's estimated that the number of children being taught at home has

[81]Chester E. Finn, Jr., "The Radicalization of School Reform," *Wall Street Journal*, February 2, 1990.

[82]Carolyn Lochhead, "A Lesson from Private Practitioners," *Insight*, December 24, 1990–January 7, 1991, pp. 34–36.

[83]Ibid.

[84]Steven A. Holmes, "In Miami, a Private Company Will Operate a Public School," *New York Times*, December 7, 1990, p. A12.

[85]Monica Norton, "Boom Times for Private Schools," *Evening Sun* (Baltimore), October 30, 1990.

risen from 10,000 to 15,000 in the 1970s to some 60,000 to 120,000 in the mid-1980s to as many as 300,000 to 500,000 today.[86]

Home schoolers predict that as more and more home-schooled students take the SAT and enter college, the education establishment is going to be faced with the embarrassing fact that most of them will be able to outperform students taught in the public schools—demonstrating that there's nothing magic about teaching children and that the public schools are thoroughly to blame for today's educational problems. Already, the establishment is preparing its response, but it's one that does not seem to make much of a claim for the educational advantages of the public schools. According to Gene Wilhoit, executive director of the National Association of School Boards, "We think that children should be in the traditional setting because home schooling takes away from a child's social skills and isolates children racially and ethnically."[87] Home-schooling parents take pains to see that their children spend time with other children, but—given that most families are indeed monoracial—they would probably have to acknowledge that during school hours their children are "racially isolated."

Of all the political challenges to the education establishment, the most important is the Milwaukee voucher plan shepherded through the Wisconsin legislature by state Rep. Polly Williams. Williams— a Democrat, former welfare mother, and Jesse Jackson's Wisconsin campaign chairman in 1984 and 1988—put the lie to the claim that educational choice is some sort of scheme of the religious right and also left Wisconsin's white liberal establishment sputtering in frustration as Republicans—including Gov. Tommy Thompson— lined up behind her legislation. As passed, the plan would give a $2,500-per-year voucher to 1 percent of Milwaukee's public school students—that is, just under 1,000 children—to be used in any nonsectarian private school. Williams reacted with scorn to fellow Democrats in the state legislature who wouldn't back her plan: "They say they're liberal, but whenever it comes to empowering

[86]William Celis 3d, "Growing Number of Parents Are Opting to Teach at Home," *New York Times*, November 22, 1990, p. A1. Some estimates run as high as 1 million. See Casey Banas, "More Parents Teaching Children Themselves," *Chicago Tribune*, May 29, 1989, p. 8.
[87]Celis.

45

black people, they stab us in the back. We want self-determination, not handouts and dependency."[88]

The education establishment wasn't willing to take the state legislature's yes for an answer. After the plan was passed, the teachers' union and State Superintendent of Public Instruction Herbert Grover went to court to get the plan overturned. Among their charges was that the plan would let schools operate without any accountability to the taxpayers. Education reformer John E. Chubb of the Brookings Institution responded:

> That's a laughable position. Milwaukee officials have been holding their public schools "accountable" for years with disastrous results. It's quite comical to say that private schools whose diplomas are recognized by state universities can't be held accountable by the parents who send their kids there.[89]

After the education establishment lost on the merits of the case, it went back to court arguing that the technicalities of legislative procedure had been violated when the bill was passed. Having grown up in Kentucky, where most of our laws passed after the biennial legislative session had legally expired—and having lived in Washington in 1982 when the biggest tax increase in U.S. history was unconstitutionally initiated in the U.S. Senate instead of the House—I know how seriously the political establishment and the courts take such technicalities when they approve of the legislation in question. Assuming Polly Williams's voucher plan survives the education establishment's counterattacks, almost 1,000 low-income black children will have a chance to get a decent education outside the Milwaukee school monopoly, and the plan is likely to spread.

After just one semester, the plan seems to be working as well as Polly Williams predicted. According to the *New York Times*:

> Wisconsin school officials say it is too early to assess the program officially. But as the program's first semester draws to a close, the parents [of the 345 students who managed to transfer to private schools] speak in jubilant tones about their children's progress, directors of the six participating private schools describe a relatively smooth transition and

[88]Quoted in "Up from Mediocrity," *Wall Street Journal*, March 29, 1990.
[89]"The Polly Williams Backlash," *Wall Street Journal*, June 14, 1990.

[seven-year-old] Javon Williams, for one, says that for the first time he looks forward to school.

Javon's mother said the public schools bored him, giving him "baby work," but that Urban Day School had challenged him and turned his energy from fighting to learning. Another parent, Fernando Delgadillo, said that the public schools gave his two daughters "rote learning" but that the Woodlands School teaches them to "reflect and analyze and be creative." And Gail Draeger said, "I'll rob a bank if I have to" to keep from sending her daughter Erica back to the public schools.[90]

In 1990 an initiative to establish an education tax credit program was placed on the Oregon ballot by a small group of parents and taxpayers, none of whom was an elected official. Although the organizers managed to get 127,000 signatures on their petitions, opponents threw every conceivable charge at the initiative: it would cost the state money, violate the separation of church and state, give taxpayers' money to "cult schools" and out-of-state schools, and so on. Television ads showed a classroom full of children in Ku Klux Klan robes. Some of the charges stuck; the voters of Oregon were understandably reluctant to make such a major change in their educational system without being sure about the idea, and the initiative lost. But most initiatives proposing new ideas fail the first—and the second—time they are on the ballot, and educational choice will be back on the ballot, in Oregon or elsewhere, in 1992.

Already, across the country, the small town of Epsom, New Hampshire, has instituted a $1,000 tax rebate for families that send their children anywhere but the local public high school; the education establishment is planning a lawsuit.[91] The latest indication of the demand for educational choice is in Chicago, where 27 low-income parents have filed suit against the state of Illinois, claiming that the state has failed to meet the state constitutional mandate to give their children "high quality public education" and asking to

<hr>

[90]Isabel Wilkerson, "For 345, Poverty Is Key to Door of Private School," *New York Times*, December 19, 1990.

[91]Fox Butterfield, "Tax Rebate in New Hampshire Town Poses Test for School-Choice Issue," *New York Times*, January 30, 1991.

be allowed to use their share of state education money at non-government schools.[92] As long as state legislatures resist making real changes in the education monopoly, parents are going to look for ways to take matters into their own hands.

Is Educational Choice a Panacea?

Toward the end of their book, Chubb and Moe wrote, "It is fashionable these days to say that choice is 'not a panacea.' Taken literally, this is obviously true." But they go on to say that only choice will address the basic institutional causes of educational failure and thus that "reformers would do well to entertain the notion that choice *is* a panacea. . . . It has the capacity *all by itself* to bring about the kind of transformation that, for years, reformers have been seeking to engineer in myriad other ways."[93]

Chubb and Moe make the point that choice must not be considered just one among many strategies for reform, as Chester E. Finn, Jr., of the Education Excellence Network did in a recent speech:

> A full policy agenda [for education reform] will entail ten or a dozen significant changes. . . . I'd draw curriculum, for example, from California and accountability [from] South Carolina and New Jersey; choice from Minnesota; school site management and parent control from Chicago and Miami; alternate certification of teachers from New Jersey; school-level report cards from California or Illinois; teacher career ladders from Tennessee and Cincinnati; "no pass–no play" rules from Texas; parent education from Missouri; increasingly hard-nosed business involvement from several places, and so on.[94]

Finn's proposal is the equivalent of telling an Eastern European reformer that his country needs double-entry bookkeeping, high-tech factories, a better telephone system, property rights and free markets, trained managers, foreign investment, and a stock market.

[92]Amy Stuart Wells, "Chicago Parents' Suit Adds New Twist to Voucher Issue," *New York Times*, December 19, 1990; Maribeth Vander Weele, "Lawsuit Asks a Voucher Program for Schools Here," *Chicago Sun-Times*, December 14, 1990.

[93]Chubb and Moe, *Politics, Markets, and America's Schools*, pp. 215–17. (Emphasis in original.)

[94]Chester E. Finn, Jr., "Real Education Reform for the 1990s," Heritage Foundation Lectures no. 256, February 23, 1990.

Creating a system of property rights and free markets will lead to the right mix of all those other hallmarks of an advanced economy. Similarly, educational choice will lead, as if by an invisible hand, to the selection of the best ideas for educational improvement—not just those currently being tried by government schools but also new ideas that bureaucrats would never dream of and that entrepreneurs will naturally discover.

Conclusion

Rising costs and slipping performance are typical of bureaucracy, monopoly, and socialism around the world. What we need is an educational *perestroika*. So far, as with Gorbachev's Soviet Union, we have had lots of *glasnost* but little *perestroika*—lots of talk about how bad the system is but little real reform. It's time for real reform. It's time to give parents the opportunity to choose the schools their children will attend, just as they choose the family's housing, food, medical care, clothing, and entertainment. Specifically, it's time to give working-class and poor families the same opportunity that rich families have to choose good schools.

A program of vouchers or education tax credits, with few restrictions on the kind of schools that parents can choose and a reasonable figure of $2,500 or so per student, will give families the clout that valued customers have. Schools will compete to attract them. Parents will be more involved in their children's education. Teachers will be freed to teach unhampered by a stack of regulations from a distant central office. Businesses will be able to hire the educated workers that a world-class economy in the information age demands. And most important, students will be able to attend schools that meet their needs and that make learning an exciting experience.

2. The Performance of America's Primary and Secondary Schools

William A. Niskanen

America's public schools are not serving us well. Over the whole period since World War II, real (inflation-adjusted) spending per student has increased about 40 percent a decade, doubling every 20 years. During much of this period, however, average test scores have declined substantially. Although test scores increased somewhat in the 1980s, American students' scores on mathematics and science tests are among the lowest of all the industrial countries. We are spending much more for schooling, but our students are receiving less education. Our public schools must bear a substantial part of the responsibility for this condition—although not the full responsibility, because a variety of demographic and social conditions have also affected these results. In an increasingly competitive world, the performance of our schools must improve. Our economic well-being, our national security, and the nature of our national community are at stake.

School Inputs and Educational Outputs

This essay compares two "snapshots" of America's primary and secondary schools—one taken in 1975 and the other in 1985, years that bracket the end of the substantial decline in student test scores.[1] Each snapshot summarizes the major inputs to our schools and several measurable dimensions of the outputs of our schools. All of the data presented in the accompanying tables are from one source, the *Statistical Abstract of the United States*, an annual publication of the federal government that is available in any public library.[2]

---

[1] The average composite scores on both the Scholastic Aptitude Test and the Iowa Tests of Educational Development (for grade 12), for example, were lowest in 1979.

[2] Bureau of the Census, *Statistical Abstract of the United States* (Washington: U.S. Government Printing Office, 1988 and prior issues). All dollar data for 1975 are adjusted to 1985 dollars by the GNP fixed-weight deflator.

Any concerned parent would have easy access to these same data. Some of my observations, however, also draw from more specialized reports and studies. A comparison of these snapshots provides a basis for identifying the major changes in the inputs and outputs of our schools.

These tables reflect the average conditions in our schools. The performance of some schools, of course, is much better than average, but that implies that the performance of other schools is much worse. A comparison of snapshots, though, is not a sufficient basis for identifying the effect of specific school inputs on educational outputs, because changes in the socioeconomic composition of student bodies and the characteristics of families and communities also affect educational performance. For a more thorough understanding of the effects of school inputs and other conditions on educational performance, we must draw on other studies, but we must also be prepared to recognize that no one understands this complex process very well.

School Inputs

The necessary inputs to a school are a building, teachers, administrators and support personnel, supplies, and students. Although these are the necessary and most measurable inputs, they are not the most important inputs that affect educational performance. Indeed, the most careful and comprehensive survey of the conditions that affect educational performance concludes that (within the range of variation of the measurable school inputs, both over time and across schools) "differences in [school] quality do not seem to reflect variations in expenditures, class sizes, or other commonly measured attributes of schools and teachers."[3] The most important characteristics that distinguish good schools from poor schools, according to a major study by John Chubb and Terry Moe, are subtle differences in the school environment that are not related to variations in the major measurable inputs.[4] Nevertheless, it is worthwhile to start this discussion by summarizing the level and

[3]Eric A. Hanushek, "The Economics of Schooling: Production and Efficiency in the Public Schools," *Journal of Economic Literature* 24, no. 3 (September 1986).

[4]John E. Chubb and Terry M. Moe, *Politics, Markets, and America's Schools* (Washington: Brookings Institution, 1990). The major findings of this study are summarized in the paper by Chubb and Moe in this volume.

changes in the major measurable school inputs. The major focus here is on public schools because nearly 90 percent of primary and secondary students are now enrolled in such schools. Nevertheless, it is also important to recognize the most important differences in the inputs to public and private schools.

Table 2–1 summarizes the major inputs to public and private schools in 1975 and 1985 and the percentage changes in these inputs over the 10-year period. The data reflect the total inputs (other than

Table 2–1
SCHOOL EXPENDITURES, EMPLOYMENT, AND PRICES,
1975 AND 1985

Category	1975	1985	Percentage Change
Expenditures (billions of dollars[a])			
Public Schools			
Total	117.7	136.5	16.0
Federal	10.9	8.9	−18.1
State	49.3	66.3	34.6
Local and Private	57.6	61.3	6.5
Private Schools[b]			
Total	13.0	12.4	−4.9
Employment (thousands)			
Public Schools			
Total	3,969	4,416	11.3
Teachers	2,055	2,210	7.5
Others	1,914	2,206	15.3
Private[b]			
Teachers	255	343	34.5
Relative Prices (1975 = 100)			
Public Schools			
Total	100	121.5	21.5
Professional Salaries	100	112.1	12.1
Other Salaries	100	110.5	10.5
Fringe Benefits	100	213.7	113.7
Supplies and Services	100	117.1	17.1

[a]In 1985 dollars.
[b]Estimated.

students) into primary and secondary schools, not the inputs per student, but by themselves they reveal some interesting patterns:

- Total real expenditures by public schools increased 16 percent over the decade. Over the past several decades, state government financing has grown most rapidly, and states have now become the major source of public school finance and regulation.
- Total employment in public schools increased by about 11 percent over the decade. The number of nonteaching employees increased twice as fast as the number of teachers and is now nearly equal to the number of classroom teachers. The number of teachers in private schools increased almost 35 percent. (Aggregate data on nonteaching employees in private schools are not available.)
- The relative price of inputs into public schools increased 21.5 percent over the decade. Real salaries increased by 10–12 percent, but real fringe benefits more than doubled. (Similar data for private schools are not available.)

During the same 10-year period, total enrollment in public and private schools changed substantially, but in different directions. For this reason, the enrollment and input ratios presented in Table 2–2 are more interesting than the data presented in Table 2–1. Over the 1975–85 decade, there were three dramatic and contrasting developments in U.S. public and private schools:

- Total enrollment in public schools declined by nearly 14 percent, but (estimated) enrollment in private schools increased by 12 percent. There was a net increase of about 600,000 in private school enrollment; this was a result (although not shown in Table 2–2) of an enrollment decline of nearly 600,000 in Catholic private schools and an enrollment increase of about 1.2 million in non-Catholic private schools. This substantial reallocation of students, during a period in which the total U.S. student population declined by about 6 million, reflects a mix of motives that are not yet well understood.
- Total real expenditures per student increased by about 35 percent in public schools but declined by about 15 percent in private schools. With respect to public schools, the decline in enrollment did permit a reduction in real spending for capital,

Table 2–2
SCHOOL ENROLLMENT AND INPUT RATIOS, 1975 AND 1985

Category	1975	1985	Percentage Change
Enrollment (thousands)			
Public	45,909	39,513	−13.9
Private[a]	5,000	5,600	12.0
Expenditures per Student (dollars[b])			
Public			
Total	2,564	3,455	34.8
Current[c]	2,104	3,211	52.6
Private[b]			
Total	2,607	2,214	−15.1
Students per Unit			
Public			
Per District	2,715	2,489	−8.3
Per School	522	470	−9.8
Catholic			
Per School	342	305	−11.7
Students per Employee			
Public			
Total	11.6	8.9	−22.6
Per Teacher	22.3	17.9	−20.0
Per Other Employee	24.0	17.9	−25.3
Private			
Per Teacher	19.6	16.3	−16.7

[a]Estimated.
[b]In 1985 dollars.
[c]Current expenditures exclude capital expenditures, interest on school debt, and other expenditures not related to the regular day-school program.

interest, and peripheral programs; excluding these spending categories, real current expenditures per student enrolled in regular public school programs increased by more than 50 percent. With respect to private schools, it should be noted that several conditions might have been expected to increase real spending: the increase in enrollment must have increased capital spending, the number of teachers increased more rapidly than enrollment, and the share of lay teachers in Catholic schools increased substantially. Clearly, the conditions that contributed to the decline in real expenditures per student in private schools are not yet understood.

- In 1975, real expenditures per student in both public and private schools were about the same, but by 1985, such spending was about 50 percent higher in public schools than in private schools. Because both the expenditures and enrollment data for private schools are estimates, some part of this difference may be attributable to sampling error. Nevertheless, the magnitude and potential implications of this difference are too large to dismiss, and the difference should be a major focus of additional research.

Two other trends were common to both public and private schools during the 1975–85 period. First, the average number of students per school district and the number of students per school in both public and Catholic schools declined by about the same percentage, despite the continued consolidation of school districts and the closing of many schools. Enrollment in the average public school has continued to be about 50 percent larger than in the average Catholic school. (Similar aggregate data on non-Catholic private schools are not available.) Second, the average number of students per teacher (a rough proxy for average class size if teaching hours per teacher are constant) also declined by about the same percentage in both public and private schools.

The average class size continued to be about 10 percent higher in public schools than in private schools. And the number of students per nonteaching employee in public schools declined substantially, reflecting the increased number of administrators, counselors, security personnel, and school bus drivers. Aggregate data on the number of nonteaching employees in private schools are not available, but selective evidence indicates that the number of such employees is relatively much smaller than in public schools; this may be one of the major reasons for the lower average cost per student in private schools, but (as mentioned above) more research is needed on this issue.

In summary, the most important changes in school inputs between 1975 and 1985 were the divergent trends in real expenditures and enrollment between public and private schools. Real expenditures by public schools increased substantially, despite a substantial decline in enrollment. Real expenditures by private schools declined slightly, despite a substantial increase in enrollment. The reasons for the substantial divergence in these trends, however, are not yet fully understood.

Educational Outputs

A school produces many types of outputs, but not all of them can be easily measured. Furthermore, they differ substantially in how they are valued by voters, taxpayers, employers, parents, and students. For these reasons, no one measurable condition suffices as an index of the outputs of primary and secondary schools or, more important, of the value of these outputs. With full recognition of this problem, this section focuses on three reported measures of school output—school completion and advancement rates, composite scores on the major college tests, and post-school employment and earnings. These data primarily reflect the outputs of public schools and do not permit a distinction between the outputs of public and private schools.[5]

Table 2–3 summarizes the percentage of the student-age population completing high school and the percentage of high school graduates enrolled in college and completing one or more years of college. These data reveal two trends:

- The percentage of teenagers completing high school by the normal age has been roughly constant for two decades. The 1985 rate, for example, is somewhat lower than the 1970 rate and slightly higher than the 1965 rate (the latter two rates are not shown in the table). The share of the population completing high school by age 29, however, increased by about 9 percent between 1975 and 1985, reflecting in part the increased attention given to adult education.

[5]The painstaking empirical studies by James Coleman and his colleagues, however, suggest that educational performance is about one grade lower in public schools than in Catholic schools, even when controlled for student, family, and community characteristics and other conditions that may lead to a selection bias. Moreover, the average public school is less integrated than the average Catholic school, and minority students generally do better in Catholic schools. For an efficient summary of these studies, see James Coleman, "Do Students Learn More in Private Schools Than in Public Schools?" *Florida Policy Review* 5, no. 1 (Summer 1989).

Table 2–3
SCHOOL COMPLETION AND ADVANCEMENT RATES, 1975 AND 1985 (PERCENT)

Category	1975	1985	Change
High School Completion			
Population Aged 17	73.6	73.3	−0.4
Population Aged 25 to 29	79.2	86.1	8.8
College Experience			
High School Graduates Enrolled	33.1	34.1	3.6
High School Graduates Completing			
One or More Years	52.1	54.3	3.4

- The percentages of high school graduates enrolled in college or completing one or more years of college each increased by 3–4 percent. This record, however, should be tempered by other data (not shown): 25 percent of college freshmen in 1984 were enrolled in one or more remedial courses, and 63 percent of colleges reported that enrollment in remedial courses increased by 10 percent or more between 1978 and 1984.[6]

The combination of these data suggests that the high schools have maintained a roughly constant graduation rate only by tolerating an erosion in the quality of schooling in the basic subjects.

Table 2–4 summarizes the composite scores and the percentage of high school graduates tested by the two major college entrance tests, the Scholastic Aptitude Test (SAT) and the American College Testing Program (ACT). The most striking finding evident in the table is that there was no net change in the composite scores on either test between 1975 and 1985, despite the large increase in real expenditures per student in the public schools. Maybe we should be thankful for small favors; during the prior 10 years, the composite test scores declined sharply, despite a similar increase in real expenditures per student. The recent stability of the composite scores on both tests is especially interesting because the tests are quite different. The SAT is primarily a test of problem-solving skills, closer to an IQ test. The ACT is primarily a test of the substantive understanding of four basic subjects. The quality of our primary

---

[6]*Statistical Abstract of the United States*, p. 142.

Table 2–4
PERFORMANCE OF HIGH SCHOOL GRADUATES ON COLLEGE ENTRANCE TESTS, 1975 AND 1985

Category	1975	1985	Percentage Change
Scholastic Aptitude Test (SAT)			
Composite Score	906	906	0.0
Percentage Tested	31.8	36.4	14.5
American College Testing Program (ACT)			
Composite Score	18.6	18.6	0.0
Percentage Tested	22.8	27.5	20.6

and secondary schools does not seem to be improving in either dimension, despite the substantial increase in real expenditures per student and the accumulation of conventional efforts at educational reform.

The interpretation of these results, however, should be tempered by recognizing two contrary trends. On the one hand, the number of students tested has increased substantially relative to the number of high school graduates (although some of this increase may be spurious if more students are taking the tests more than once). To the extent that a broader student population is being tested, the recent composite scores somewhat understate student performance. On the other hand, many schools increasingly "teach to the tests," and many students take supplementary test-preparation courses. For this reason, the test scores of college-bound students may overstate the performance of the average student. This issue is not easy to resolve. A more accurate indicator may be the scores on the tests taken by all high school seniors in several states. In both California and Iowa, for example, the average test scores of high school seniors have also been roughly constant over the 1975–85 period.[7] The results of these tests of high school seniors suggest that the composite scores on the SAT and ACT may not be significantly biased. On balance, the data indicate that average student performance on objective tests of both problem-solving

[7]Congressional Budget Office, *Trends in Educational Achievement* (April 1986), pp. 104 and 109.

59

skills and substantive understanding is no longer declining; the
current problem is that student performance is not increasing, or
not increasing very much, despite the substantial increase in real
expenditures per student.

Table 2–5 summarizes the employment and earnings records of
high school graduates who are not enrolled in college and also of
high school dropouts. To put these data in context, it is important
to understand certain changes in the general U.S. economy between
1975 and 1985. Nineteen seventy-five was the trough year of the
severe 1974–75 recession, and 1985 was the third year of recovery
from the severe 1981–82 recession. Total employment as a share of
the total adult civilian population increased by 7.3 percent during
the 10-year period. The population aged 16–21 not enrolled in
college declined from 6.9 percent to 5.1 percent of the total adult
civilian population, a condition that should have tightened the
market for low-skilled labor. The real foreign-exchange value of the
dollar increased by about 40 percent, increasing the competitiveness
of foreign products and labor. And the average real hourly wage
rate in the total nonagricultural economy increased 4.5 percent.
These changes in the general economy provide context for understanding the following two trends in the post–high school employment and earnings of those not enrolled in college:

- The employment rates (through age 21) for high school graduates not enrolled in college and for high school dropouts each

Table 2–5
EMPLOYMENT AND EARNINGS AFTER HIGH SCHOOL,
1975 AND 1985

Category	1975	1985	Percentage Change
Employment Rate (percent)			
Graduates	70.5	73.1	3.8
Dropouts	43.7	46.4	6.3
Annual Earnings (dollars[a])			
Graduates	13,048	12,680	−2.8
Dropouts	12,285	11,407	−7.2

[a]In 1985 dollars.

increased, but by a lower percentage than the 7.3 percent for the total adult population.

- The real annual earnings for full-time work (for ages 18–24) declined for both high school graduates and dropouts, compared to an increase of 4.5 percent for the total adult population and 8 percent for new college graduates.

Because employment and earnings are functions of both supply and demand conditions, these data are not sufficient by themselves to identify whether the job-related skills of young workers declined or whether the demand for such skills declined; the probable answer is that the data reflect a combination of these two effects. The substantial increase in the proportion of college freshmen enrolled in remedial courses suggests that the skills of the average high school graduate declined. This period, however, was also unusual in one other respect: for the first time since World War II, the earnings of new college graduates increased relative to the earnings of young workers with only high school training. One study suggests that the substantial change in foreign trade conditions in the early 1980s increased the demand for high-skilled labor and increased the effective supply of low-skilled labor.[8] (The tightening of the teenage labor market associated with the sharp decline in the foreign-exchange value of the dollar since 1985 is also consistent with this interpretation.) More research is necessary to sort out these two effects. In summary, it appears probable, but not certain, that the average job-related skills of young workers without college training declined over this period. It is clear that the value of these skills declined. In either case, our schools, despite a substantial increase in real expenditures per student, are not adequately preparing young workers for the contemporary job market.

The several types of measures of educational output reviewed above present a disturbingly consistent record. The percentage of students completing high school by the normal age did not change. Although the percentage of high school graduates entering college increased slightly, the percentage then required to take remedial courses increased substantially. The composite scores on the two major college tests did not change. And the real earnings of new

[8]Kevin Murphy and Finis Welch, "Wage Differentials in the 1980s: The Role of International Trade" (unpublished manuscript, 1988).

high school graduates not enrolled in college declined. On net, based on these measures, the level of educational output per student did not change much between 1975 and 1985, despite the substantial increase in real expenditures per student. It is only small consolation to recognize that educational output declined in the prior decade. These types of measures, of course, do not exhaust the many dimensions of educational output. One might hope, for example, to know how much our students understand our shared history and culture or our contemporary economic and political systems. The recent tests by the National Assessment of Educational Progress (NAEP) indicate a dismally low average understanding of these subjects but do not provide a basis for estimating whether performance in these areas has improved or declined.[9]

International Comparisons

The results of international comparisons of student performance on mathematics and science tests have been even more dismal. On a 1982 test involving 17-year-old students, the United States was in the lowest fourth of 15 countries on five of six basic mathematics subjects; even the best U.S. students did not score well, placing last in tests on algebra and calculus. A 1988 test of science skills had similar results: among 14-year-old students in 17 countries, the United States placed 14th, and among advanced science students in their senior year in 13 countries, the United States ranked 9th in physics, 11th in chemistry, and last in biology.[10] This record must be improved if the U.S. economy is to maintain its leadership in industrial technology.

Developments since 1985

Many of the data for the categories covered in the accompanying tables are not yet available for the years since 1985. The available data, however, are not encouraging. Real expenditures per student have continued to increase at about the same rate. Since the 1983 report *A Nation at Risk*,[11] the pace of school reform efforts has increased. And the composite score on the SAT was constant from

[9]For a summary of these tests, see Department of Education, *American Education: Making It Work* (April 1988), pp. 12–14.

[10]Ibid., pp. 12, 13.

[11]National Commission on Excellence in Education, *A Nation at Risk* (1983).

1985 through 1987—and declined slightly in 1988 and 1989. The increasing concern of parents, employers, and politicians about the quality of our schools has not yet had much effect on school performance.

Demographic and Social Conditions

Our schools, of course, operate in an environment of changing demographic and social conditions that also affect educational performance. A careful recent study by the Congressional Budget Office (CBO), however, concludes, "It appears that the contributions of these factors were generally less substantial than many observers have thought, ranging from very small to modest."[12]

The most important demographic changes appear to be the increasing proportion of minority students and the changes in average family size, but the CBO study attributes only one-fifth to one-fourth of the decline in test scores to the sum of these conditions. Among the social conditions that appear to have had no significant effect are changes in single-parent households, maternal employment, and television viewing. There is more controversy, however, about the effects of drug use. The patterns of current drug use by people aged 12–17 are mixed. From 1974 to 1985, the percentage of this age group that was currently using marijuana remained about constant; the percentage using inhalants, cocaine, and other stimulants increased slightly; and the percentage using alcohol and tobacco declined.[13] The supply of illegal drugs may have significantly disrupted the school environment, but the mixed patterns of current drug use probably has little net effect on educational performance. On net, most of the changes in the performance of America's schools appear to be attributable to changes in the school environment, not to the other major changes in the country's population and social conditions.

Conclusion

The time for excuses is over. All of the conventional proposals for school reform have been implemented—and have failed. Real

---

[12]Congressional Budget Office, *Educational Achievement: Explanations and Implications of Recent Trends* (August 1987).

[13]*Statistical Abstract of the United States*, p. 112.

expenditures per student in our public schools have increased rapidly for 40 years, average class sizes have declined, average real teacher salaries have increased, the centralization of public school finance by state governments has substantially reduced the variation in spending per student among school districts, and there has been a gradual consolidation of the smallest school districts and schools.[14] Although average student performance increased somewhat in the 1980s, the average composite score on the SAT is now about the same as in 1974 and is much lower than it was in 1963. And the absolute level of understanding of basic subjects is dismally low, even among our best students, in terms of both our own standards and international comparisons.

There remains a legitimate controversy about the appropriate directions of future school reform. The beginning of wisdom, however, is to recognize that the current system of financing, organizing, and regulating America's public schools has failed.

---

[14]My own study of the California public school system concludes that student performance is a negative function of the size of the school district, after controlling for expenditures per student and for student, family, and community characteristics. This study was also the first to develop a proposal for a school-choice plan within the public schools. See William A. Niskanen and Mickey D. Levy, "Cities and Schools: A Case for Community Government in California" (Graduate School of Public Policy, University of California, Berkeley, 1974).

3. Inside Chicago's Schools

Bonita Brodt

One afternoon, not long after I began what was to be nearly a four-month-long odyssey as a *Chicago Tribune* reporter stationed inside one of America's troubled public schools, I happened upon an eighth-grade boy who should have been in his remedial reading class but was instead wandering aimlessly in the halls. He began to chuckle as he spotted a laborer down on his hands and knees. The man in workclothes was replacing black and maroon checkerboard squares of floor tile with light-colored squares that would make the hallways look brighter but would certainly show dirt.

"What a joke," the boy muttered, shaking his head from side to side.

"What do you mean?" I asked.

"It's like when your mom tells you to clean up your room and you put all your dirty clothes in a closet," he explained. "That's not going to make this a good school."

I often thought about this young boy's words as I followed in the footsteps of the children, parents, teachers, and administrators whose lives came together but often collided at Goudy Elementary School, one of the Chicago public school system's 402 regular elementary schools. His wisdom struck me as far beyond his years. Indeed, what a mixed-up world it was where the system's central bureaucracy would neglect this school's academic and social framework to the point of virtual collapse and yet pump $1 million into physical renovations to make sure that the building did not fall apart.

Over time, I began to see that Goudy Elementary School stands as a brick-and-mortar metaphor for a lot of what has gone wrong with U.S. public schools.

Behind the walls of this hollow educational warehouse on the North Side of Chicago, I saw firsthand how the futures of nearly 700 children were being silently but certainly shaped by an antiquated system wherein education was often secondary to a maze of other interests and each day was a test of endurance in which the most important lesson to be learned by anyone was how to survive the five-and-a-half-hour school day. I saw how the one institution that has the greatest potential to break the cycle of urban poverty had degenerated into an institutionalized case of child neglect. I saw how the racial politics of a city, the misplaced priorities of a centralized school bureaucracy, and the vested interests of a powerful teachers' union had all somehow taken precedence over the needs of the very children the schools are supposed to serve. Most of all, I saw that children—all children—deserve much better than a Goudy school.

Over the last decade or so, we in the news media have probably done a very good job of shedding light on the sorry state of U.S. public education. We've reported the grim statistics that show alarmingly high dropout rates, low teachers' salaries, embarrassing academic and social accomplishments by the students who manage to stick to it for 12 years. We've chronicled studies and reports that analyze the deficiencies in U.S. public education and we've quoted public officials, civic leaders, and caring professionals who ask tough questions and challenge the system to accomplish more. But while we may have covered the news events well enough, it was our feeling at the *Chicago Tribune* that there was a much deeper story that begged to be told. What's wrong with this country's public schools is not spot news. It didn't happen overnight.

And so, in the fall of 1987, the *Chicago Tribune* launched a seven-month examination of the third-largest public school system in the United States, the Chicago Public Schools. Our series of articles, published in May 1988, was called "Chicago Schools: 'Worst in America.' " I was the principal reporter on the project, one of seven reporters who undertook the assignment, and our stories—many of which came from inside Goudy Elementary School—provided a telling glimpse of what public education has come to mean.

When we began, the time was ripe for an unflinching look at the schools that fail Chicago. That fall, the city's 419,537 public school children were shut out of their classrooms when the Chicago Teachers Union flexed its considerable muscle and carried out a record 19-day teachers' strike. The public outcry was huge.

Then the national spotlight shone on the city's troubled schools. During a visit to Chicago that November, William Bennett—then

66

the U.S. secretary of education—surveyed the wreckage and called the Chicago public school system "the worst in America," a stinging rebuke that drew fire from defensive city politicians and school bureaucrats but hit right where it hurt.

"How can anyone who feels about children not feel terrible about Chicago schools?" Bennett asked. He was talking about a school system that boasts some dismal statistics: nearly half the children who enroll in Chicago schools drop out before graduation, and ample information suggests that many of those who manage to endure 12 years do not fare altogether well. The average high school graduate in Chicago reads like an eighth grader. And if that isn't bad enough, in 1989, once again, half the city's public high schools placed in the bottom 1 percent of U.S. schools in the ranking of how their students scored on the standard college entrance exam, the American College Testing Program (ACT).

Tolerating Failure

Our reporting revealed that Bennett's message was stitched together with more than a single strand of truth. We found overwhelming evidence that the Chicago Public Schools were a disgrace.

Indeed, not all of the 595 elementary and secondary schools in Chicago were failures, nor were all of the 28,675 teachers and 419,537 students below par. We saw flashes of excellence, children who were learning and happy to be in school, and teachers who cared. But success was the exception. Failure was not necessarily encouraged but it was tolerated to an inordinate degree.

In the early stage of our reporting, I talked to dozens of teachers and administrators throughout the school system to try to get a handle on how things could have gone so wrong. Comments from two school principals—one who led one of the city's most successful public elementary schools and another who was at the helm of an all-black public high school with more than its share of problems— told me a great deal about the bureaucracy that was responsible for both schools.

One of the schools, Bell Elementary, is a neighborhood school with a selective-admission program for children who can test into the school system's program for "gifted" students. Children in this program routinely test two to three years above grade level on the standardized tests. That year, although Bell's eighth-grade children had led the city in their reading scores, parents and teachers expressed disappointment when this became another accomplishment that went unnoticed by the central bureaucracy or the school board. "Wouldn't it have been nice," the principal told me, "if we would have had a letter from somebody congratulating us for our achievement that I could have displayed on the school bulletin board?"

Then there was Crane High School on the city's West Side, a school responsible for educating students whose lives are mired in poverty and savaged by social problems. Ninety percent of the student body comes from nearby high-rise public housing projects. Here, reading and mathematics scores are among the lowest in the city, and the dropout rate is among the highest.

That school's principal had been in charge of the school for several years, long enough to see that the problems that beset his student population had been festering for a long, long while. I asked him if school officials had ever done anything to recognize Crane's obstacles or had given him the kind of resources that would help him reach out to the needy children who depend on his school. He thought for a moment. Then he shook his head. "No," he said. "I can't think of one thing."

It was this lack of concern that piqued our curiosity. How could the system have become so unresponsive to the staggering needs of students?

The most basic civics lesson about Chicago would have to explain that the public schools have been something of a political playground ever since the city's first public school opened its doors in 1834. As Chicago developed into a major northern industrial city, and immigrants and blacks migrated to settle and look for opportunity, Chicago took shape as a city of factories and stockyards and of segregated neighborhoods with boundaries often defined along racial and ethnic lines.

Three decades ago, the majority of Chicago's public school population was white and came from middle- or working-class homes. Then came the massive exodus of families out of the city amid the racial turmoil of the 1960s and 1970s. Parents of tens of thousands of schoolchildren, fearing proposals that might call for busing to maintain racial integration, either transferred their children to private schools or moved to the suburbs. Although many have dubbed this transition "white flight," the term "bright flight" might be more accurate because there was a similar exodus of the city's middle-class black children.

Today, nearly 70 percent of the children who depend on the Chicago Public Schools for an education come from impoverished homes. They are the children of the families who have been left behind. Overwhelmingly, they are minority children. Enrollment today has not changed markedly since we did our research: about 60 percent of Chicago public school students are black, 24 percent are Hispanic, 2.9 percent are Asian, and 0.2 percent are American Indian or Alaskan. About 12.9 percent are white.

Although it is clear that all Americans have a stake in the quality of their country's public education systems, one of the most revealing facts we learned about Chicago was that the city's power structure has never had much of a personal stake in the public schools. City leaders, school officials, and a long succession of mayors have long bypassed the deteriorating school system in favor of sending their children to private or parochial schools. Not surprisingly, we found that only 15 of the city's 50 aldermen depended solely on the public schools for their children.

Only a few of them explained why. "We're Catholic and we want the religious instruction," said city alderman Edward Burke in explaining why his four children attend parochial schools. Then he paused and added: "Nobody in his right mind would send kids to public school."

But what about the families that have no other options? What about the children for whom there is no other choice? As a reporting team, we fanned out to scour the system. We found disturbing facts at every turn.

We found high school students using a popcorn popper to heat their science experiments or sitting in classes that were being taught either by a parade of substitutes or by no one at all.

We found a bloated school bureaucracy, headed by a man who described himself as "probably the most gifted urban administrator in this country," that paid $200 a month for a suburban company to water and trim the plants that adorned its beautifully refurbished central office complex. Yet, at the same time, the funds for the year's educational supplies had been slashed to as little as $13.76 at one elementary school as a way of generating money to fund the pay increases that settled the teachers' strike.

We found a teachers' union that had grown so powerful in the years when the central bureaucracy was becoming dangerously out of touch with the needs of the classrooms and financial woes were crippling the system that the protections built into the teachers' contract had taken away much of the local school principal's ability to choose and assign staff. Terminating teachers for inferior performance was a process that had become so time consuming, so cumbersome, and so fraught with legal minefields that a teacher with a record of poor performance in many cases was simply transferred to another school.

We found a business community that was just beginning to fear for the workers of the year 2000 but was already hit by a shortage of well-qualified public school graduates for entry-level jobs. And we found taxpayers who in a *Tribune* poll said they would be willing to pay more in taxes to improve the city's school system.

Goudy Elementary School

But our most telling answers came from inside Goudy Elementary School. Although some observers often look at high schools as a barometer of the success of an educational experience, we felt that the underpinnings of failure begin early in elementary school, during the years when a child may be turned on to the idea of an education—or may be forever lost.

Goudy was not the best of what the Chicago public school system had to offer, but it was by no means the worst. It was a schoolhouse that was overwhelmed by the kinds of problems that tax public school systems throughout the country, festering in academic and spiritual distress. Nearly 73 percent of the children who attend public school in Chicago depend on the regular neighborhood schools such as Goudy, schools that often sit in segregated neighborhoods and have precious few resources to spare.

Americans have long accepted the belief that the public schools provide a stepping stone to something better. But we found that the Chicago public school system fails utterly to meet the challenge of educating the children left behind, a staggering number of whom are at risk of failure even before they walk through the schoolhouse doors.

There is nothing selective about a school like Goudy. Its doors are open to anyone—not only to all the children who happen to live in the neighborhood but also to all teachers that the system assigns, no matter what their ability or expertise. Some of the children who go to school here come from stable homes. Some are reared in families with one or two working parents. But almost all of the children who depend on this school for a grounding in the basic academic and behavioral skills are like 68 percent of all the children in the city's public schools: they are poor. When we did our research, 45 percent of Goudy's students were Hispanic, 34 percent black, 11.2 percent Asian, and 2 percent American Indian. Seven percent were white.

I will never forget the lessons I learned during the nearly four months I spent inside Goudy Elementary. My time there was an Alice in Wonderland journey through a world in which things were not always what they seemed.

For nearly 700 children, there was no recess. No swings. Not even a rusted jungle gym. The play lot was a buckling expanse of pavement that spilled into a back alley without the benefit of a protective fence. Goudy was a place where the principal was also a truant officer and social worker because the system did not provide enough of those kinds of support. It was a place where an eighth-grade girl came to school with scratch marks on her face after a fight with a female classmate, then went home with a spelling book tucked under her arm to take care of her 10-month-old son.

In one classroom, on which the federal government was spending nearly $75,000 so that students could receive remedial instruction in reading and mathematics, the teacher explained that she did not actually "teach" because her elaborate computer system told children how to chart their own course of study. That teacher was paid $34,110 a year and had enough of a budget to pay for a full-time aide to help her with the six groups of 16 children each that came to her room each day, a luxury the system did not otherwise provide.

Regular classroom teachers struggling to meet the needs of their needy students found themselves responsible for classrooms of up to 39 children. Often, they were short of supplies and books, and seldom had more resources than a note pinned to a child's shirt to bridge the distance between the classroom and the home. The building engineer, earning $34,301 a year, made more money than many of the teachers.

Because of a purported lack of space, some children attended reading class in a noisy auditorium. Others got their lessons in the school's garagelike annex, seated at desks shoved together in a narrow hall. Two remedial classes of first graders, many of whom had already flunked a year of school, shared one confusing classroom in which bulletin boards served as a makeshift and hardly soundproof divider between the groups.

But children were often secondary to other considerations when it came to doling out the rooms. Except for the small reading group she taught each morning, the teacher whose mother was a former school board member—the teacher with the "political clout"—had a classroom virtually to herself. It was her office, complete with a telephone.

All kinds of "lessons" were taught at Goudy School. Behind each door there was a story about public education, and the images were powerful ones to see firsthand. I often sat in on a third-grade class, which consisted of a roomful of children, most of whom had already flunked a year of school, being taught by a teacher who had been transferred to Goudy after having received an inferior rating at another school. Often, I would find the children eating, fighting, running around the room, and stealing supplies out of the oblivious teacher's briefcase or desk. The teacher, who had little rapport with the children and got not much respect, often resorted to construction-paper activities or bribing them with fully stocked glue pots to take home. I spent a lot of my time talking with children. One day, I asked a young boy what it was like to be in this class. "She thinks we're stupid," the boy told me. "She gives us all the answers. She don't know how to make us act, so we tear up the place."

In the room for the school's most motivated fourth and fifth graders, I found children reading Greek mythology, playing instruments in a rhythm band, writing their own compositions, or practicing ballet, using the eraser tray beneath the chalkboard as the barre.

The first and second graders assembled in another classroom had all flunked a year of school. Most did not know their colors and numbers and only a few could read. In this class, children rarely talked. They sat at their desks stiffly, with hands clasped on desktops. Even pencil sharpening was regimented: the teacher would position herself at a small table where she kept the sharpener, and then one by one, each child would hand the teacher a pencil and she would sharpen it and hand it back. One day, I happened to be observing the classroom when the children were quietly coloring a mimeographed handout. One by one, each of them walked up to the teacher's desk, but she just waved them back to their seats. The teacher, I discovered, was a 25-year teaching veteran who was teaching the children with terribly out-of-date materials. I wonder how many young children, in the 1980s, would recognize a "muff"?

Because Goudy's children were so uniformly poor, the school was "rich" in federal funds for remedial education. Although some principals in other Chicago public schools use this money to divide oversized classes and hire additional teachers, this money is often used for "pull out" programs. The idea is that the lower achievers can be pulled out of their regular classrooms, regrouped with a smaller number of children, and benefit from remedial education in a more intimate setting for a few minutes of the school day. At Goudy, however, such regroupings were often chaotic adventures that broke up the children's attention span, disrupted teaching plans, and caused more harm than good. Goudy's fourth-grade teacher was an energetic young man who had a wonderful rapport with children. The trouble was, he never had them in his room. All day long, small groups of children drifted in and out of his classroom, making it next to impossible for him to bring continuity or a sustained lesson to the school day. One day, in a fit of anger, he sat down with a piece of paper, did some figuring, and confirmed his worst suspicion: he had all of his students in his room, uninterrupted and still fresh enough to respond to his best shot, for only 30 minutes each school day!

There was a M*A*S*H-like atmosphere about Goudy. All day long, voices crackled over the public-address system. The principal interrupted one afternoon to alert the whole school to the fact that a group of boys was running wild in the second-floor corridor. The clerk sent her voice into classrooms when she needed to know something, when she wanted to continue an argument after a teacher had stormed out of the office, or on paydays when she ordered some teachers to come to the office during class time to pick up their "negotiables," the school's euphemism for paychecks. (The word had been used ever since a teacher had complained that she did not feel secure when the word "paychecks" was said in the presence of the low-income students who attended Goudy.)

School administrators often sent out all-points bulletins over the public address system for students who walked to their morning reading class and then kept on walking, right out of the school.

"Reading is horrible. Boring," explained one 13-year-old boy who often skipped reading class and went down the street to McDonald's to pass the time. "The same old thing every day, story after story in this dumb book. You just want to escape sometimes. There's nothing to do in this school that's fun."

The children cried out for something better, but they did not get it in this neighborhood school. There was no science laboratory. No art teacher. The school was rich in remedial programs that drew attention to a child's failures. But there were no real extracurricular activities that might help children excel in something either before or after the school day.

Organized team activities came on a good day in gym class that took place on a hardwood floor that begged for a good varnishing and under huge windows protected by steal mesh and framed by heavy mustard-colored curtains that hung in shreds.

Although private washrooms reserved for the principal and teachers were kept well stocked, soap, paper towels, and toilet paper were not always available for the children. For the better part of the year, there wasn't even a working toilet-paper dispenser for the boys. The school was cut down to only two working washrooms for nearly 700 children to accommodate a contractor's renovation schedule. By Thursday, the entire second floor would be permeated by the smell of the boys' washroom. On Fridays, the odor would be gone.

Fights were common in one of the classrooms. The teacher there was the first to admit something was wrong. "I have a room of 39, overage, unmotivated sixth and seventh graders," she explained. "Most of them have already flunked one year of school. And I am not prepared for this. I have absolutely no idea what to do." The teacher, I learned, had been given the responsibility of teaching a roomful of the school's most abysmal achievers—not because anyone thought she would do well at it, but because it was her turn.

Though the two eighth-grade classrooms were side by side, the teachers seldom shared their plans. Still smarting from political battles about who would get to teach the most motivated students, they did not always speak to each other. In the history book used by the brighter class of eighth graders, Ronald Reagan was president. The slower class read from a text in which Richard M. Nixon was still in office.

One sixth-grade teacher had no real geography books. He improvised, partly with the benefit of scenes of America depicted on the calendars that hung over his chalkboards.

The first-grade teacher had been asking to have writing lines painted on her chalkboard since 1964.

Dedicated teachers cried out for something better.

"I want to be a part of something I believe in," said one teacher, a veteran of 33 years of teaching in the public schools. When she was younger, she said, she did things like visit homes and try to provide a social connection for her needy students. Sometimes, she even invited students to visit her house. But so many children with so many needs simply became too much. "You try," she told me. "If you care, you always try. But I am constantly amazed by how little I am able to do."

A generation or two ago, many of the children who depended on a school like Goudy might have left school at an early age to work in an economy that needed unskilled people willing to dig holes by hand or carry heavy things around. But now machines do that, and there is almost no demand for the unskilled, so these children must depend on the schools for whatever hope they have for a better life.

One of the most important lessons I learned while at Goudy is that it is these very children—and the school system's unwillingness to find a way to effectively reach them—that cause deep concern. Many of them come from desperately poor and unstable families, lack positive role models, and are being raised by parents who work rarely, if at all, and move several times a year in search of affordable housing.

Some children come to kindergarten still not toilet trained. There are first graders who come from homes where there is so little nurturing that they haven't learned colors and numbers. I learned of eight-year-olds who tore pages out of school books that had been taken home so the family could use the pages for toilet paper. I learned of sixth graders who didn't know offhand how many inches are in a foot because they had never worked with a ruler.

One day, a teacher told me she had been tickled once to see one of the boys in her class for children with behavior disorders teetering playfully on an inside window ledge. She said she had called him Humpty-Dumpty and had recited the nursery rhyme. But none of the preteen boys had known what she meant. "They thought it was a rap," the teacher remembered. "They had never heard it. They didn't even believe me until I brought in a book of nursery rhymes and pointed to the page and said, 'Look! Here it is!' "

A first-grade teacher at Goudy had taught at the school for 24 years. Although she herself had attended the school as a child when the neighborhood had been different, and she has seen firsthand some of the troubling changes in the families that send their children to Goudy, she told me that she still has not gotten used to what they tell her about their family life. "They talk about fights, knifings, arguments where furniture is thrown and where people are drunk. Many insist there are guns in the house. You really have to step back and think that these are the children you are so desperately trying to teach."

Losing a Generation

We are at risk of losing an entire generation of children because our public schools are not responding to the desperate needs. But this is not true just at Goudy Elementary School. Nor is it true only for the Chicago Public Schools. It is true of virtually every urban school district in the country with a significant poverty population. Though there have been flashes of wisdom and some programs that work, no U.S. educational system has found a way to reach impoverished children effectively and consistently.

One of the most remarkable facts I learned while reporting this story was that too many administrators and teachers still tried to hide behind what I came to think of as "the Great Excuse." When I asked them about the broken bridge between home and school, they would throw up their hands and ask what they were supposed to be able to do when the children came with so many problems. Granted, education does not occur in isolation and the job can be difficult when lessons taught in the classroom are not reinforced at home. But I keep coming back to one question: is enough being done to make the distance between school and home a shorter one?

Since our articles were published, some things have changed in Chicago. No one has tackled what many consider to be some of the fundamental problems plaguing the school system, including class sizes of up to 39 children to one teacher, too few early-education programs, and schools staffed so poorly that thousands of students are taught by a pool of uncertified teachers of uneven ability. No one has come up with fresh, innovative programs that might help the school fit the needs of the children rather than have the children fit the needs of the school.

Instead, Chicago is once again in the national spotlight, the site of one of the country's most far-reaching experiments ever in what some call school reform. State lawmakers, responding to our articles and to the public outcry to fix the system's troubles, passed new laws that dismantled the Chicago system's central bureaucracy and instead created more than 500 mini–school boards, called "school councils," that now have the authority to run each of the city's public schools.

Each council is made up of parents, community members, and teachers. The council members are supposed to have the power to hire and fire the principal, develop strategies for improving the school, and decide how a lot of discretionary money is spent.

How effective these councils can be in making meaningful change remains to be seen. The most basic question cannot yet be answered: will any of this change what happens inside the schools? What the school-reform legislation did was to give a lot of power and responsibility to a lot of parents, many of whom are poorly educated themselves and do not have in their arsenal the basic tools that many observers believe will be necessary to bring about real reform.

Already, the councils have complained that they are receiving little direction and cooperation from the central administration when they need answers. How and where they will hold their meetings is now anyone's guess in the wake of revelations that the financially strapped school board has enough money to keep each school open for a council meeting after the regular school day but twice a year.

But there is hope. One interesting development in the saga of the "Worst in America" was the refusal of the system's newly appointed interim school board to pay for $37,000 for commemorative paperweights that a bureaucrat bought to give to the newly elected school council members. The president of the school board, however, said he would try to find private donors to pay for the commemorative pieces.

In Chicago, I think this is called "reform."

4. The View from the Third Floor

Ben Peterson

> There are certain queer times and occasions in this strange
> mixed affair we call life when a man takes this whole uni-
> verse for a vast practical joke, though the wit thereof he but
> dimly discerns, and more than suspects that the joke is at
> nobody's expense but his own. However, nothing dispirits,
> and nothing seems worth while disputing. He bolts down
> all events, all creeds, and beliefs, and persuasions, all hard
> things visible and invisible, never mind how knobby; as an
> ostrich of potent digestion gobbles down bullets and gun
> flints. And as for small difficulties and worryings, prospects
> of sudden disaster, peril of life and limb; all these, and death
> itself, seem to him only sly, good-natured hits and jolly
> punches in the side bestowed by the unseen and unaccount-
> able old joker. That odd sort of wayward mood I am speak-
> ing of comes over a man only in some time of extreme
> tribulation; it comes in the very midst of his earnestness, so
> that what just before might have seemed to him a thing
> most momentous, now seems but a part of the general joke.
>
> Herman Melville, *Moby Dick*

At the age of 15, Herman Melville became a school teacher. He couldn't have liked it very much; three months later he was a cabin boy on a vessel bound for Liverpool. By 1841, his father dead and the family fortune gone, Melville was desperate enough to try teaching again. The school closed without paying him. He never returned to the classroom, preferring instead to ship as a common seaman on the whaler, *Acushnet*, a job so dangerous, hard, and dirty that men deserted when the ship put in at a cannibal-infested island.

I have no proof of this, but somehow I feel that Melville was reflecting on his life as a teacher when he wrote the lines quoted above. Earnestness combined with tribulation is a perfect job description for high school teachers. Eventually, you even get the joke.

Three years ago I was poised for what I believed would be a breakthrough in my writing career. I had just sold an hour-long TV episode. My second screenplay had been optioned. My agent opined that I was destined for greatness, or at least some substantial paychecks, if only I could produce more than my customary one screenplay per year. To write more I needed to work less—60-hour weeks are not conducive to reflection. Not that I needed a lot of reflection to write the kind of stuff I specialized in, but I am a slow typist. I needed a sinecure or a patron. The Medici were not hiring. The Los Angeles Unified School District was.

The ad read, "Wanted: Teacher. Call. . . ." I was impressed by its brevity. When selecting organizations to work for, I favor the terse ones.

An hour later I was attending a "job fair" at a downtown hotel. I guess I should have been suspicious of an organization that rents a fancy ballroom to conduct 15-minute interviews. I was to learn that only the French Foreign Legion processes recruits faster than the LAUSD—and for many of the same reasons.

I was asked if I would teach in an inner-city high school. I said that I would. The fact that I had not been in any high school classroom since I graduated from my own little country school some 19 years earlier didn't faze me. After all, I had spent 10 years riding the New York subways.

My assignment was ninth- and tenth-grade English at Douglass High School, a Molotov cocktail's throw away from the site of the Watts riot. The school looked foreboding—low, Panzer-gray buildings surrounded by tall fences topped with wire and accessed through heavy metal gates. Our embassy in Teheran should have been as well constructed.

I met the principal and the head of my department. Neither of them seemed the slightest bit concerned that I had never spent a day teaching high school. Their sole interest seemed to be, is this guy a racist? Good breeding and a lifetime in public education (a field that encourages circumlocutions) prevented them from just asking me. After 15 minutes of hypotheticals like "A black child and a Hispanic child get into an altercation. The Hispanic calls the black a 'nigger.' How do you handle it?" and "Name three black

Americans you admire and tell why you admire them," I was prepared to be asked if I liked chitlins. Finally, I simply said, "I'm not a racist. I can teach here." Everyone was embarrassed for a moment. We stumbled through the rest of the conversation like blind people in unfamiliar rooms. Eventually, I was hired. The principal took me to lunch in the cafeteria. He had the fruit salad. I ate the chitlins.

The next day I picked up my keys and was given a room assignment. Two minutes later I was hopelessly lost in a labyrinth of dark corridors reeking of industrial cleaner. Then the bell clanged, the sound ricocheting off the graffiti-scarred walls and the thin metal lockers. Doors burst open and the students boiled into the corridors. Instantaneously, the air was filled with curses, shouts, laughter, and Run DMC turned to maximum volume. The institutional smells were lost in a riot of sweat, salsa, chili dogs, vomit, and pheromones. Students rushed up, down, and over the staircase, crushing me against the wall. I couldn't move. Faces were thrust against my own, eyes sullen, dull, or defiant, breath full of fast food or slowly rotting teeth. Girls chewed gum so hard I thought their jaws would dislocate. The snapping sounded like distant forest fires. I began to feel like Bambi.

The bell rang again. The tide disappeared, rolled away behind the steel bulkheads. I approached two teenagers who were trying to make love standing up. I asked them where Room 209 was, but it is difficult to talk when you have two tongues in your mouth. I saw two policemen leading a young man down the stairs. I stopped and asked them. The student pointed down the corridor with both manacled hands. Down the hall, the lovers looked up when they heard his chain clink.

My first two days were spent as a substitute. Substitutes are the migrant workers of the teaching profession. They get up at six a.m. to wait for a call that may never come. Often they are summoned 20 minutes before the first bell to a school halfway across the city. When they arrive late, their pay is docked.

Subs aren't treated any better in the classroom. Since they don't know students' identities, the kids sign anybody's name they can spell on the roll sheet and torture the sub with impunity. Just try keeping Bill Cosby, Michael Jackson, and Fuck You after school.

Lots of teachers don't bother with lesson plans, so the poor sub is left to his own devices with a group of screaming teenagers.

Classes swell as the kids who are supposed to be there are joined by their friends, all of whom are invariably more poorly behaved than the average Hun.

I was not abused as a sub, merely ignored. Occasionally, I would make some gesture of controlling the class, something like "Excuse me, would you please put her clothes back on?" The student would pause and stare, all slack jawed and sullen, and maybe shake a hairy fist at me. Then her boyfriend would stop her and they would resume performing acts contraindicated in the Bible.

During those two days, I read a lot and longed for the day when I would have my own class, know the students' names and the names of their families, and lead them out of the depths of their ignorance toward a more intimate acquaintance with the mysteries of deconstructionism. They went on deconstructing the room and often one another. I read Proust and worked the *New York Times* crossword puzzle, except during the periodic power shortages that plagued the school. Something about lab animals dropped on power grids.

My big day came at last. Another teacher had cracked, drawn a .25-caliber Beretta, and waved it around a crowded classroom. All of the students turned in their homework the next day. The teacher, however, had already been transferred to another, less stressful job, probably fighting oil-well fires. Who would grade those papers? I picked up my keys, checked my beneficiaries, and headed toward the third floor.

Third floors are bad places to be in public high schools. Since there are no elevators, access to them is restricted to those who walk. That immediately precludes all security guards and most administrators.

The third floor is not unlike an archaeological dig. One experiences the same dust, heat, and confusion of artifacts. One meets the kinds of strangely garbed people speaking incomprehensible languages that one imagines inhabited Baalbek, Pompeii, or any other ancient city. Middens dot the landscape promising all sorts of interesting finds for those brave enough to risk cholera.

Anyway, I got to the third floor, found the classroom (no mean feat considering the wattage of the three unbroken bulbs in the corridor), and greeted my class. They were a remarkably attentive group, more so than any other I had encountered in my brief stay at Douglass. I sketched my goals for the remainder of the year, then asked for questions.

One of the students raised his hand. He was a short, handsome boy with a curl. Since it was May and air conditioners in high schools are as rare as elevators, the Jeri curl spray had already melted out of his hair and was soaking through the collar of his ski parka.

"What kind of gun you carry?" he asked.

I had been trained for precisely this moment during the two-day "So You Want to Teach High School" course I had been given by the district. The answer to that question could determine the relationship I would have with this class for the rest of the year. I had to be friendly, yet firm, creating the trusting, caring atmosphere that would allow me to lead those children out of the educational morass to which poverty, racism, and an aloof bureacracy had condemned them.

"I don't carry a gun," I replied.

A shout went up. They rushed from their seats to embrace me, pounding me on the back, pumping my hand. I felt like Mr. Chips, Mr. Novak, and Gabe Kotter all rolled into one. Then they left.

Fifty minutes later, the bell rang. I left. On my way home, I discovered that my wallet was missing. The next day I returned. About half of my students did. I would lecture and they would talk with their friends, curse their enemies, leave the room, and get into shouting matches with people of other racial subsets. Many slept. I tried to get them to sit up, pay attention, take notes. By the end of the second week, I was negotiating with them not to snore.

I begged, I threatened, I called their parents, sent them to the deans. I cajoled them, showed them movies, bought them candy that I traded for correct answers. Attendance got worse; grades plummeted. The candy melted in my drawer as May turned into June.

The composition of the class was very interesting. Since "tracking," that is, placing students in homogeneous classes according to IQ or achievement, has been determined to be discriminatory, the students ranged from the mentally retarded to boys and girls who read two or three levels above their grade level. The heterogeneity of the group was enhanced by the Los Angeles Unified School District's "no retention policy." That policy encourages teachers to pass any student in grades one through eight to the next level no matter how poor his performance or how deficient his skills. The educational doctrine currently in vogue holds that the student will learn the skills in the next higher grade. The average reading level at Douglass High School is fourth grade. Teaching *Julius Caesar* to fourth-grade readers is very difficult.

Yet teaching English is only a small part of what I'm called upon to do at Douglass. School has become the last hope for imparting values that were once taught by families, churches, and society. The school's mandate has grown too large. A teacher is called upon to be policeman, judge, jury, and jailer, psychologist, social worker, minister, nurse, mother, father, and big brother. I have no training for most of those roles and little inclination to perform them.

America's original mandate for its educational system was to inculcate working-class values in students, educate the newly enfranchised masses, and create avenues for social mobility. Most of my students aren't interested in getting ahead; that prospect is too vague, too uncertain, too foreign to their experience. They're interested in staying alive. They know they are targets; they don't want to become statistics.

I once polled a class of 30 kids, asking them how many personally knew someone who had died by violence in the last year. Only two students did not. Most of the others had lost a family member or close friend.

A year ago I asked my tenth graders to write an essay describing the most difficult thing they had ever had to do. In the midst of dozens of essays describing the tortures of taking the driver's test and complaints about plane geometry finals, one essay stood out. It was a simple, unemotional discussion of the trauma the writer had endured telling her mother that the mother's boyfriend had assaulted her. Again.

The first incident had happened about three years before. The boyfriend had gotten into a fight with Marsha's mother. During the argument, the man had forced both mother and daughter into the same bed and held a pistol on the older woman while he raped Marsha. After that he assaulted the 13-year-old girl regularly while her mother stood outside the locked door, wringing her hands and threatening to leave him. Marsha complained to a neighbor, and the man was arrested. Recently, the man had been paroled, returned to their home and was eyeing Marsha's youngest sister, a child of 10.

84

I would be creating a false impression of Douglass High School if I dwelt on the headline aspects of life in the inner city. That's grist for the minicams, "News at Eleven," and *Colors*. And it's not the reason that faculty members leave every year in droves, or that last year 1,000 kids dropped out of a school with an enrollment of over 2,000 while only 24 students went to college. The true story is much smaller, and much, much worse.

The Douglass story is constant rudeness, a world in which "please" and "thank you" are as rare as a 600 on the SAT. It's the trash that fills the corridors with every change of classes no matter how much the custodians clean. It's the fact that no matter what you affix to your door—message, happy face, postcard, student art—it's torn down almost immediately. It's children being beaten in the corridors for wearing the wrong color trousers. It's dictionaries that are destroyed almost immediately, to be replaced two or three years later from ever-shrinking school budgets. It's parent conference nights in which the teachers outnumber the parents. It's racial skirmishes between blacks and Hispanics as the latter become more and more of a factor in what is one of the last predominantly black high schools in Los Angeles. It's teachers who use their position and power to sexually exploit children. It's the ceiling that collapsed in my room in February and hasn't been repaired yet, and the heat that never works. It's working 80 hours a week at three jobs to support my family and dreading the three summer months when there are no checks.

During my first year at Douglass, I had a student in one of my freshman classes who never completed an assignment, turned in any homework, or took a test. That in itself was not terribly unusual. Still, there was something about Franklin that made him different from the scores of angry, bored, or beaten children who populated my classes.

There were pain and bewilderment in Franklin's face whenever he began to read in class. He stammered badly, his tongue stumbling and falling over the simplest words. The other kids hooted at him and tortured him by calling him the vilest names imaginable. Franklin would pause, look at them, and then continue his slow crawl across the line. Nothing I could do to the others, no threats, detentions, referrals to the deans, or calls to their parents could deter them from making cutting comments as Franklin struggled with the simplest word.

Nothing seemed to work with Franklin and I tried everything: student tutors, after-school sessions, one-on-one sessions, reading labs. One day I saw him tracing a map for a history class; it was totally reversed, with Florida where California is. Franklin was dyslexic.

It took two months for the visiting social worker to see the child and another two months for her to diagnose him. All that time he continued coming to my class. His grades bottomed out; the other children got crueler and crueler. He became more angry, more sullen, more defiant.

I was becoming more intimate with anger too. I was angry at my wife for staying home with the kids while I worked three jobs to support them, angry at myself for taking this low-paying job teaching a group of people who couldn't read and didn't care, who insulted me and menaced each other, who carved their gang graffiti in my desk, and stole anything in the classroom that wasn't locked up. Most of all, I was angry at myself for not having written a word in over a year.

I became angry at Franklin every time he raised his hand and volunteered to read. He would begin, stumbling and fumbling with every word. Soon the others would be bored with him. The comments would begin, quiet at first, then louder and louder until I would have to throw one of them out of class. One day I told Frankling to stop reading. I couldn't bear to hear him anymore. He was so absorbed in what he was reading that he just went on and on. He didn't stop until I screamed, "Shut up, damn you!"

The room was quieter than I had ever heard a classroom at Douglass. Franklin closed the book slowly, painfully, as though he were closing the casket lid on the face of an old friend. He put his head down on the book and turned his face toward the door. He may have cried; I didn't want to know.

Five months after our problems began, the social worker called to tell us that she had secured a place for Franklin in one of the special education classes that treated dyslexia. Franklin smiled at me again; together we went to call his mother to tell her the good news, that the system worked, that together we could reverse the damage that the years of neglect had done to her son.

"I'm not putting that boy in no retarded class," Mrs. Wilson announced. "He was in one of them when he was a little fella and I believe it set the boy back, being in amongst them loonies."

I was sure I could change her mind. After all, I was intelligent and educated; I could reason and persuade. Most of all, I was right. However, Mrs. Wilson was his parent and she prevailed. Franklin didn't get to go to special ed. Three years later, he's made it to the tenth grade. His teachers tell me he still can't read. His mother still watches over him; recently she's been joined by a parole officer. Franklin and I don't look at one another when we pass in the corridors.

In Exodus the Israelites endure many hardships at the hands of Pharaoh. Their land is despoiled, and they are taken away in chains. Once in Egypt, they are forced to work long hours under barbaric conditions. Pharaoh even orders the midwives to kill the male children.

The Israelites endure all this. The one thing they do not, cannot, endure occurs when Pharaoh refuses to provide them with straw for the bricks they are making for his pyramids. Without straw, the bricks are useless. Gathering their own straw forces the Israelites to fall far behind Pharoah's ever-increasing quotas. He makes a mockery of their labor, and the Israelites rebel.

After three-plus years of teaching in the inner city I have concluded that my work is meaningless. Few care, least of all the students and their parents. Perhaps those children of the streets knew too much when they came to me. It's very difficult to teach someone as full of pride and pain as the average Douglass High student. For me it's time to quit. I've learned that my stomach is not nearly as strong as I thought it was.

5. Public and Private Choices for African-American Parents

Joan Davis Ratteray

During the discussions of education reform over the past decade, one of the most prominent issues has been whether parents should have the freedom to choose which schools their children attend. However, the concept of choice in education has a number of different interpretations, depending on whether we are talking about public choices or private choices, and whether we are talking about the impact of conservative or liberal ideologies on education policymaking.

Because the idea of choice now has become the fulcrum for the debate on school effectiveness, it appears that African Americans in the inner city are on the front lines of yet another educational battle. African-American children once more will become pawns of well-intentioned policymakers who seem to spend an inordinate amount of time reinventing square wheels and ignoring wheels that work.

At the crux of the problem is the idea that conservative and liberal policies are separate and distinct solutions for education in the United States. The truth is that when they are put into practice in U.S. classrooms, their effects on African Americans are similar and their ideological differences become blurred.

Conservative and Liberal Approaches to Choice

The pursuit of liberty through choice in education is an idea that, on its face at least, offers great promise for inner-city schools. However, disputes between conservative and liberal educators in at least four areas may prevent the idea of choice from fulfilling its promise to African Americans.

First, conservatives argue that people have a right to choose with whom they should associate and when, and that voluntarism is the implementing strategy by which this right becomes a reality. In urban education, this means that parents can choose whether their children will be the ones to integrate or not integrate the classroom. Liberals, on the other hand, appear unwilling to address head-on the issue of choice as an inalienable right. Instead, they take a more oblique approach. They contend that if we provide equal opportunity in education, choice becomes irrelevant and unnecessary. Furthermore, equality of opportunity leads to another virtue, that of equity or fairness. For liberals, the implementing strategy that makes equity a reality is the coercive involvement of the state.

On the one hand, conservatives leave open the possibility of re-segregation and the continuation of what became known in the South as "segregation academies," which met the academic needs of a few. Such schools were in fact the first schools of choice, allowing Euro-Americans (Americans of European descent) to choose to separate themselves from African Americans.

That previous linking of choice with racial separatism is at the root of why African Americans often perceive that the idea of "choice" is not in their best interest. They also fear that choice would drain funds from public schools—taking resources from the majority, giving them to the few who are able to benefit from choice plans, and destroying the possibility of having equality and equity.

On the other hand, the goal of liberals is to produce a society in which all citizens are equally literate, self-sustaining, and productive, and generally they have been prepared to accomplish this through forced integration. However, in light of political realities, liberals also promoted the use of incentives to stimulate choice in education. They created inner-city magnet schools, which, when compared with other urban public schools, had an enhanced curriculum, extra supplies, more highly compensated personnel, and superior facilities. The objective was to direct money and other resources to a select group of schools that would attract whites and other middle-income families back to inner-city schools.

In reality, the proportions of whites and blacks allowed in magnet schools were prescribed by courts and regulators, which effectively decreased the meaningfulness of individual choice. Some educators now have cooled in their support of magnet schools and begun looking for alternative vehicles for desegregation because the schools are not sufficiently integrated with whites.[1] Therefore, the

[1] Michele L. Norris, "Magnet Idea Outdated, Says P. G. Official: New Desegregation Methods Are Sought," *Washington Post*, January 5, 1990, p. A1.

material "advantage" of magnet schools is that they are instruments of state coercion disguised with economic incentives. They are hiding behind the artificial, painted smile that sometimes calls itself parental choice.

The second conservative/liberal distinction involves accountability. This is the process by which educators are held responsible for the quality of education that children receive. Billions of dollars are pumped annually into school systems, and accountability enables policymakers to determine whether such large expenditures produce the intended educational outcomes.

Liberals prefer to use public money as a lever to achieve accountability, but the pursuit of public money has destroyed independence in the African-American community. In 1916, over 650 schools had been identified as serving most of the African-American youngsters in this country, but only 28 of them were public schools; today, the ratio is completely reversed.

Not only do liberals consider money to be ideologically pure if it is public, but they want lots of it. They contend that the chronic inequality of resources among schools is a major reason for the failure to educate the working class and the poor and that choice would exacerbate differences of funding and quality among schools. In spite of the fact that funding for U.S. education has continued to rise, educators continually demand more money to correct the problems of our schools.

Conservatives believe that schools should be accountable directly to consumers, rather than to elected representatives or appointed bureaucrats, regardless of whether the funds supporting those schools are disbursed by the public or private sector. This is a process conservatives call accountability through the marketplace. Vouchers and tuition tax credits, they say, would make schools more accountable.

The third distinction between conservatives and liberals involves the relationship between equality of opportunity and equality of results in education. Conservatives insist that they believe in equality but assert the Darwinian concept that unequal results are natural outcomes of the educational process. In other words, success follows a normal curve in which some excel, become affluent, and assume leadership positions; a large number of people remain in the middle; and some find themselves at the bottom. To conservatives,

91

excellence can be pursued without reference to equality, and choice facilitates achieving excellence.

Liberals contend that education should be opened up, rather than restricted to a few. Not only should each child have an equal opportunity upon entering the system but there must also be equality of results; these two conditions produce a state of equity or fairness. Every child has the inalienable right to be literate, employable, and a full citizen, so the state must not only guarantee this equality of opportunity and outcome but also restrict the choices that would facilitate the pursuit of excellence.

The fourth distinction between conservatives and liberals is in their approaches to the role of culture in education. Conservatives accept the fact that people come from different cultural backgrounds but argue that all groups must work to build "one America" that is a "color-blind society." However, as immigration policies continue the infusion of new cultures, the idea of "one America" has become increasingly remote. John Jay, one of this country's European Founding Fathers, might not have understood the pace of this change, because he wrote:

> Providence has been pleased to give this one connected country to one united people, a people descended from the same ancestors, speaking the same language, professing the same religion, attached to the same principles of government, very similar in their manners and customs, and who, by their joint counsels, arms, and efforts, fighting side by side throughout a long and bloody war, have nobly established general liberty and independence.[2]

Today, several leading conservative spokesmen also have defended the need for Western civilization to be at the center of curricula in U.S. schools because, they claim, the Western tradition has demonstrated itself to be superior to all others. The effect of this approach is to subsume cultural differences and to create a one-way process by which nonwhites are expected to move closer to, if not be indistinguishable from, the orientation, value system, and traditions of whites.

Liberals have a similar objective but a different strategy. They initially encourage students to explore their cultural differences but

[2]John Jay, *The Federalist Papers*, no. 2. (1787).

soon define many ethnic-minority students as "disadvantaged," "deprived," and in need of help. Liberal educators especially discourage such students from developing a worldview that is grounded in those differences. Liberals do this because of their notion of universality— that people are all the same and that cultural differences are externalities that can be modified. Therefore, liberals feel justified in molding differences until they fit mainstream life, which at this point happens to be defined in the Euro-American tradition. To make the universal "brotherhood of man" a living reality, the liberal doctrine usually relies on the power and financial resources of the state.

Both conservative and liberal approaches to choice, however, have major deficiencies. First, neither voluntarism nor coercion alone has proven to be an effective strategy for integration, and the United States still is a nation of unmeltable differences. No matter how many laws are introduced to regulate behavior, no way has been found to change the hearts of men and women except by the will of men and women themselves.

Both groups profess an interest in accountability, but neither seems overly concerned about being accountable to the African-American community, primarily because most African Americans have not accumulated the "private money" that traditionally demands accountable behavior.

Both groups strive for excellence, but they define it strictly by the standards of the European intellectual traditions. Neither the conservative nor the liberal agenda adequately addresses what can be a source of strength for African-American youth: learning environments that are nurturing *because* they are culturally affirming and self-initiated. The result has been intellectually unsatisfying; African Americans find themselves with many unmet academic needs.

Unmet Needs of African-American Students

There is ample evidence that both conservative and liberal ideological frameworks for choice, as well as their implementing strategies, do not meet the intellectual needs of African Americans, and this dilemma cries out for a fresh approach.

The evidence of systemic failure can be seen in the state of African-American education today. After the enslavement of African

Americans ended,[3] their education got off to a roaring start but quickly lost momentum. At the close of the Civil War, over 90 percent of the freedmen could not read or write, but by 1900, illiteracy had been reduced to 45 percent. Today, illiteracy among all "minority" youngsters is approximately 48 percent. In spite of the fact that different measuring sticks are applied, the African-American subset of these minorities probably is not much better off now than in 1900. Mired in failed educational policies and beset by inherent weaknesses in conservative and liberal ideologies, progress seems to have ground to a complete halt.

The Institute for Independent Education recently examined test scores in elementary schools, as well as the enrollment patterns of each of the major ethnic and cultural groups, for eight urban areas: Baltimore, Prince Georges County (Maryland), Detroit, Indianapolis, Rochester (New York), New Orleans, Chicago, and Houston.[4] Figure 5–1 shows that when we consider the first six,[5] approximately 74 percent of African-American elementary school students attend schools at which the median percentile rank is below national norms in reading, mathematics, or both. Only 26 percent are in schools that are above the norm in both reading and mathematics. Therefore, young African Americans in these urban areas do not have equality of results.

The data also show that the record for various cultural groups is mixed. Table 5–1 examines student enrollment and achievement in three areas: Baltimore, Detroit, and New Orleans. In Baltimore, the schools appear to be equally "good" for both African Americans and whites; in Detroit, the schools are equally "poor" for both groups; and in New Orleans, African Americans and whites are at opposite ends of the quality spectrum. The persistent intractability of this problem over the years invites us to develop a new vision for its resolution. Public schools as they are presently constituted always will do serious intellectual damage to the African-American

[3]The term "slave" is not used because it seems to suggest that there is something wrong or inferior about the slave, whereas the proper focus of guilt is on those who have done the enslaving.

[4]Institute for Independent Education, "What's in a Norm? How African Americans Score on Achievement Tests," *Research Notes on Education*, Paper no. 3, July 1989.

[5]Only the first six urban areas are comparable because they report scores in percentile ranks. Chicago and Houston report only grade equivalents.

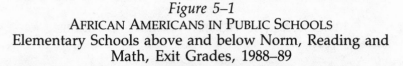

Figure 5–1
AFRICAN AMERICANS IN PUBLIC SCHOOLS
Elementary Schools above and below Norm, Reading and
Math, Exit Grades, 1988–89

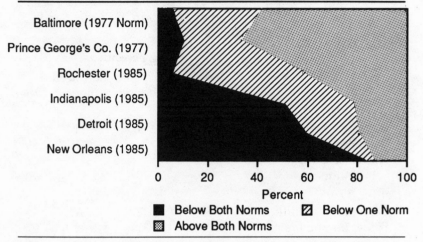

SOURCE: Institute for Independent Education.

children in their care because the deficiencies are systemic and closely linked to the underlying conservative and liberal constructs that now define U.S. education.

One ray of hope takes the form of magnet schools. However, that approach is at risk. In another report, the Institute for Independent Education looked at magnet schools in Chicago.[6] In these schools of choice, African Americans are numerically dominant, whether the schools are below norm, slightly above norm, or far above the norm (Figure 5–2). Clearly, there is the prospect of equal opportunity, but there is no equality of results because African Americans in these special schools of choice are concentrated in schools that are either below norm or barely above norm.

This report also shows that at least one high-performing magnet school has an enrollment that is 81 percent African-American, with more than one-third of the students from low-income families. Conversely, one of the worst-performing magnets has a large white

[6]Institute for Independent Education, "Magnet Schools in Chicago: Achievement at Risk if Policymakers Retreat," *Research Notes on Education*, Paper no. 2, July 1989.

Table 5–1
PERCENTAGE OF STUDENTS ENROLLED IN PUBLIC ELEMENTARY SCHOOLS FOR THREE URBAN AREAS, BY ETHNIC GROUP, 1988–89

(Schools Ranked below and above Norm in Reading and Mathematics at Exit Grades)

	Percent			
	African American	Hispanic American	European American	Other
Baltimore				
Below on two indicators	6	1	1	1
Below on one indicator	29	29	15	29
Above on both indicators	65	70	84	70
Detroit				
Below on two indicators	59	32	37	47
Below on one indicator	21	31	35	27
Above on both indicators	20	37	28	26
New Orleans				
Below on two indicators	84		22	
Below on one indicator	6		28	
Above on both indicators	10		50	

SOURCE: Table 2, "African Americans Enrolled at Elementary Schools in Eight Urban Districts, 1988–1989." In Institute for Independent Education,"What's in a Norm?" *Research Notes on Education*, Paper no. 3, July 1989, p. 3.

population and fewer low-income families. Therefore, African Americans are indeed capable of high achievement. We also know that the distribution of African-American students among good and poor schools is not entirely a matter of talent and ability; it can be the artificial result of specific school policies.

Unfortunately, public-sector magnet schools are at risk because liberal educators, white and black, are turning their backs on the idea of choice. When the Bush administration offered $100 million in aid that is not limited to desegregation efforts, the National

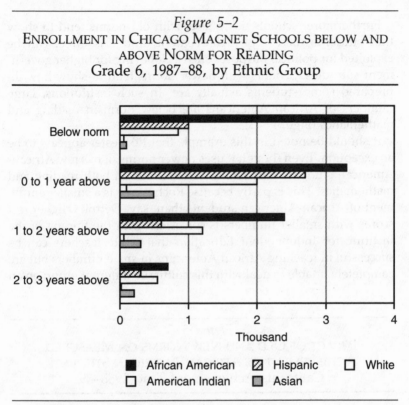

Figure 5–2
ENROLLMENT IN CHICAGO MAGNET SCHOOLS BELOW AND
ABOVE NORM FOR READING
Grade 6, 1987–88, by Ethnic Group

SOURCE: Institute for Independent Education.

Education Association passed a resolution supporting programs that offered choice at the local level but rejecting programs mandated by federal and state governments. By rejecting such federal and state support, the NEA is effectively threatening to dismantle magnet schools. Although magnet schools do not now serve large numbers of African Americans, they have the potential to be a major instrument for attaining high achievement by African Americans in public schools.

Leading African-American educators met in June 1989 at Hunt Valley, Maryland, and announced that they too were opposed to choice. For them, it had the potential of discriminating against poor families whose children attend nonmagnet neighborhood schools, and they feared that the poor might not be welcome in certain schools of choice.

Furthermore, schools using tests with old norms tend to show that students have high achievement, and this effect can be exploited for political purposes such as lobbying for higher government subsidies. Schools with newer norms tend to show how ill-prepared some students actually are. In such institutions, large numbers of African Americans are below norm in reading and mathematics (Figure 5–3).

It should be noted in this example that Rochester appears to be an exception. Even though it uses newer norms, it has few African-American students performing below norm on both reading and mathematics. This is partly because Rochester has a smaller enrollment of African-American students than, say, Detroit. Higher test scores with smaller numbers is consistent with the finding of the Institute for Independent Education that white teachers can be successful in teaching African Americans in small numbers but are completely unable to deal with this culturally different group on an

Figure 5–3
IMPACT OF OLD AND NEW NORMS ON MEASURED ACHIEVEMENT OF AFRICAN-AMERICAN STUDENTS
California Achievement Test, 1988–89

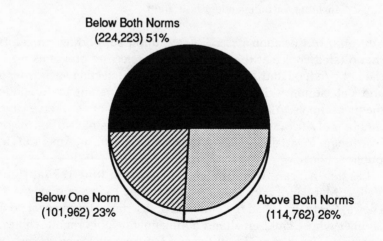

Below Both Norms
(224,223) 51%

Below One Norm
(101,962) 23%

Above Both Norms
(114,762) 26%

SOURCE: Institute for Independent Education.

intellectual level when the numbers are large.[7] Rochester also has smaller teaching units and a large number of schools of choice. Thus, administrative decisions can drastically alter the academic fate of African-American students, but few districts seem to have the will to put their resources squarely into such efforts.

Both conservatives and liberals now can take credit for the tragic state of African-American education in inner-city schools. Neither has addressed the basic intellectual needs of these particular children. However, there are some ideas currently being practiced in schools throughout the United States that have not yet become part of mainstream educational theory, practice, and policymaking. Some of these ideas have proven to be successful in meeting the needs of African-American students and therefore deserve further consideration in settings where there are large numbers of African-American youngsters.

Reconstructing a Vision for African-American Education

The attitude of the public school establishment toward African Americans has changed in recent years, but only in superficial details. There have been important advances in individual achievement by African Americans. For example, we have had an astronaut-physicist, a chairman of the Joint Chiefs of Staff, an ambassador to the United Nations, and an elected governor. However, there has been little substantive change in what public schools have done for African Americans over the past two centuries.

In 1796, Prince Hall, a Revolutionary War veteran and one of the Founding Fathers of the African-American community, pleaded with the Boston school board either to educate Africans in the Americas or to send them back to Africa. The school board declined to do either. Today, school boards still are in a chaotic state of indecision about how to promote effective education for African Americans.

In America's inner cities, where most African Americans live, academic underachievement is well documented. Nevertheless, a new understanding is beginning to emerge among educators in

---

[7]Institute for Independent Education, "The Final Blow! African-American High School Students and Advanced Placement Examinations," *Research Notes on Education*, Paper no. 4, July 1989.

both public and private schools that the European intellectual tradition in the United States has failed to recognize that the children of Africa have made major contributions to civilization. Nor has the European intellectual tradition encouraged students to examine knowledge from an African frame of reference, especially if the underlying assumptions might be fundamentally different from traditional European assumptions. It is because of this type of neglect, which some would say has not been benign, that Prince Hall started the first African-American independent school in his son's home in 1798. Thus began an independent school movement that has continued for 200 years and still holds promise for a brighter tomorrow.

Hall's efforts began the debate over whether African Americans should rely on public or private choices. Unfortunately, the debate in the African-American community has followed the European intellectual tradition, favoring either/or propositions. The debate has been framed in terms of whether we should create our own schools of choice in our own communities, or whether we should use the coercive power of government to force other people to accept us into the mainstream educational system. This is the same dichotomous thinking that has so stifled conservative and liberal deliberations in education policymaking.

In fact, it may be just as incorrect to view the proper education of African Americans as an either/or, conservative/liberal proposition as it is to view contemporary political ideologies on a left/right continuum. The most effective African-American education may have a little of both and some of neither because it comes from a completely different frame of reference.

Five years ago I was intrigued to discover several independent elementary and secondary schools across the country, and I was heartened to find that they stood as beacons of hope in the devastated landscape of so many inner-city communities. These schools were created by African Americans, Hispanic Americans, American Indians, and Asian Americans. They often replaced the hope that many families lost when they became disillusioned by the failure of inner-city public schools to educate their children. These schools of choice in the private sector have been built by educators who have high expectations for urban youth. Many of the schools that serve African-American youth have begun to move Africa back toward the center of their educational theory and practice.

Since my first introduction to these schools, I have begun to delve more deeply into this vision of independence in education and the need to have options in education available to broaden educational opportunities in urban communities. As I talked with groups of principals, teachers, parents, and students across the country, it became clear to me that the quality of education for African Americans could be improved significantly if independent neighborhood schools gradually could replace most, if not all, inner-city public schools. Change and innovation can be implemented in these schools because they are not tied in knots by the ideologies that form the operating environments of public institutions. Independent schools may not be the panacea for all our woes in contemporary society, but they are an important part of the answer to the enormous waste of human potential that now takes place in urban public education.

Independent neighborhood schools embody the right to choose and are viable options for many low-income and moderate-income families. Parents choose them not only because of what they teach and how they teach it but because often they are safe havens from the violence and chaos that affect so much of inner-city life. At the more than 300 schools we have identified so far, over 87 percent of the families served are African Americans.[8] Over one-third of the schools found so far are in the Northeast.

Such schools are living examples of direct accountability to consumers. Approximately half the schools are owned by families, community organizations, or businesses, while the remainder are affiliated with churches or other religious organizations.[9] These schools often are cautious about accepting resources from the public sector because they fear their independence might be threatened, so they rely on private money instead. They are more comfortable being accountable to parents than to bureaucracies. The parents are supportive as long as the school does a good job but take their children out when the school fails to meet parental expectations.

[8]The enrollment at some schools is predominantly African American, Hispanic American, American Indian, or Asian American, while other schools have a broader mix, including Euro-Americans, which reflects the neighborhoods in which the schools are located.

[9]Joan Davis Ratteray and Mwalimu Shujaa, *Dare to Choose: Parental Choice at Independent Neighborhood Schools* (Washington: Institute for Independent Education, 1987).

Although some schools do go out of business, some of the existing schools have had a long tradition of service dating back to the end of the 19th century.

Independent neighborhood schools demonstrate their commitment to equal opportunity because they are supported by families from a broad range of socioeconomic groups. Their mission seems to be inclusive rather than exclusive, and their generous enrollment policies create a wide range of abilities in each classroom. The schools have an average enrollment of 49 at the elementary level and 110 at the secondary level, with a range of from 22 to 1,000. Over half their students come from families of four or five members in which the total family income is less than $30,000, although from 11 to 16 percent of the families in fact earn more than $50,000.

While there have been no formal studies of student outcomes in these schools, we can say that most such schools accept the notion that individual achievement falls along a normal curve that stretches from excellent to average to poor. They do not expect equal results because their enrollment includes students from a broad range of home and school experiences, as well as those who have experienced various levels of success in their past.

Culture plays an important role in independent neighborhood schools. The major reason parents give for supporting these schools is their dissatisfaction with the way in which inner-city public schools treated African Americans in the curriculum and in the classroom. This dissatisfaction peaked in the 1970s, at the same time that independent schools began to flourish. In fact, at least 59 percent of the existing independent neighborhood schools have opened since 1970.

An equally important attitude toward achievement is that in many instances, the group is more important than the individual. Independent schools often operate literally as extended families, nurturing children in both the academic and nonacademic aspects of their lives, even though the children are from diverse nuclear families. Furthermore, even though parents choose such institutions because of their reputation as places where children in fact learn, parents accept the shift in emphasis from the individual to the group.

For example, parents say they choose independent schools because of their disciplined environments, and discipline may be

102

one way in which the rights of the group can take precedence over the rights of the individual—on a voluntary, noncoercive basis. The schools also are places where a child's cultural background will be affirmed and where values, including religious values, will be taught. In some schools, cooperative learning, in which members of the group help each other learn, is stressed more than the aggressiveness that so often accompanies competitive learning.

The paradox of the independent neighborhood school is that parental choice gives individual parents the ability to patronize groups that will nurture the social and academic lives of their children. Such environments make it possible for children to find themselves and to move into the world from a position of strength, secure in what they have to offer the community, the nation, and the world.

6. Profit-Seeking Schools

Myron Lieberman

The most overlooked issue in discussions of educational improvement is the need to encourage schools for profit. In the space available, it is impossible to convey the importance of this issue adequately; it may be helpful, however, to explain how I came to adopt my views concerning this matter.

In 1986 I published a book entitled *Beyond Public Education*.[1] The main thesis of the book was that conventional school reform was, is, and would continue to be a futilitarian effort. By "conventional school reform" I refer to reforms that do not involve basic changes in the governance structure of U.S. education. As I explained in the book, the basic obstacles to improving U.S. education are its monopoly status and the fact that the services are overwhelmingly provided by government. Reforms that do not address these issues are unlikely to lead to significant improvement.

Beyond Public Education devoted a great deal of attention to the way in which various interest groups, primarily the public education lobby, are able to veto or sabotage desirable changes under our existing system of public education. In part, their veto power defines the problem: how do we change from a system in which producers have a stake in inefficiency to one in which they have a stake in higher levels of efficiency? With all its limitations, the free-enterprise system appears to be the most effective way to get interests working for, instead of against, a more efficient educational system.

Nevertheless, the focus of *Beyond Public Education* was on demonstrating the inherent deficiencies of the existing system. The question of what to do about them was largely deferred to my 1989 book entitled *Privatization and Educational Choice*.[2] The latter is an effort

[1]Myron Lieberman, *Beyond Public Education* (New York: Praeger, 1986).

[2]Myron Lieberman, *Privatization and Educational Choice* (New York: St. Martin's, 1989).

to analyze the various modes of privatization from educational, economic, and political perspectives.

The modes of privatization include contracting out, vouchers, tuition tax credits, home schooling, and private learning centers. Each mode can be implemented in several different ways. As matters stand, however, these modes do not emphasize for-profit enterprise. The overwhelming proportion of private schools are nonprofit organizations.

One of the issues that has concerned me is the claim that vouchers or tuition tax credits would bring the benefits of competition to education. Specifically, one of my concerns was whether we can or should expect the benefits of competition from nonprofit enterprise. This led me to review the literature on nonprofit organizations—a literature that is growing rapidly owing to the fact that our economy has been devoting a larger share of resources to the nonprofit sector in recent years.

On the basis of this review, I reached two tentative conclusions: First, there are strong reasons to doubt whether we can expect the benefits of competition in an industry dominated by nonprofit enterprise. Second, to the extent that we can expect the benefits of competition from nonprofit enterprise, there may be reasons to question why such enterprise should be nonprofit. For example, in the hospital field, nonprofits compete with for-profit hospitals. An analysis of their operational similarities, including services provided for the indigent, raises the question: what is or should be the justification for nonprofit status? Significantly, research on nonprofit organizations suggests that, in some important respects, they are more like government bureaucracies than competitive, for-profit enterprises. This is especially true of managerial incentives, a much-neglected issue in the educational reform movement.

Before elaborating on this point, let me comment briefly on our information about for-profit schools. As far as I have been able to determine, very little information on the subject is available. The states typically classify schools as either public or private, making no distinction between private schools that are run for profit and those that are nonprofit. Consequently, we lack reliable data on the number of for-profit schools, as well as their enrollments, costs, expenses, profits, programs, and educational effectiveness. Even the national organization of for-profit schools (the National Independent Private School Association) lacks reliable information on these issues. In addition to the fact that most states do not collect separate data on for-profit schools, difficult technical problems have yet to be resolved. Comparisons with public schools would normally have to be based on comparable grade levels to be useful, but the data are not always available in this form (for example, a for-profit school might offer two years of preschool and first grade). Obviously, allocations of income and expenses might be misleading if the grade levels are not comparable; likewise, educational comparisons are not likely to be useful if the grade levels are not comparable. In fact, the states do not define "school" in the same way. If "school" is defined as an enterprise that enrolls one or more grades as required by state law, 96 to 99 percent of private schools are probably nonprofit.

Advantages of For-Profit Schools

Despite the lack of systematic data on for-profit schools, anecdotal evidence about them is suggestive. Day care provides an illustration. In 1985 my interviews with operators of for-profit schools in the San Francisco area revealed that most schools provided day care as an add-on or were seriously considering doing so. Frequently, both parents worked and were not available to supervise their children between the close of school and parental arrival from employment. Many other children were from single-parent families in which after-school care was essential to enable the parent to continue working. For the most part, the issues involved were normal business issues: how many parents would be willing to pay how much for various services? School management then had to decide its risks and costs and make a decision. The schools showed an interesting divergence on the issue of add-ons. Some offered a low basic rate with several options for additional services; others, reluctant to "nickel and dime" their parents, tended to fold more services into the basic rate.

The point is that the decisions to offer day care were made in the same way as other business decisions. Significantly, at the time the for-profit schools were providing day care for an additional fee, public schools were not doing so, even when many parents clearly would have paid for it.

The differences between the two situations were especially evident when I visited a school that required its students to wear uniforms. This school policy was a business decision. The owner of the school did not have to put the issue on the school board agenda, conduct interminable hearings, defend the policy against the objections of opponents, get bogged down in deciding about the color and design of the uniforms, and otherwise devote substantial resources to the policy or its implementation. If parents wanted to enroll their children, they had to accept the policy; if they didn't like it, they could enroll their children in a different school.

It requires little imagination to appreciate the differences between the decisionmaking process in this for-profit school and a public school. In a public school, the issue could drag on for years; like sex education, it could be a never-ending source of community controversy over public school policy. If such a decision is to be made in the economic system, the service provider does not have to satisfy everyone or even a majority of parents; it is necessary only to satisfy enough parents to achieve profitability. The superior responsiveness of the for-profit sector in this situation is hardly debatable, yet it is all the more impressive in view of the fact that responsiveness is allegedly a major virtue of public education.

Note that the parents who object to uniforms or who cannot afford them have no cause for complaint. After all, most schools do not require uniforms. Indeed, the above example illustrates one of the public policy advantages of for-profit schools over both public and nonprofit schools. Even among nonprofits, such as Catholic schools, the school constituencies are sometimes deeply divided on such matters as curriculum, dress codes, and extracurricular activities. In the nonprofit setting, it is often necessary to reach an accommodation on such matters, and the efforts to do so can be as divisive as in the public sector. In the for-profit sector, however, such differences would constitute a market niche. Instead of being forced to reconcile conflicting views within a single school or system, the entrepreneurial educators would tend to view the differences as an opportunity, not as a problem.

Significantly, existing for-profit schools do not necessarily serve the most talented or the most affluent students. On the contrary, the largest group of for-profit schools are the schools serving the disabled; in fact, there is a national organization of such schools for profit. This is especially interesting because of concerns frequently expressed that public schools would become a "dumping ground" if we strengthened parental power to choose a private school. The evidence available suggests that a variety of private markets would emerge—or could emerge, depending on the specifics of the situation. It is worth noting that another emerging market is college counseling; proprietary counseling services have emerged as a result of dissatisfaction on the part of both high school counselors and parents.

It should also be noted that many parents spend a great deal for educational services for children outside of formal schools. Private music lessons are just one example. We do not have systematic data on the size of the school market for education, but undoubtedly it could run into tens of billions of dollars annually. For example, more and more summer camps offer educational services, such as mathematics, science, computer education, foreign languages, and sports of various kinds. The specialized educational services offered in summer camps provide additional support for the viability of a market approach. Significantly, one finds very little criticism of out-of-school, or nonschool, instruction for profit; indeed, the subject receives very little attention in the literature on educational policy. One might suppose that if the evils of for-profit education were so inevitable, they would have surfaced in the nonschool markets for educational services. In this connection, it would be interesting to track the extent to which public school teachers provide educational services on a for-profit basis either after school or during vacation periods.

Let me now illustrate the point about incentives by drawing on my experience with for-profit learning centers. In writing *Privatization and Educational Choice*, I visited the headquarters of the three major companies: Sylvan Learning Centers, Huntington Learning Systems, and Britannica Learning Centers. With Sylvan and Huntington, I spent a day going through the program arranged for potential franchisees, that is, people interested in investing $100,000 or more in a learning center.

Let me describe Sylvan's operation briefly. In general, its centers operate from the time schools close to 9:00 p.m., Monday through Thursday. They are also open on Saturdays and during the summer and extended vacations.

In the centers, the mode of operation is one teacher for three students. Each teacher sits at a table with three students, so there is a high degree of interaction between teacher and students. Fees are set by the franchisees, but we can use $25 an hour as a reasonable average. The teachers are paid $8 to $10 an hour; they may be retired teachers, former teachers seeking part-time work, graduate students, or others deemed qualified. Sylvan uses only certified teachers; Huntington tries to do so, but accepts qualified exceptions.

The centers have space for only a small number of tables, perhaps four. Thus if operating at capacity, such a center would have 12 parents paying $25 an hour for instruction, and 4 teachers receiving $32 an hour in toto. If operated six hours a day, the center would gross $1,800 and pay $192 for instruction. The difference ($1,608) must cover rent, utilities, supplies, equipment, advertising, insurance, and salaries and profits for the franchisee. This summary is oversimplified, but accurate enough for present purposes.

On the way home from Montgomery, Alabama, where Sylvan's headquarters are located, a question arose in my mind. During the program for potential franchisees, company representatives frequently referred to differences between their program and the programs of competitors. The competitors, though, never included the public schools themselves. On the face of it at least, the public schools could have offered the same program to parents for $10–$12 an hour instead of $25. After all, the facilities and equipment were in place, and many overhead costs, such as insurance on the buildings, were already paid. If public school teachers refused to work for $8 an hour after school, the school district could hire the same teachers who were willing to work at this rate for the learning companies. If union opposition or legal obstacles rendered this impractical, the school system could make the buildings available and provide parents with a list of teachers whom the parents could hire. In other words, the school district could serve as a middleman; the rates charged parents could include a small surcharge to cover school district costs, such as additional custodial or maintenance costs. In short, I could find no obvious reason why school districts could not make these instructional services available for less than half the amounts charged by the learning centers—and at no additional cost to the school districts.

The next morning I called the company officer who had served as my host. I pointed out that in all the discussion about "the

110

competition," no reference had ever been made to the possibility that school districts would become part of the competition. Given that school districts could provide identical services at less than half the price paid to the learning centers, had the possibility of competition from school districts been considered?

The response was that the company was not concerned about competition from school districts. We did not discuss the reasons in detail, so I decided to conduct a brief investigation of the issue. At the time, I was teaching graduate courses at the University of Pennsylvania. Most of my students were public school administrators or teachers who planned to become public school principals or superintendents. When I asked why the public schools did not make similar services available, the answers were consistently inadequate. The answer that best explains the situation is one that was never cited by any student: there are no personal managerial incentives to initiate such a change and there are managerial incentives to avoid such action. For example, union opposition was cited, but as someone who has negotiated over 150 school district contracts in six states, I believe union opposition could not block any school board that sincerely wanted to offer the services.

It is always possible to weaken a valid argument by a poor example. I hope I have not done that in this case. To me, the example illustrates some of the inherent advantages of for-profit schools over public and/or nonprofit schools. These advantages include the following:

- The producers have a direct personal stake in increasing productivity.
- Education for profit is much more responsive to parental inquiries, needs, and interests. For example, secretaries in the learning centers are trained to record inquiries and to respond to them properly. The learning centers must sign up a certain percentage of parents who call for information, hence considerable attention is devoted to telephone procedures.
- Instructional services can be eliminated, modified, or added much more expeditiously than in public schools.
- For-profit schools are not subject to the enormous burdens of state regulation and prescription, such as tenure laws, bargaining laws, and employee benefits. Most of such legislation is

111

intended to maximize teacher benefits, even at the cost of student learning.

- For-profit schools would probably reduce the tremendous litigation costs of public education. These costs arise largely over the need to interpret statutes that are not clear and are often deliberately ambiguous. To the extent that education is provided privately, contractual arrangements would tend to obviate problems generated by unclear statutes.
- For-profit schools would provide a more accurate guide to parental preferences. Markets are clearly superior to political systems on this issue.
- For-profit schools would not carry redundant employees on their payroll, whereas public schools are often required to do so by law. In one recent case, the California Supreme Court held that a school district could not refuse to rehire a teacher on the basis of anticipated declines in enrollment; the dismissal could be effectuated only after the enrollments actually declined. Needless to say, inability to act on the basis of anticipated demand would be disastrous to a private company.

These are not the only advantages or potential advantages of for-profit schools. In fact, I may have omitted the most important. About 50 percent of our high school graduates go on to college; of those who do, about 80 percent enroll in public institutions of higher education. In my opinion, the fact that so many of our young people spend so much of their time in institutions that emphasize redistribution instead of generation of wealth has been harmful. Persons educated in not-for-profit institutions in which teachers and textbooks emphasize the value of redistribution are not as likely to be aware of the benefits of a market system—which is indeed the case with our present educational system. Few high school or college students understand the dynamics of a genuine market economy, so enactment of policies that would strengthen a market approach—in education or elsewhere—is difficult. Thus the paradox is that the failure of our educational system to educate is one of the main reasons why the system cannot make the changes that are needed.

Why Aren't There More For-Profit Schools?

What explains the extremely small number of schools for profit? Obviously, the availability of tax-supported education underlies the fact that only 10 percent of our schools are private. Still, it does not fully explain why such a small proportion of private schools are for-profit schools. One reason is that most private schools are denominational; religious organizations provide the funding and the supply of students for the majority of them. Inasmuch as religious organizations are overwhelmingly nonprofit, and must be to enjoy the tax exemptions and other benefits associated with nonprofit status, the fact that most private schools are not for profit is not surprising.

Nevertheless, the proportion of for-profit schools would be much higher if state and federal laws did not discriminate against them in various ways. For-profit schools typically are not eligible for benefits provided for both public and nonprofit schools. Significantly, public and nonprofit schools have sometimes joined forces to exclude for-profit schools from competing on an equal basis; indeed, in the leading case on the issue, a regional accrediting association composed of public and nonprofit schools refused even to consider a for-profit school for accreditation. The refusal was successfully defended in court despite the fact that accreditation was essential for the proprietary school to participate in various federal programs.

Although for-profit schools face some cultural bias, such bias is probably not the major barrier to their expansion. In health care, the number of for-profit hospitals has increased dramatically under Medicare and third-party payments by health insurers. In addition, for-profit enterprise dominates most independent health services, such as laboratory testing. The increase in for-profit health care has cut into the market share of both public and nonprofit providers, and for reasons that would apply to education if and when educational vouchers are enacted.

In my view, failure even to consider the statutory restrictions on for-profit education must be viewed as a major weakness in conservative policies on education. This is evident not only with regard to the statutory restrictions on for-profit schools but also in terms of the limitations on the authority of school boards to contract for instructional services. The availability of contracted services is heavily influenced by the statutory framework governing the duration of contracts, banking and bidding requirements, bidding procedures, and a host of other matters. Nonetheless, neither the

Reagan administration nor the Bush administration to date has evinced any interest in fostering a more hospitable environment for for-profit education.

Overall, for-profit schools are in a Catch-22 situation. Because they are weak politically, they are not able to block legislation that weakens their ability to compete. Because such legislation continues to be enacted, they are less and less able to compete. The sad truth is that many private school personnel who do support vouchers and/or tuition tax credits have only a rhetorical interest in competition; their underlying interest is in increased public support, not in increased competition among schools, public or private. Furthermore, of those who seek public assistance for parental choice, most do so to retain an existing constituency, not to expand it as an entrepreneurial enterprise would normally try to do. In short, plans offering parental choice must provide for-profit schools with an equal opportunity to compete with public and nonprofit schools. Unless profit-making schools have a level playing field, parental choice will not generate the benefits associated with competition in the for-profit sector.

7. Give Choice a Chance

John E. Chubb and Terry M. Moe

A new wave of school reform is beginning to sweep the nation. From coast to coast, school boards and state legislatures are looking at ways to use parental choice, an innovative concept in school organization, to improve education. This change is exciting because parental choice represents a genuinely promising approach to school improvement. Properly implemented, parental choice would eliminate the most critical source of school failure in the United States today and create powerful new forces for school success in the years ahead.

However, parental choice may never fulfill its promise. Like so many past waves of reform, it may wash over the country's educational systems without making a desirable difference.

Parental choice may not fulfill its promise for precisely the same reason it has so much promise. A basic premise underlying the concept of parental choice is that the nation's educational systems are a large part of the reason that U.S. education is mediocre. Organized as public monopolies, schools and school systems have come to exhibit many of the potentially serious problems—excessive regulation, inefficient operation, and ineffective service—that are inherent in this form of organization. If these problems are to be more than temporarily alleviated, America's educational systems will need to be reorganized fundamentally. Public school monopolies will need to be opened to competition, and social control over schools will need to be exercised less through politics and central regulation and more through markets and parental choice.

There are many reasons to believe that such reforms will promote school improvement. But what makes parental choice an especially promising idea is that it tries to get at the root of the problem of educational mediocrity. Unlike so many past reforms that treated symptoms and were eventually undone by our systems of education, parental choice tries to eliminate a basic source of mediocrity—

115

the systems themselves. By aiming to do so, however, parental choice may ultimately never be able to fulfill its great promise in that really changing any system as thoroughly institutionalized as public education may be more than today's reformers are willing or able to do.

Still, parental choice has been incorporated into political and government agendas around the country, has been endorsed by the Bush administration, and is in limited use in many places already. In the next few years, it is bound to be implemented, in one way or another, in more states and districts. The opportunity does exist for parental choice to make a desirable difference in public education. But the opportunity could easily be squandered or lost if reformers fail to appreciate that the basic reason choice has so much promise is that it provides the means to restructure the way U.S. education is provided. If reformers do not understand this, if they see choice as just another reform to be turned over to our educational systems to implement and to control, choice will not make much of a difference. Fortunately, there are many sound reasons why reformers sincerely concerned about the quality of U.S. schools should favor systemic change and should support a system of educational choice. Our purpose here is to supply a good number of those reasons.

We have already written many professional and popular articles on the causes of effective and ineffective schools. And the Brookings Institution recently published a book in which we elaborate on our initial findings; report in detail on the final results of our nationwide study of 400 high schools and over 20,000 students, teachers, and principals; and offer a blueprint for reform. That work has generated a great deal of interest among reformers and a great many questions too. Accordingly, here we try to answer the questions that we are asked most frequently by politicians, journalists, administrators, and educators who have read our work on school performance and reform or who are otherwise interested in educational choice. And in doing so, we also try to show why reformers should give choice a chance.[1]

[1]Because this paper was written primarily to inform education reformers about the practical implications of our research on public and private schools, and not to report the results of our research directly, it does not provide extensive primary or secondary documentation of our arguments or findings. Readers interested in detailed supporting material can find it in our other publications, especially John E. Chubb and Terry M. Moe, *Politics, Markets, and America's Schools* (Washington:

1. Are the nation's schools really performing so poorly that wholesale changes in them must be considered?

Yes. Schools in the United States appear to be doing a worse job than schools in this country did in the past and than schools in other countries are doing now. We say "appear" because there are many factors that influence the accomplishments of students besides schools—factors that have never been adequately controlled in analyses of U.S. students over time or in comparisons of U.S. and foreign students. Nevertheless, a number of relevant indicators are disturbing.

The academic achievement of U.S. students may be significantly lower today than it was 25 years ago. On the best-known indicator of student ability, the Scholastic Aptitude Test (SAT), the average total score of college-bound seniors fell more than 90 points between 1963 and 1981, and it remains more than 75 points below its high-water mark today.[2] Although some of this decline can be explained by increases in the size of the test-taking population (a growing proportion of the population is attending college), similar declines were registered on many other tests that do not present this problem of comparability.[3] For example, scores on the Iowa Achievement Test, administered to students in grades six, eight, ten, and twelve, dropped about as much as SAT scores during the late 1960s and 1970s. The same can be said of the tests administered to students at ages 9, 13, and 17 as part of the periodic National Assessment of Educational Progress (NAEP). True, not all test trends over the last 25 years have been bad. The gap between minority and nonminority test scores has closed significantly. And during the late 1970s and early 1980s, depending on the test, U.S. students recouped some of their earlier achievement losses. Unfortunately, those gains have now stabilized and may well have ended.

Brookings Institution, 1990); John E. Chubb and Terry M. Moe, "Politics, Markets, and the Organization of Schools," *American Political Science Review* 82, no. 4 (December 1988): 1065–87; and John E. Chubb, "Why the Current Wave of School Reform Will Fail," *Public Interest* 90 (Winter 1988): 28–49. In this paper, we document only those arguments or conclusions not documented in our other published work.

[2]Congressional Budget Office, *Trends in Educational Achievement* (Washington, April 1986), ch. 3; Office of Educational Research and Improvement, Department of Education, *Youth Indicators 1988: Trends in the Well-Being of American Youth* (Washington, August 1988): 68–69.

[3]Congressional Budget Office, *Trends in Educational Achievement*, ch. 3.

SAT scores, to cite a clear example of this, have not risen since 1985—and they suffered a two-point fall in 1988.[4]

Another troubling trend is the persistently high rate of high school dropouts. Again, the facts depend to an extent on how the measurement is done. If dropouts are taken to include those young people of normal high school age who either are not in school or are out of school and do not have a regular high school diploma (not equivalency credentials), the average dropout rate is currently about 25 percent, and as much as 50 percent in some cities with high percentages of minority enrollment.[5] If the dropout rate is taken to count only those students who have failed by their late 20s to receive either a regular diploma or a high school equivalency credential, the rate is not as bad—13.9 percent in 1986.[6] But the disturbing fact about the dropout rate is that, however it is measured, it has not declined significantly since 1970. After making great strides in increasing school attendance in the immediate postwar era—half of all adults did not have a high school education in 1950—U.S. schools have stopped making progress, far short of success, in reaching this modest educational objective.[7]

Trends aside, the accomplishments of average U.S. students today are also very unimpressive. The NAEP classifies fewer than 10 percent of all 13-year-olds as "adept" at reading, and fewer than 1 percent as "advanced."[8] Large percentages of the 17-year-olds taking the NAEP tests incorrectly answered questions requiring only basic skills or knowledge. For example, 47 percent could not "express 9/100 as a percent." Only 5 percent could calculate the cost per kilowatt on an electrical bill that charged $9.09 for 606 kilowatts of electricity. Twenty-six percent of the students did not know that Congress is part of the legislative branch of government. The same proportion could not define "democracy." On other NAEP tests, 43 percent of all high school students could not place

---

[4]The College Board, *News from The College Board*, September 20, 1988; see table entitled "College-Bound Seniors, SAT Score Averages, 1967–1988."

[5]"Data Bank," *Education Week* (February 18, 1987): 19–21.

[6]Office of Educational Research and Improvement, Department of Education, *Youth Indicators 1988*, p. 52.

[7]Ibid., pp. 52–55.

[8]This and the following examples are discussed in Congressional Budget Office, *Trends in Educational Achievement*, pp. 43, 46.

118

World War I in even the broad historical period of 1900–50, and 75 percent could not place Abraham Lincoln's presidency in the era 1840–80.[9]

By international standards that kind of performance also fails to measure up. Eighth-grade students in the United States placed next to last on a 1981–82 mathematics test administered in 12 advanced industrial democracies.[10] The averages of Japanese students, the highest in the world, were about 15 percent higher than those of American students. In a 1982 comparison of the best mathematics students in 11 nations, including many nations with which the United States competes economically, American students came in dead last in calculus and algebra, scoring at the same level as the median of all Japanese 17-year-olds.[11]

The most recent comparisons tell the same story. A new study conducted by the Educational Testing Service for the National Science Foundation and the Department of Education found American 13-year-olds performing worse or no better in science and mathematics than students in all of the other countries in the study—the United Kingdom, Ireland, Spain, Canada, and South Korea.[12] In mathematics, South Korean students, the highest performers, are achieving levels four times those of American students—an alarming statistic indeed, but far from an isolated one. By most measures, U.S. students are doing rather poorly, and their schools must bear some responsibility for this.

2. What have U.S. schools been doing about the troubling trends in student performance?

For the last 20 years U.S. schools have been trying in many and varied ways to improve student performance. Educational systems did not wait until the 1983 presidential report, A Nation at Risk, warned of a "rising tide of mediocrity" to begin seeking improvement. The national decline in test scores was apparent by the early

[9]William J. Bennett, American Education: Making It Work (Washington: Government Printing Office, April 1988), p. 13.

[10]Office of Educational Research and Improvement, Department of Education, Youth Indicators 1988, pp. 64–65.

[11]Bennett, p. 12.

[12]Barbara Vobejda, "Survey of Math, Science Skills Puts U.S. Students at Bottom," Washington Post, February 1, 1989, pp. A1, A14.

1970s, and efforts to turn that decline around—to boost student achievement—began in earnest at that time. For example, the 1970s saw a strong nationwide movement to hold schools accountable for student performance. The 1970s also brought innovations in curriculum, instruction, and special programs almost as numerous as the state and local systems of education that implemented them. To be sure, the 1980s saw stronger waves of reform sweep across the nation. But the important point is that the nation's school systems began introducing reforms attacking educational mediocrity a long time ago, and they have continued to pursue such reforms over the last two decades.[13]

This experience should at least make reformers skeptical of new efforts to improve education through the existing school systems. Although it would be premature to pass final judgment on the school reforms of the last five years, it is fair to say that U.S. school systems can provide little evidence that their last two decades of reform efforts have paid off. And there is ample evidence that the dominant approaches to reform that the schools have used— approaches that rely heavily on spending and regulation—have not been working out.

It may come as a surprise to some participants in the current educational debate, but public schools are increasingly well-funded institutions. Between 1970 and 1987, current expenditures per student increased 407 percent in nominal terms against an inflation rate of 177 percent.[14] That represents a real increase of 83 percent. Total expenditures per student in daily attendance reached $4,300 by 1987.[15] For the sake of comparison, that amount is almost twice the cost of educating a student in a Catholic school, where— research indicates—the education is superior.[16] Even during the

[13]On school reform in the 1960s and 1970s, see especially Diane Ravitch, *The Troubled Crusade: American Education 1945–1980* (New York: Basic Books, 1983).

[14]Calculated from the following tables: Table 217, "Public Elementary and Secondary School Estimated Finances, 1970 to 1987, and by State, 1987," in Bureau of the Census, *Statistical Abstract of the United States: 1988* (Washington, 1988); Table 181, "Estimated Public School Expenditures, 1970, and Personal Income, 1968, by States," in Bureau of the Census, *Statistical Abstract of the United States: 1970* (Washington, 1970).

[15]Bennett, p. 45.

[16]Per-student current expenditures in Catholic high schools averaged $2,690 in 1987–88; based on conversation with Fred Brigham of the National Catholic Education Association, Washington, February 8, 1989.

120

1970s, the period of steepest decline in student achievement, current expenditures per student in the public schools increased 44 percent in real terms.[17]

What were these increased financial resources being used for? Some portion of the additional money was being used for two things that educational systems have long argued are vital to school improvement: teacher salaries were increased, and class sizes were decreased. Between 1970 and 1987, the average teacher salary in the United States increased from $8,560 to $26,700, and the average ratio of students to teachers (a proxy for class size) fell from 22.3 to 17.6.[18] Moreover, the increases in teacher salaries purchased at least nominal gains in teacher quality. The percentage of teachers with master's degrees doubled between 1970 and 1983, reaching 53 percent.[19]

These "improvements" account for about half of the 83 percent real increase in education spending per student over the period. Although the increase in average teacher salaries amounted to only 12 percent in real terms, the increase had to be paid to 27 percent more teachers per student. Therefore, the cost of teacher salaries rose 42 percent per student between 1970 and 1987. If the returns on this investment have been meager—and this apparently is so—there are three immediate reasons. One is that reductions in student/teacher ratios, or class sizes, of the magnitude achieved during

[17]Calculated from the following tables: Table 271, "Public School Finances, 1975 to 1981, and by State, 1981," in Bureau of the Census, *Statistical Abstract of the United States: 1982–83* (Washington, 1982); Table 181, "Estimated Public School Expenditures, 1970, and Personal Income, 1968, by States," in Bureau of the Census, *Statistical Abstract of the United States: 1970* (Washington, 1970).

[18]Salary figures were obtained from Table 211, "Public Elementary and Secondary Schools—Number and Average Salary of Classroom Teachers, 1960 to 1987, and by State, 1987," in Bureau of the Census, *Statistical Abstract of the United States: 1988* (Washington, 1988); Table 185, "Public Elementary and Secondary Schools—Estimated Number and Average Salary of Classroom Teachers, States: 1970," in Bureau of the Census, *Statistical Abstract of the United States: 1970* (Washington, 1970). Student/teacher ratios were obtained from Eric A. Hanushek, "The Economics of Schooling: Production and Efficiency in Public Schools," *Journal of Economic Literature* 24 (September 1986): 1148; and, for the most recent year, telephone conversation with Nancy Protheroe, Educational Research Service, Arlington, Va.

[19]Hanushek, p. 1149.

the 1970s and 1980s simply may not produce systematic improvements in student achievement. Another reason is that these reductions were not achieved through careful efforts to increase student-teacher contact but rather as a by-product of efforts to minimize teacher layoffs during a period of declining student enrollments. A final reason is that the higher average salaries—actually 7 percent lower during the 1970s—were not being used to attract more talented teachers into the profession but to compensate those already in the aging teaching force for increasing experience and educational attainment.

If the increased investment in teacher salaries did not pay off as hoped, however, it had—and still has—a better prospect of improving education than most of the rest of the increase in public school spending that occurred between 1970 and the present. Schools are not spending more today than 20 years ago because of better books, materials, laboratories, equipment, or other obvious improvements in instructional facilities. Rather, at least half of the 83 percent real increase in educational spending per student between 1970 and 1987 was consumed by such things as more expensive employee fringe benefits (which doubled their share of school system budgets); rising fixed costs, such as rent, maintenance, and insurance; increasing use of auxiliary teaching services provided by aides and counselors; and last, but not least, educational administration.[20] Indeed, after teachers (with their higher salaries and fringe benefits), the school bureaucracy may be the single largest beneficiary of the substantial increase in educational expenditures over the last two decades.

Because of problems of data availability and comparability, it is impossible to estimate with confidence the size of the real increase in all administrative costs per student in U.S. public schools since 1970. But the data that are available describe very significant growth in public school bureaucracy during this period. For example, during the period from 1977 to 1987, when the ratio of students to teachers nationwide fell 8.4 percent, the ratio of students to central office professional personnel dropped 21 percent.[21] In other words,

[20]Glen E. Robinson and Nancy J. Protheroe, *Cost of Education: An Investment in America's Future* (Arlington, Va.: Educational Research Service, 1987).

[21]Ibid., p. 18.

122

administrative employment outside the schools was growing at two-and-a-half times the rate of instructional employment inside the schools. Between 1960 and 1980, local school spending on administration and other noninstructional functions grew by 107 percent in real terms, almost twice the rate of instructional expenditures per student.[22]

More instructional matters were also being taken out of the classroom. Between 1960 and 1984, the number of nonclassroom instructional personnel in U.S. school systems grew 400 percent, nearly seven times the rate of growth in the number of classroom teachers.[23] In 1983 (the last year for which such figures are available), full-time classroom teachers represented barely half (54 percent) of all local school employment; administrators represented 13 percent.[24] Whatever its precise magnitude, though, the recent growth in public school bureaucracy may have harmed more than helped the academic performance of schools. And, if the growth in bureaucracy was not generally beneficial, it partially explains why two decades of growth in school expenditures was not very effective.

In due course, we will provide many reasons for concern about school bureaucracy, but an immediate reason has to do with the role of bureaucracy in school reform. Two decades of school reform have substantially increased the regulation of public schools. Schools are more constrained in their use of personnel, design of curriculum, choice of instructional methods, maintenance of discipline, and provision of special programs. School reform is not solely responsible for this constraint. Collective bargaining with increasingly powerful teachers' unions has helped to constrain schools. And the school systems, for their own reasons, have seen fit to take authority out of schools and to centralize it in school headquarters.[25]

[22]Bennett, p. 46.

[23]Ibid.

[24]National Center for Education Statistics, Department of Education, *Digest of Education Statistics 1985–86* (Washington, September 1986), Table 47 ("Staff Employed in Public School Systems, by Type of Assignment and by State: Fall 1983").

[25]On centralization and consolidation in U.S. public education, see especially David B. Tyack, *The One Best System: A History of American Urban Education* (Cambridge: Harvard University Press, 1974); and Roald I. Campbell et al., *The Organization and Control of American Schools*, 5th ed. (Columbus, Ohio: Charles E. Merrill, 1985).

Still, from the countless special programs of the federal government—for example, compensatory education—to the curriculum specifications of state departments of education, to the implementation of these innovations by district offices, school reform has increased the regulation of local schools.

During the past decade, moreover, this tendency toward more regulation has picked up pace. The powerful waves of school reform that have swept the nation since 1983 have followed well-worn paths. First, educational spending has been increased more than anyone thought possible when *A Nation at Risk* called for a long list of expensive reforms. Between 1983 and 1988, aggregate spending on public elementary and secondary education increased by $56 billion—an amount greater than 1 percent of the gross national product.[26] Second, many new regulations have been written. Some of these regulations may be desirable (although research does not encourage optimism). For example, almost all states have imposed higher graduation requirements on high schools, and many states now require competency tests of new teachers. But much of the regulation—as we explain below—has the prospect of backfiring. The increased regulation of student and teacher performance, now being widely implemented through evaluation and accountability systems composed of tests and a host of other so-called objective criteria, could easily rob schools of vitality and undermine their performance. This is a fairly well-known danger, but it is a danger that educational systems, now so heavily dependent on central administration, seem willing to accept. It is also a danger that politicians, who ultimately are responsible for these systems, can hardly avoid. With education organized as it is, politicians interested in improving school performance have little choice but to provide educational systems with more money and then try to regulate how those systems use it. Within the existing systems, reform options are limited.

3. What do other researchers have to say about the recent trends in learning and schooling?

The decline in student test scores over the last 25 years is one of the most researched and least understood phenomena in education.

[26]Bennett, p. 45.

As yet, researchers have produced no simple or adequate explanation for it. The trend appears to be the product of many factors, some educational but many noneducational. The most important factor, accounting for perhaps a fifth of the total decline, appears to be a change in the socioeconomic composition of the test-taking population.[27] U.S. schools were taking in different kinds of students, students who were more difficult to educate than students in the past. Influences in the home were also changing. For example, the second most important factor in the decline (and brief upturn) appears to be change in family size, with larger families initially hampering achievement and then smaller families encouraging it.

It is also clear that the decline did not affect all grades equally. The decline consisted primarily of worsening scores among students born before 1963, the "baby-boom" generation.[28] As these students moved through the schools, test scores declined, pushing SAT scores down from 1964 to 1979. But as the baby boomers began to be replaced, around 1970, by a new cohort, test scores in the early grades began to climb. By 1980, the younger cohort, now in high school, was taking the SAT and posting the modest increases in SAT scores observed during the early 1980s. Unfortunately, further gains have not been posted by subsequent cohorts, leaving achievement generally below the levels of 25 years ago.

The significant contribution of so-called compositional and cohort effects to changes in test scores highlights the importance of factors beyond the control of schools that affect student achievement. Yet, even when additional noneducational factors are taken into account—alcohol and drug use, and exposure to environmental lead (both of which had small effects on test scores); and single-parent households, maternal employment, and television viewing (none of which had any measured effect on test scores)—no more than a third of the variation in test scores over time can be explained.[29] That leaves a lot of room for educational factors to make a difference.

---

[27]Congressional Budget Office, *Educational Achievement: Explanations and Implications of Recent Trends* (Washington, August 1987), pp. 30–31.

[28]Congressional Budget Office, *Trends in Educational Achievement*, pp. 31–39.

[29]Congressional Budget Office, *Educational Achievement*, pp. 32–35.

However, researchers have made little progress in identifying significant educational factors. The most comprehensive study to date, made by the Congressional Budget Office in 1987, found some evidence that schools might have undermined achievement by watering down the content of courses, assigning less homework, and using less-challenging textbooks.[30] But the study found no impact, positive or negative, from such other educational factors as teachers' test scores, teachers' educational attainment, or state graduation requirements. The fact of the matter is that most of the relationship between schooling and learning over the last 25 years remains a mystery.

Some clues about the relationship can be found, however, in other kinds of research into student achievement, research that has not focused on test score trends but on differences in tests among schools at given times. This research has reached some fairly strong, though negative, conclusions about the connection between schooling and learning. It implies that there is no surprise in the fact that test scores declined or stagnated while school resources and certain school conditions improved. A recent survey of 147 statistical analyses of school performance, for example, found no consistently positive and significant relationship between student achievement and any of the major factors popularly assumed to influence achievement: student/teacher ratios, teacher education, teacher experience, teacher salaries, and per-student expenditures.[31]

Nevertheless, we know that factors outside of schools do not adequately account for student achievement either. And we know—from casual observation, as well as from careful case studies—that some schools are much, much better than others. The challenge remains to find out why. The research in which we have been engaged takes up that challenge.

4. Why does your research have anything new to say about the mysteries of student achievement and school performance?

There are two distinguishing qualities of our research, the first having to do with the kinds of causes of school performance we are looking at, the second having to do with the data we are using

[30]Ibid.
[31]Hanushek, pp. 1141–77.

to study those causes. Research into the determinants of school performance and student achievement has been dominated by what are often called input-output studies.[32] Based on the economic concept of the production function, these studies have tried to explain educational "outputs," such as student test scores, with conventional economic "inputs," such as expenditures per student, teacher salaries, class sizes, and the caliber of school facilities. The fundamental idea behind these studies is that schools, like any economic enterprise, ought to produce their products—educated students—with varying degrees of effectiveness and efficiency as the combination of capital and labor used in production varies. Years of study now suggest, however, that schools may not be like just any economic enterprise. Beginning with the famous Coleman Report of 1965, input-output studies have been unable to establish any systematic relationship between school performance and a wide range of indicators of school resources.[33]

The research that we have been doing takes a different approach from input-output studies. It focuses more on the production process itself. It considers how schools are organized and operated—in other words, how inputs are actually converted into outputs. The production process may well be more important in public education than the economic theory of production functions would suggest. Schools are not part of a market in which competitive forces can be assumed to encourage managers to organize their firms to use capital and labor efficiently. Rather, they are part of political and administrative systems in which the forces that managers—principals and superintendents—are exposed to cannot be expected to encourage efficient organization. It therefore becomes especially important in analyzing the performance of a public enterprise such as a school to study its organization. It is also important to examine those noneconomic forces that lead schools to organize as they do. While our research also considers the conventional economic determinants of school performance, our emphasis is on the production process—how it works and what causes it to work in different ways. Because of this emphasis, our research may well have something new to say.

[32]For the most recent comprehensive review of this literature, see ibid.

[33]James S. Coleman et al., *Equality of Educational Opportunity*, Department of Health, Education, and Welfare (Washington: Government Printing Office, 1966).

Our research is also distinguished by the data it employs. We are far from the first researchers to suggest that school organization is important, that it can help explain the weak link between school resources and school performance. Indeed, over the last 10 years, many researchers have completed studies that show that successful schools have distinctive organizations. Better schools appear to be characterized by such things as clear and ambitious goals, strong and instructionally oriented leadership by principals, an orderly environment, teacher participation in school decisionmaking, and collegial relationships between and among school leaders and staff. However, the studies that have identified these characteristics—studies known collectively as Effective Schools Research—have not settled the issue of school performance.[34] There are serious doubts about the magnitude of the impact that school organization has on school performance and, indeed, about whether organization is a cause of performance at all; healthy school organizations may be a consequence of successful students, and not vice versa. It almost goes without saying that Effective Schools Research has provided few clues about the causes of school organization; the focus of that research has been on organizational consequences.

A primary reason for the doubts about Effective Schools Research is the methods that have been used in most of the studies. Research has been dominated by qualitative case studies of small numbers of schools, usually reputed to be unusually successful. The few studies that have used somewhat larger numbers of schools and employed quantitative analysis have still not examined representative samples. From one study to the next, there has been considerable variation in the particular organizational characteristics said to be important. And the conclusion that organization is important, however frequently it has been drawn, is still based substantially on impressionistic evidence, uncontrolled observation, and limited numbers of cases. In sharp contrast, input-output research, however negative its conclusions, is based on rigorous statistical analyses of hard data in hundreds and thousands of schools nationwide. There is consequently more reason at this point to believe that the relationship between school resources and school performance is

[34]For a friendly, comprehensive critique of the Effective Schools Research literature, see Stewart C. Purkey and Marshall S. Smith, "Effective Schools: A Review," *Elementary School Journal* 83, no. 4 (March 1983): 427–52.

unsystematic than to believe that there is a strong link between school organization and school performance.

In our research, we explore how strong that link may be by employing the methods that have been used in input-output analyses. Unlike most researchers engaged in Effective Schools Research, we investigate the resources, organization, and performance of a large, random, national sample of schools in which all characteristics are measured with quantitative indicators, all relationships are estimated with statistical controls, and all inferences are drawn carefully to try to distinguish causes from effects.

Our data base is the result of merging two national surveys of U.S. high schools—High School and Beyond (HSB), a 1980 and 1982 panel study of students and schools, and the Administrator and Teacher Survey (ATS), a 1984 survey (which we helped design) of the teachers and principals in half of the HSB schools. The merged data set includes over 400 public and private high schools— the private ones providing a valuable look at school organization in a market setting—and approximately 9,000 students, 11,000 teachers, and the principals in every school in the sample. Although no single piece of research is ever definitive, and this is certainly true of research as new as ours, our work is a step in the right direction methodologically, and therefore a contribution that may well make a difference.

5. What have you found out about the relationship between school organization and school performance?

If school performance is gauged by student achievement, school organization is a major determinant of effectiveness. All things being equal, high school students achieve significantly more—perhaps a year more—in schools that are effectively organized than in schools that are not. Indeed, after the aptitude or entering ability of the student, no factor—including the education and income of the family or the caliber of a student's peers—may have a larger impact on how much a student achieves in high school than how a school is organized to teach its students.

We reached these conclusions after analyzing the gains made by roughly 9,000 students on standardized tests—in reading, writing, vocabulary, mathematics, and science—administered first during the sophomore year of high school and then again at the end of the senior year. It is important to recognize that by analyzing the gains on these tests, as opposed to analyzing only the final level of achievement on the tests, we have probably improved our chances of measuring the effect that schools actually have on achievement. Most studies of student achievement analyze test score levels, not gains. By high school, however, levels of achievement are heavily influenced by a host of factors preceding the high school experience. Our study looked at a variety of factors besides the school experience too, but our measures of student achievement were not contaminated by prior influences; the gains in scores reflect only the learning that has taken place during the high school years.

The influences on student achievement, besides school organization, that we examined included several that are generally beyond the control of schools—the education and income of the parents, the race of the student, the education and income of the families in the school (a proxy for peer-group influences), and the aptitude of the student. We also examined some of the conventional influences over which the school has control—student/teacher ratios, expenditures per student, teacher salaries, graduation requirements, homework loads, disciplinary policies, and more. When all of these influences were examined simultaneously, and in various combinations, most did not have a significant impact on student achievement. School resources and prominent school policies were not systematically related to student performance. This finding is consistent with the results of countless input-output studies that preceded ours.

In the final analysis, only four factors consistently made a significant difference in achievement gains by high school students. In order of importance, they were student aptitude, school organization, family background, and peer-group influence. Over a four-year high school experience, the differences in achievement that would be expected to result from being in the top quartile rather than the bottom quartile on each of these factors, all other factors being equal, are as follows: aptitude, one-and-a-half years of achievement; school organization, a little more than one year of achievement; family background, one year of achievement; and peer-group influence, less than a half year of achievement. In short, school organization may be as important to student achievement as the influence of families, a major influence indeed.

6. What are the organizational characteristics that seem to make schools effective?

Three general characteristics most distinguish effective school organizations from ineffective ones. The first is school goals. The objectives of effective, or successful, schools are clearer, more consistently perceived, and more academically ambitious than the goals of ineffective schools. More than twice as many effective schools as ineffective ones make "academic excellence" their top priority. In contrast, the unsuccessful schools place more priority than do the successful ones on such objectives as basic literacy skills, good work habits, citizenship, and specific occupational skills. Overall, effective organizations seem more likely to possess a sense of mission, something that many other observers of effective schools have also noted.

The second distinctive characteristic of effective organizations is leadership. The better schools have principals who are stronger educational leaders. Specifically, effective organizations are led by principals who, according to their teachers, have a clear vision of where they want to take the school and the firm knowledge needed to get the school there. This is consistent with the sense of mission that characterizes school goals. But there is more to effective leadership. There is a strength in the better principals that comes through in their reasons for wanting to head a school. Principals in effective schools are much more likely than their counterparts in ineffective schools to report that they took the job of principal to gain control over the educational performance of the school—over personnel, curriculum, and other school policies—and they are much less likely to admit that they simply preferred administration to teaching. In much the same vein, the successful school principals have more teaching experience and less ambition to leave the school for a higher administrative post. Overall, the principals in the successful schools seem to be more oriented by teaching and less by administration. The successful principals seem more like leaders, the less successful ones more like managers.

Finally, effective organizations are more professional in all of the best senses of that much-abused term. Principals in the effective schools hold their teachers in higher esteem and treat them more as equals. Teachers in such schools are more involved in decisions about various school policies and are given more freedom within their classrooms. They also treat each other more like colleagues, cooperating with one another, coordinating their teaching more regularly, and holding one another in relatively high regard. The teachers in effective schools behave in another important way like professionals too; they come to school regularly and present less of an absenteeism problem for principals. Finally, the teachers in effective schools exhibit stronger feelings of efficacy and beliefs that they can really make a difference in the lives of their students. And it is no wonder. In a school in which everyone is pulling together, working as a team—the concept we think best captures the effective school—and in which teachers are respected and trusted to do their best, it stands to reason that teachers would tend to believe that they can actually succeed.

7. What causes some schools to be more effectively organized than others?

This is a very important question, and one that has been asked too seldom. If school performance is ever to be lastingly improved, it will not be enough to know what effective schools look like. Knowing that effective schools should have clear goals, strong leadership, and a professional structure will not necessarily help reformers make schools more effective. It may not be possible, for example, to train principals to be stronger educational leaders, or to encourage them to treat teachers like colleagues or true professionals. Yet reformers in every state are trying to do precisely these kinds of things today. On the basis of Effective Schools Research, many state departments of education have established effective-schools programs to encourage or force their schools to develop more effective organizations. Schools are being instructed to raise their expectations, establish priorities, make decisions more cooperatively, and so on, but this approach assumes that they have become poorly organized because they did not know any better. Once schools know how to organize themselves more effectively, it is assumed, they will do so. This assumption, however, is likely to be very wrong.

Unlike Effective Schools Research, which has shown little interest in those things that might cause schools to become ineffectively or effectively organized in the first place, our research is extremely interested in the determinants of school organization. We have been struck by the fact that many schools have become effective organizations without the benefit of any research that would show them the way. By the same token, we find it hard to believe that many of the worst school organizations have reached their sad state because their superintendents, principals, or teachers did not know any better. More likely, schools have organized—effectively or ineffectively—in response to various political, administrative, economic, and educational forces that demand organizational responses. If this conclusion is correct, the key to school reform in the United States is understanding how those forces work and then making adjustments to them.

We examined simultaneously the effects of a large number of such forces on school organization. Many mattered little or not at all. For example, when all else is taken into account, higher teacher salaries and increased expenditures per student do not produce more effective school organizations. Even if expenditures are used to reduce student/teacher ratios, there is no significant impact. More effective organizations do not have more teachers per student—or, by extension, smaller classes. Ultimately, more effective organizations are distinguished from less effective ones by but two kinds of forces. One kind emanates from the students in the school, and the other is applied by politicians and administrators outside the school.

High schools are more likely to organize effectively—to set ambitious priorities, practice vigorous educational leadership, and operate professionally—if their students are well behaved, have above-average entering ability, and come from relatively well-educated and affluent families. If the students in a school exhibit any one of these traits, the organizational effectiveness of that school is likely to rank one or even two quartiles above that of a school whose students do not have that trait. This is not to say, however, that the impact of school organization on student achievement is artificial. Students still register higher gains in schools that are effectively organized, all things being equal. But a school is more likely to get organized to provide this academic boost if its students are more academically inclined to begin with.

Nevertheless, not too much importance should be attached to the organizational advantage of educating bright kids. The single largest determinant of whether a school is effectively organized is not the influence of the students in the school but the strength of the pressures outside the school. Specifically, the more a school is subject to the influence of administrators, unions, and—indirectly—school boards, the less likely the school is to be effectively organized. Schools that have relatively little control over curriculum, instruction, discipline, and especially hiring and firing are likely to fall more than two quartiles in overall organizational effectiveness below schools with relatively great control over these matters. This is true, moreover, when the influences of students and parents are held constant. Schools with less academically able students can be organized quite effectively—and can succeed—if they are given the freedom to do so by politicians and bureaucrats.

8. Why is autonomy from outside authority so important for effective school organization?

Autonomy is vital for many reasons, but two seem to be paramount. First, and clearly most important, schools that have control over their personnel are far more likely to develop many of the qualities of organizational effectiveness than schools that lack control. A principal who has the power to staff a school—to hire teachers and, if need be, fire them—is likely to fill the organization with teachers whose values, ability, methods, and behavior are compatible with his or her own. In other words, such a principal is likely to create a team whose members are deserving of trust. Team members are therefore more likely to be involved in school decisions, to be delegated more authority, and in general to be treated like colleagues. Because of all of these influences, teachers are also likely to treat each other more like colleagues. The result, then, of vesting more control over personnel in principals is to increase the prospect that a school will pursue a coherent mission as an integrated, professional team.

The result of withholding control over personnel from principals is much the opposite. Stuck with staff members who have been assigned to the school and cannot be easily removed, a principal will discover that teachers disagree with his or her educational objectives and with each other's objectives and methods. In this setting of conflict and disagreement, which the principal ultimately can do little about, the principal is going to be reluctant to involve teachers in school decisionmaking or to delegate additional authority to them. Teachers are also less likely to feel great affinity for each other and therefore less likely to work together closely. The school will tend, then to operate not as a professional team but as a bureaucratic agency managed by explicit rules and careful supervision. Unfortunately, the personnel systems of many public schools give principals so little discretion that the schools do tend to operate much like other, less professional government agencies.

The other general reason that school autonomy is essential to effective school organization is that successful teaching is probably more art than science; it is a highly contingent process, having results that depend on the interaction of the methods used and the students those methods are used on. No one method, employed inflexibly, will work for all students. Unfortunately, when officials outside of schools try to direct teaching, they inevitably push teachers toward using one best method. In the extreme, the well-intentioned regulation of curriculum and instruction so limits teacher flexibility that the quality of teaching deteriorates for many students, especially those whose needs are not met by the one best method. And this is not just a hypothetical problem: many researchers have identified the overregulation of curriculum as a serious problem in today's schools.[35] Ours is hardly the only research to find that schools with too little autonomy from external control often perform badly.

9. Because school-level autonomy seems to be so important for effective school organization and performance, why do some schools have autonomy, but most do not?

To aid us in figuring out how America's schools might be given more autonomy, we investigated why some schools already enjoy it. Much as we concluded when thinking about how schools could be led to organize effectively, we decided that school autonomy was probably not a virtue that would come to schools just because researchers or reformers thought it was a good idea. Rather, it seemed that autonomy stood a better chance of being increased if the forces that reduced it were understood and then attacked. Thus, we examined a number of factors that we suspected would influence the degree of autonomy that a school would experience. Our

[35]For example, see Linda Darling-Hammond, "The Over-Regulated Curriculum and the Press for Teacher Professionalism," *NASSP Bulletin* (April 1987).

results support two generalizations, one about public schools, the other about private ones.

Public schools are given relatively high levels of autonomy only under very special conditions. All things being equal, public schools fall at least two quartiles below private schools in autonomy from external control. To enjoy the kind of autonomy that the average private school receives, the public school must exist in the most favorable of circumstances. To be permitted to control its own destiny, the public school must be located outside a large city in a suburban school system. Its students must be making significant gains in achievement, and its parents must be in close contact with the school. In other words, when the public school is performing well, being monitored by parents, and not part of a large administrative system, it will be given relatively great control over its policies, programs, and personnel.

Unfortunately—and predictably—the public schools that now enjoy autonomy are not the ones that are most in need of improvement. And the inner-city public schools that most desperately require improvement are the ones that have so little of the autonomy they arguably need. It may even be that urban public schools are caught in a vicious circle of deteriorating performance, increasing control, and eroding organizational effectiveness. Under political pressure to do something about city schools that are failing, school boards, superintendents, and administrators tend to take the only actions they can: they offer the schools more money, if it is available, but then crack down on underachievement with tougher rules and regulations governing how teachers must teach and what students must learn. But crackdowns are seldom carried out deftly. And any intervention that responds clumsily to the real needs of teachers and students may undermine school organization rather than build it up.

Private schools, even in urban systems with high percentages of poor students, generally do not face these troubling pressures. Rather, almost regardless of their circumstances, they tend to be free from excessive central control by administrators, school boards, and unions. The main reason appears to be market competition. In a process much the reverse of the one in public schools, wherein political pressure leads to an increase in central control, competitive pressures lead to an increase in autonomy in private schools. To stay in business, private schools must satisfy parents—and satisfy them more than the public schools or alternative private schools. Private schools are therefore forced to organize themselves in ways that, above all else, respond to the demands of parents. One thing this clearly means is that private schools must vest a lot of control over vital school decisions—about personnel and curriculum, for example—at the school level, where the wishes of parents can be more clearly perceived and accommodated. Strong external control is incompatible with the imperative that private schools either satisfy parents or lose them to other schools. In contrast, strong central control fits public schools very nicely. They need not satisfy parents first; indeed, they must ensure that parents are not satisfied at the expense of other legitimate groups such as unions, administrators, and various special interests. Policymaking is therefore taken out of the public schools themselves in instances in which parents would have a political edge.

Because public schools are ruled by politics and private schools by markets, public schools may be at a decided disadvantage in developing effective organizations and promoting student achievement. Private schools, without the benefit of any reform at all, are encouraged by competitive forces to operate autonomously and to organize effectively. And indeed, the private schools covered in our research have more of the attributes of organizational effectiveness than public schools, regardless of the quality of their students. Public schools, however, are usually not granted the autonomy they need to organize effectively—political forces discourage this— and therefore they must be periodically reformed from the outside.

10. What does your research suggest will be the consequences of the many school reforms and improvements of the 1980s?

Our research suggests that the school reforms pursued so aggressively during the 1980s will have disappointing results. We offer this assessment with some caution because our research does not examine the consequences of specific reform efforts. Nevertheless, it is fair to assume that the consequences of reform will depend on how reform affects those attributes of schools that are most strongly related to student achievement. Most current reforms either fail to influence school characteristics that seem to matter most for student achievement or influence those characteristics in counterproductive ways.

Public school reform in the 1980s had essentially two thrusts, one to spend more money and the other to impose more standards. Thus, teacher salaries and per-student expenditures were increased by large amounts (as we explained above in answer to question no. 2), and graduation requirements, teacher certification and performance standards, and student-achievement objectives were raised substantially too.

Spending reforms obviously do not have a very good track record. For example, per-student expenditures increased nearly 50 percent in real terms during the 1970s (see our answer above to question no. 2), while high school achievement slid downward. If our research is correct, the record of the 1970s will be repeated. All things being equal, the amount that a school spends on each student or on each teacher is unrelated to the amount that students in a school achieve. Many schools succeed in this country with relatively low levels of funding and many others fail with relatively high levels of funding. Because so many forces more powerful than money influence how well a school performs, spending more money on schools will probably not transform the bad ones into good ones. In the very long run, higher teacher salaries ought to attract more talented people to teaching and provide some overall improvement. But there is no evidence that, in the short run, higher teacher salaries, paid to poor and excellent teachers alike, will spur improvement. And there is little evidence that the small reductions in class size that might be purchased with greater school revenue will boost achievement either. Schools can succeed with relatively high student/teacher ratios and fail when those ratios are low. In sum, if schools are given more funds to employ in essentially the same ways funds have been employed in the past, there is little reason to believe additional spending will bring about improvements.

Of course, many school reformers are wary of throwing good money after bad. They recognize that past investments in public schools have not produced their expected returns. Many reformers understand that giving poor schools and incompetent teachers more money will not turn either around. Reformers during the 1980s, therefore, got tough with the schools, holding them to higher standards and telling them more explicitly what to do. Some of this may be helpful. It is hard to argue with competency tests that prevent the truly unprepared from becoming teachers.

138

But most of the well-intentioned crackdown that reformers have launched on mediocrity over the past decade may not help at all. Our research shows that student achievement is not promoted by higher graduation requirements or more demanding homework policies—two favorite targets of school reforms. And more fundamentally, our research shows that the regulation of teachers and teaching can be detrimental to school performance. Current reforms employ more extensive teacher-evaluation systems, use more frequent standardized testing to keep track of student performance, and impose more detailed curricula and instructional methods. Yet, these are precisely the kinds of reforms that can rob schools of the autonomy they need to organize and perform effectively.

School reformers are not ignorant of the dangers of excessively regulating schools, however. And some reformers are taking small steps to provide schools with autonomy. School systems are experimenting with school-based management and other forms of decentralization. For example, the entire Chicago school system is converting to a system of community control over schools. However, there are at least three problems with such efforts. First, the so-called autonomy that schools are being given is being circumscribed by regulations governing precisely how decentralized policies must be made—specifying, for example, decision processes and participation rules. Second, the use of autonomy is being monitored with elaborate performance-accountability systems—for example, employing standardized tests—that threaten to distort how autonomy is used. Finally, autonomy is always vulnerable to political pressures that it be reduced. If schools use their increased authority in ways that are unwise or displeasing—and some inevitably will—school authorities such as superintendents and school boards will be pressured to intervene in school decisionmaking and to return to the pre-autonomy ways of doing things. Increased school autonomy is simply not consistent with public education as it is now organized. Unfortunately, autonomy, not spending and regulation, seems to hold the key to school improvement.

11. Does your research suggest any promising approaches to school improvement?

Our research suggests that the key to better schools is more effective school organization; that the key to more effective school organization is greater school autonomy; and, finally, that the key to greater school autonomy is school competition and parental choice. We believe, therefore, that the most promising approaches to school reform are those that promote competition between schools and that provide parents with choice among schools—for example, through magnet school programs, open enrollment systems, and scholarship plans.

However, not just any reform that increases competition and choice will do. To succeed, an arrangement employing competition and choice must ensure that the systemic forces now discouraging autonomous and effective school organization are fundamentally weakened. In effect, this means restructuring today's systems of public education.

The greatest virtue of a system of competition and choice, and the virtue that sets such a system apart from current systems of public education, is that competition and choice make it possible to provide schools with autonomy without their having to relinquish accountability. In a school system organized according to the principles of competition and choice, the responsible government authority can permit the schools to make virtually all decisions for themselves yet be confident that they will not generally abuse the vast discretion delegated to them. If the principles of competition and choice are followed closely, no school is guaranteed students or funds; rather, its enrollments and finances derive solely from students and their parents choosing that particular school. Schools that use their control over personnel, curriculum, discipline, and instruction to organize in ways that are displeasing to parents and students—and to teachers—will quickly find themselves struggling to stay open. Schools that use their authority to organize effectively, to provide the kinds of educational gains demanded by parents, will be well supported. In a system of competition and choice, autonomous schools, schools that are substantially free from top-down regulatory control, are held accountable for their performance indirectly and from the bottom up.

In public education as it is currently organized, autonomy and accountability work at cross-purposes. Efforts to enhance autonomy come at the expense of accountability, and vice versa. If public education were reorganized so that schools were forced to compete for the support of parents given the freedom to choose, autonomy and accountability would work in harmony. Competitive pressures would encourage educational authorities to delegate power to the school level where it could be used most effectively to meet the demands of students and parents. The ability of parents to leave schools that were not meeting their demands would work as a powerful force on schools, holding them accountable for their performance.

To be sure, the accountability that would be provided by market forces in a reorganized system would be different from the accountability provided by administrative and political forces in the current systems. In a system of competition and choice, schools would be more accountable to students, parents, and teachers, and less accountable to bureaucrats, politicians, and the interest groups that influence them. Although that may not be the kind of accountability that school reformers want, it is the only kind of accountability that is fully consistent with school autonomy and, by extension, with more effective school organization and performance.

12. In practical terms, how would a system of competition and choice work?

In an ideal world, one in which a new system of public education could be created from scratch and previous systems would be of no consequence, a system of competition and choice would use educational scholarships. The government would still fully fund education with tax revenues, but the money would be distributed to students and their parents in the form of scholarships, and not distributed directly to the schools. The schools would receive their funds when they cashed in the scholarships from the students they were able to attract. Beyond acting as a public education bank of sorts, the government's direct role in the system would be limited. The government would establish the criteria that a school would have to meet to qualify for scholarships—obviously, racial nondiscrimination in admissions, and probably basic accreditation standards having to do with course offerings and graduation requirements. But most of the rest of the decisions—about curricula, personnel, discipline, instructional methods, and priorities—would be made by the schools themselves—teachers and principals—responding to their clients. Although the government might want to be more involved in decisionmaking for schools and might

141

well get more involved, it would come under strong pressure not to intervene from most schools and parents, for whom competition and choice would be working effectively.

Unfortunately, we do not live in an ideal world in which we can easily organize public education anew. This means that we may need to employ less sweeping reforms than the one just outlined to implement competition and choice. The leading alternatives include districtwide or statewide open enrollment systems and magnet schools. These practical choice alternatives can work. Mechanisms other than scholarships can bring about many of the changes in school organization and performance generally promoted by competition and choice. But if the practical alternatives to scholarships are to make a significant difference in school performance, they too must make basic changes in the way our systems of education are currently organized. They must make substantial changes on both the demand side and the supply side of public education.

On the demand side, the changes are straightforward. Parents and students must be given the right to choose the school that the student will attend. Students must not be assigned to schools on the basis of geographic proximity or for other strictly administrative reasons. All students should attend schools they have chosen. This is not to say that all students would get into the school that is their first choice, in that schools for which there is excess demand would have to turn some students away. But those students who are unable to have their first choice should not automatically be consigned to schools closest to their homes—or to any other schools they have not chosen. Rather, each of them should have the chance to attend the school that is his or her second choice—or third or fourth choice, if necessary. If students are denied the right to make more than one choice, the system will not work for those students turned away because of excess demand. Present-day magnet school programs generally suffer from this defect. Although students who do win acceptance to the magnet schools are made better off, those who are not accepted are left behind—sometimes are worse off— in their neighborhood schools.

The shortcoming of magnet school programs points up a deeper problem in grafting a system of competition and choice onto an established educational system: although it is relatively easy for a school system to restructure its demand side—to provide parents and students with some choice—it is very hard for a school system to restructure its supply side. Unfortunately, if the supply side of public education is not restructured, changes on the demand side will not generate many benefits.

For a market to work properly, there must be enough suppliers, and also enough potential for the entry of new suppliers into the market, so that suppliers cannot dictate to consumers. If there are too few established suppliers, and no prospect of new suppliers, consumers will have no choice but to take what existing suppliers provide (assuming the good or service has no substitutes—that is, it is a necessity—which is true of education). In a system effectively controlled by suppliers—a monopoly or oligopoly—the consumer is not sovereign; the demands of consumers are not driving the production of the good or service. The very point of creating an educational system of competition and choice, however, is to change the system of control—to increase the influence of the consumers of education and to decrease the influence of the suppliers. This cannot occur if parents and students are given the right to choose schools, but the schools from which they must choose are tightly controlled by a single authority.

So, how must the supply of schools be changed? To begin with, no school should be entitled to students. Schools that are not chosen by students—say as a first, second, or third choice—should be closed. No student should be forced to attend a school that is so bad that no parents would voluntarily have their child attend it. Closed schools could then be reopened under new management, with new objectives, new programs, and perhaps even a new teaching staff. Of course, this raises the question of what should be done with the principals and teachers in schools that students reject and that therefore are not entitled to financial support. In a private market, the employees of a failed business must seek employment elsewhere. In a public school system, where tenure and other rules negotiated by unions protect the jobs of teachers according to seniority, many of the staff of closed schools are likely to be reassigned to successful schools, however unwelcome those people may be. If a school system maintains all of the rules of job protection established prior to the installation of competition and choice, the supply of schools will ultimately fall far short of satisfying parent and student demand and of raising system performance. This has been a problem in magnet school programs in which the most talented teachers win assignments to the magnet schools and the less talented teachers are permitted to continue toiling in the traditional schools.

An obvious way around this kind of rigidity in the supply system, the kind that may force students to attend undesirable schools, is to allow teachers, principals, or any qualified entrepreneurs, including parents, to start schools on their own. If the only schools that are created are the ones that central educational authorities permit to be created, the sovereignty of parents and students will be undermined. If, on the other hand, schools are free to be created by any educational entrepreneurs that can win parental support (and meet government standards of eligibility as a school of choice), the demand for the kinds of schools that are wanted will ultimately be satisfied.

So-called entrepreneurial schools might exist within established educational systems and therefore be subject to the same personnel rules as other schools. But if this were so, the kinds of rules—for example, tenure and seniority—that can impede the efforts of principals and teachers to organize effectively would come under strong pressure for change. If entrepreneurial schools operated outside established systems, the staff in those schools would have the right to vote to bargain collectively for the same job protection. But chances are the staff of autonomous entrepreneurial schools would not want or need the kinds of personnel rules found in public school systems. In any case, once students are not forced to attend schools they and their parents have not chosen, and educators are permitted to create schools that they believe students and parents will choose, the key changes in the supply of public education will have been made.

There is one other important change in the supply of education that should accompany basic changes in the structure of educational supply and demand. Decisionmaking about school personnel and policy should be delegated to the school itself. Where truly basic changes have been made, decentralization will tend to occur naturally. Competition induces decentralization. In a public system of educational choice in which basic changes in the structure of supply and demand have not been made, decentralization will not be as strongly encouraged, but it will be vigorously pursued nonetheless.

144

In a system in which schools know that their resources are dependent on their ability to attract students, the schools will insist that they have the authority to organize and operate according to their best judgments of what students want and need. Central authorities will be hard pressed to retain control over many of the matters that they now dictate.

The sooner central authorities recognize that only decentralized decisionmaking—school autonomy—is consistent with the new kind of accountability provided by competition and choice, the better the chances that a new system will work. In a competitive system of relatively autonomous schools, central authorities will still be able to contribute. They will be able to learn from the market who the weak principals and the less competent teachers are, and which schools are ineffective. Authorities can then use this information to work constructively with—or ultimately to eliminate—problem personnel, and to preserve the autonomy of successful teachers and principals. Systems of open enrollment could readily operate with central authorities performing in this new capacity.

13. How successful have actual systems of competition and choice been?

Genuine systems of competition and choice do not yet have much of a track record. Magnet schools and limited forms of open enrollment have been tried in hundreds of school systems around the country. These experiments have generally proven popular with parents and students, and have been credited with improving the education of the students fortunate enough to attend schools of choice.[36] Magnet school programs have also had some success in promoting desegregation, a goal that first brought many of them into existence. But whatever the virtues of these innovations, they only hint at the prospective consequences of competition and choice. Virtually none of the existing innovations have made the kinds of changes in the demand and supply sides of public educational systems that are necessary for the results of competition and choice to be adequately observed. The results of the many

[36]For a survey of educational choice experiments, see Mary Anne Raywid, "The Mounting Case for Schools of Choice," unpublished manuscript, Hofstra University (May 1988).

experiments with competition and choice are encouraging, to be sure; but they are only encouraging, not confirming.

Nevertheless, there have been a few experiments with competition and choice that have made more radical changes in existing systems. These experiments support the concepts of competition and choice rather strongly. In New York City's East Harlem district, one of the poorest areas in the country, student achievement has been raised from the lowest in the city to the median using a system of competition and choice that has multiplied the number, variety, and effectiveness of schools while reducing the size and central control of them. In Minnesota, students have been free to choose to attend any public school in any district in the state since the fall of 1987. The most comprehensive system of competition and choice in the United States, the Minnesota plan has not been operating long enough to gauge its effects on school performance. But the plan has proven to be workable administratively, and it has already resulted in abundant efforts by schools to reach out to students and parents. It has also encouraged school improvement without the actual transfer of many students. The mere threat of student departures seems to influence schools significantly. Finally, the Cambridge, Massachusetts, educational system, faced with the increasing flight of affluent parents to private schools, created a system of elementary school choice in the early 1980s that has won back parents and satisfied the first or second choices of the overwhelming majority of students.

14. What kinds of results should we expect from a genuine system of educational competition and choice?

In an educational system in which schools compete for their funding from parents and students who are free to choose among a range of existing and new schools, a number of desirable consequences are likely to result. Our research suggests, first, that the management of schools would be substantially decentralized. Schools would be given the autonomy to chart courses more consistent with the directions in which clients want schools to go. Second, this autonomy would be used by the schools to shape their organizations in whatever ways prove most effective in meeting demands. All indications are that schools would tend to become more focused and mission oriented, recruit stronger educational

146

leaders, and develop more professional teaching staffs. Finally, schools and students would become more closely matched. A constellation of schools—different schools serving different kinds of students differently—would probably emerge. Each school would still accomplish the minimum goals set by the government—for example, providing four years of English, three years of mathematics, and so on, to high school graduates—but each school would meet the requirements in different ways and pursue its own objectives as well. Some schools, for example, might stress the fine arts, others the liberal arts, others mathematics or science, and still others business and assorted occupations. And whatever the academic orientation of the school, it would tend to match the interests of its students.

These kinds of developments are likely to lead schools to perform those educational functions desired by parents more effectively than they are now being performed by public schools. For example, high schools whose very reason for being is to teach computer science should be able to prepare students better in that subject than comprehensive high schools do today. There are also three major reasons to believe that schools of choice will better promote student achievement more generally. First, our research shows that autonomous, effectively organized schools are more successful in bringing about student achievement, regardless of the caliber or family attributes of the student. Second, the experiences of magnet schools suggest that students achieve more when the school motivates students according to their diverse interests. Finally, parents are likely to become more interested in and supportive of schools when they have gone to the trouble of selecting the schools their children attend—as has already occurred in magnet school experiments. The sum total of these forces—organizational, motivational, and parental—stands to be higher student achievement.

15. In a system driven by the demands of parents and students, many of whom do not really know what is best for them, won't schools that are unsound but superficially attractive flourish?

A system of choice, driven partly by the demands of some frivolous parents, might encourage the development of academically unworthy schools offering easy courses, no homework, and diplomas for all who stay four years. However, competition would tend

147

to drive such unworthy schools out of business over time. Parents and students would quickly learn that the schools conducting flashy, superficial programs award diplomas that employers and colleges do not respect, and provide "educations" that leave students unable to function effectively as adults. Parents and students would quickly discover that schools offering more effective and no less interesting programs are more deserving of support. Ultimately, there is no reason to believe that parents would not choose those schools with a proven record of success in educating children such as theirs.

16. Even if a lot of frivolous schools do not flourish in a system of choice, won't the children of uninformed or disinterested parents end up in mediocre schools?

A properly designed system of educational competition and choice would not relegate the children of apathetic or uneducated parents to mediocre schools. First of all, many of the benefits of a market can be enjoyed by consumers regardless of their sophistication or level of information. In a competitive system, schools would recognize that because many parents and students are making informed choices, a school that does not strive to meet demands for quality risks losing financial support. Hence, all schools would be encouraged to improve, and parents who know little about school quality and enroll their children in schools only on the basis of geographic proximity would nonetheless know that their schools had survived the competitive test. The uninformed parent would be served in much the same way as the hasty shopper in a supermarket: even the shopper who pays little attention to unit prices or to other indicators of value is well served by the market—by the informed choices of millions of shoppers and the competitive pressures on producers to serve those shoppers best. This is not to say that some uninformed parents would not be taken advantage of by some schools in the short run. But in the long run, competitive pressures would tend to force out of the market those schools that do not serve parental needs relatively well.

Uninformed parents would not be served as well as informed ones, however. Those parents who care most about education would strive harder to match their children with the most appropriate schools. Of course, this happens in today's educational

148

system too. Parents who value education choose their homes on the basis of the quality of local schools or send their children to superior private schools. But the inequities in the current system are no excuse for permitting inequities in a new system.

To reduce inequities in a system of competition and choice, the government should take two measures. First, it should give schools a financial incentive to attract the children of uneducated, uninformed, and unconcerned parents. Schools that enroll students from such educationally disadvantaged families should receive additional support, perhaps $1,000 more per student per year. The government would need to decide what set of circumstances puts a student at an educational disadvantage, but it could use as a reasonable approximation the poverty standard it uses now for programs of compensatory education. The government could also use the money now spent at the federal and state levels for compensatory education to offer annual bonuses of $1,000 per student to schools enrolling the truly economically disadvantaged. These bonuses not only would encourage schools to reach out to those parents who would not make informed choices but also would encourage schools to take on the greater challenge of serving students who do not come to school already well prepared to learn.

The second step that government should take is to assume responsibility for informing parents about the choices available to them. The government could provide all parents with detailed information about school programs, orientations, faculties, and students. It also could provide statistics on school performance, such as graduation rates or test scores. Such statistics would have to be assembled with great care, however; the government could easily distort school programs by imposing narrow achievement measures that encourage schools to "teach to the tests."

As an alternative, and one that we believe would prove superior, the government could allow schools to provide whatever information they thought most useful for attracting parents and regulate the accuracy of the information provided. Recognizing that schools of choice would have strong incentives to communicate their virtues to prospective students and their parents—and this might well include the publication of test scores and graduation rates—the government could opt to ensure "truth in advertising" rather than to provide the information itself. In either case, by ensuring that

149

parents are informed and by providing schools with financial rewards for enrolling the educationally disadvantaged, the government could go a long way toward reducing inequities in a system of choice.

17. Because of the costs of transporting students away from neighborhood schools, won't systems of educational choice be more expensive than current systems?

A system of educational choice need not cost more than current educational systems, and it might cost less. Transportation raises costs significantly only if the supply of schools is restricted to public schools as they are now constituted. If the supply of schools is allowed to respond to demand, the supply is likely to expand, with relatively small numbers of large comprehensive schools being replaced by larger numbers of small, specialized schools. This expansion could easily occur without the construction or acquisition of new facilities if several schools share a building. "Schools within a school," as this concept is usually known, were used to more than double the number of schools in East Harlem's system of choice. However the supply might be expanded, though, students would find a significant number of choices within a distance that is now served by the transportation arrangements of public education systems.

Of course, if the supply of schools were not expanded, transportation would cost more, and either taxpayers or parents would have to pay for it. But these costs might not prove to be onerous, for they could be offset by administrative savings in operating a decentralized system. There is every reason to believe that the administrative structure of a public-choice system would be less bureaucratized than today's public school systems, and that it would look more like private educational systems, in which competition compels decentralization and administrative savings. Although the efficiency of a public-choice system might not reduce the costs of education substantially (depending on how it is measured, administration represents only 5–20 percent of the costs of public education), the savings ought to be enough to offset any increased transportation costs.

18. Should private schools be permitted to participate in a public-choice system?

Private schools would not have to be included in a system of educational choice for such a system to work, but including private schools would raise the probability of success. The greatest obstacle to a successful system of educational choice is a restricted supply of schools. If students who are unable to attend the schools they chose are compelled to attend schools that they would never choose, a public-choice system is not working fully. Rather, the system is mostly benefiting those students fortunate enough to attend their chosen schools. And the students forced to attend the schools that every student and educator who really cares about education is trying to flee may be made worse off. The solution to this problem (as we explained in our answer to question no. 13) is to decontrol the supply of schools—to allow unwanted schools to close and to encourage new, more responsive schools to open. However, decontrol will be exceedingly difficult to accomplish within established systems of public education. It would be much easier to implement if private schools were made part of the educational supply.

If a system of educational choice is implemented without private school participation, a provision would need to be made to permit new schools to organize in response to parental demand. If schools can be organized only by central educational authorities, the chances are great that the supply of new schools will not be adequate to meet parental and student demand. Central authorities will be pressured by teachers' unions and constrained by the rules of personnel systems not to close old schools or create new schools by transferring, dismissing, or even "counseling out" unwanted teachers. Although competitive pressures will make it more difficult for central authorities to protect and maintain ineffective schools, the authorities will certainly not permit the supply of schools to respond to demand in the way a market of autonomous schools would respond. Unfortunately, to the extent that a system of competition and choice fails to shift school organization and control from top-down regulation to bottom-up self-determination, the new system will fail to improve school performance. Thus, it is essential for even a fully public system of educational choice to permit principals, teachers, or entrepreneurs, free from central administrative control, to organize schools when they see the demand for particular kinds of schools going unfilled.

If any group of parents or any educational entrepreneur is free to organize a school to be funded by the public system of educational choice, however, it is but a small step further to include private schools. To illustrate, what would be the difference between a public school of choice organized autonomously by a group of educators and parents and a private school? The autonomous public school would need to satisfy eligibility criteria—for example, requiring particular courses and meeting safety standards—but private schools must already satisfy many state regulations, too. Indeed, a public-choice system might well adopt the minimal kinds of regulations now imposed on private schools to specify what autonomous public schools of choice would have to do. But however autonomous public schools of choice came to be regulated, they would actually look a lot like private schools—provided the new public schools were genuinely autonomous. In an effective system of public educational choice, then, there would be little difference, besides funding, between public and private schools, and less reason for prohibiting private school participation.

There is, moreover, a very good reason for including private schools in a choice system. Private schools would immediately expand the educational supply, the range of educational options. They would ensure that the educational supply would not be dependent entirely on the entrepreneurship of educators willing to bear the risks of starting new schools or on the responsiveness of central educational authorities. Private schools would immediately inject competition into the educational system, for in most states private schools are in abundance. Nationwide, one out of every five schools is private.[37] If tapped, the ready supply of educational options in the private sector would ensure that more parents provided with school choice would actually have their demands fulfilled. Without private school participation, a public-choice system could easily prove less responsive.

[37]National Center for Education Statistics, Department of Education, *Digest of Education Statistics, 1985–86* (Washington, September 1986), Table 8, "Number of Schools, by Level and Control and by State: 1982–83".

19. Wouldn't private school participation in a choice system destroy public education?

In contemplating the effects of private schools on a system of educational choice, it is important to distinguish between public schools and public education. Private school participation in a system of educational choice might indeed cause some public schools to go out of business; in fact, some public schools could be destroyed. But this is not the same as saying public education would be destroyed. Far from it. The objective of a system of educational choice is to strengthen public education, to improve the quality of education that is provided with government funds under general government supervision. If a public-choice system were to raise the average level of achievement of U.S. students by encouraging competition among and between public and private schools, that reform would be revitalizing public education, not destroying it. Educational reform should ultimately be evaluated in terms of its effects on students, not on schools.

It should be pointed out, moreover, that private schools might be changed as much as public schools by a system of educational choice. Private schools that elect to participate in a choice system would become wholly, or almost wholly, supported by public funds, and fully subject to the (preferably minimal) regulations imposed on public schools of choice. Participating private schools would therefore be hard to distinguish from public schools. And the distinction would literally disappear if participating private schools were not permitted to charge tuition on top of the payment received from public education authorities. Because most private schools now operate with far less revenue per student than public schools, many private schools would probably not object to operating without supplementary tuition. Any system that awarded private schools a sum approaching the current per-student expenditures in public schools would make most private schools better off.

Still, some schools, public and private, might want to charge tuition in excess of their per-student allotment. Whether this should be permitted is not a question we can answer, for it depends heavily on value judgments that can be made only by the political process. Permitting participating private schools to charge tuition beyond the public expenditure would permit those parents wanting "more" education for their children, and able to pay more, to purchase a

153

more expensive education without having to foot the whole bill themselves. The virtue in this is that more children would be able to avail themselves of a potentially (though not necessarily) superior education than are able to currently—either because they cannot now afford tuition at elite private schools or mortgage payments in the neighborhoods of elite public schools. But there is a possible price to pay for satisfying parents with high educational demand. Permitted to charge additional tuition, schools would have an increased incentive to try to attract affluent students, and the means to create large inequities in the student composition and financial resources of schools. These inequities may not be as large as those that plague public education today, but it would remain the responsibility of the political process to decide whether they are too great to justify the benefits that tuition add-ons might provide for many students.

It is also the job of the political process to settle one other issue of private school participation. The majority of private schools in this country are parochial or religiously oriented institutions. Although there is plenty of reason to believe that these schools provide very good academic educations, better on average than public schools,[38] there is at least some reason to exclude parochial schools from participation in a public system of educational choice. Americans may still believe, as they once did, that religion can interfere with the social integration that schools are trying to accomplish, and that religious schools should not therefore be aided by the government. The Constitution provides additional support for this view. But there are enough constitutional precedents for public support of students who choose to be educated in religiously oriented institutions—for example, government grants for private higher education, and special government programs for poor or handicapped children attending religious schools—to indicate that the courts might permit parochial school participation in a system of choice. Ultimately, the question of parochial school participation probably hinges more on the views of the public and less on the views of the courts, in that the courts have no clear-cut precedents

[38]See especially James S. Coleman and Thomas Hoffer, *Public and Private High Schools: The Impact of Communities* (New York: Basic Books, 1987).

to guide them. Be this as it may, before parochial school participation can be urged, value judgments must be made. We cannot say whether the potential benefits of opening up many good (and currently under-enrolled) religious schools to public school students are worth the potential costs of providing some public encouragement to the dissemination of religious values.

20. What, in conclusion, are the most important points for school reformers to bear in mind?

If our research into the causes of school performance is basically on target, it holds several simple but important lessons for school reformers. The first is that school performance can easily be undermined by school reformers. If reformers believe, as many certainly do, that greater effectiveness can be obtained from schools through enlightened regulation and training, they are likely to be proven wrong. The qualities that effective schools most need to possess—ambitious academic goals, strong educational leadership, and professional staff organization—cannot easily be imposed or taught by education reformers or government authorities. Indeed, external efforts to force school change, however well-intentioned, can make schools worse. The reason is that the organizational requisites for effectiveness tend to develop not when schools are told how to operate but, rather, when they are given the autonomy to develop their organizations themselves.

The second lesson of our research, then, is that school reformers should provide the schools with more discretion and authority. More decisions about personnel, curriculum, instruction, and discipline should be made by principals and teachers, and fewer decisions should be made by state legislatures, school boards, and superintendents. Educational policymaking should be substantially decentralized.

The third lesson, however, is that decentralization must involve more than the restructuring of public school administration. If schools are to be provided with meaningful autonomy—the kind that gives them more adequate flexibility to tailor their staffs and programs to the needs of their students, and thereby to improve the performance of their schools—decentralization cannot be accompanied by elaborate administrative accountability systems. To the extent that schools are required to make decisions and produce outputs according to the specifications of central education authorities, the value of autonomy for school improvement will be reduced. The only way to preserve autonomy and accountability too is to move to an alternative system for ensuring accountability. If our research is correct, the most promising alternative to a system of political and administrative control is a system that controls schools through the use of market forces. Public educational systems governed by the forces of school competition and parental choice are far more likely than current educational systems to encourage the development of autonomous schools that perform effectively.

There is a fourth and final lesson, however. If a system of educational choice is to make a significant difference in school performance, it must be freed from a key source of control now exercised by public school authorities. It will not be enough for reformers to grant parents the right to choose their children's schools. If the schools from which parents must choose remain under the firm control of central education authorities, parents will not have a real choice, and the system will not be subjected to the market forces that promise to change school organization and performance. Choice is relatively meaningless if the choices are not permitted to change. Hence, reformers should recognize that the most critical reform for them to make, if parental choice is to promote real school improvement, is to end the monopoly that public school systems have long exercised over the supply of schools.

Limited forms of parental choice are steps in the right direction, to be sure. But partial measures are precisely the kinds of measures that public education systems are most likely to undo. If educational choice is to make a real difference, it must be given a real chance.

8. The East Harlem Story

Sy Fliegel

The debate over federal school vouchers has died down, but the search for alternative mechanisms that promote successful schools continues. I have always felt that youngsters in private and parochial schools are in a system that provides them and their families with a choice of schools, and that it would be beneficial if students and parents in public schools could also have an opportunity to select a high-quality school that meets their interests and abilities. In New York City's School District No. 4, we hold the general belief that what is good for the children of the rich is good for the children of East Harlem.

The elements of successful schools have been decoded. The emphasis now has to be on the structure or system that promotes change.

Parental choice of schools can provide the catalyst for educational reform by introducing a market mechanism to the public educational system—a marketplace for ideas, innovations, and investment. It also can increase the sense of ownership for parents, students, teachers, and administrators. Although choice in itself is not a panacea, it does provide a framework for school improvement efforts.

When I was principal of P.S. 146 in Manhattan's East Harlem school district, I found one year-end ritual particularly disheartening: each June, a number of parents of graduating sixth graders would find my office to express trepidation about the zoned junior high school to which the students would now be assigned. They invariably were the best-informed parents whose information about the local junior high schools provoked some well-founded concern. And yet the best suggestion I could make, the best the system could offer, was, "Why don't you use someone else's address?"

A version of this article appeared in *Public Schools by Choice*, ed. Joe Nathan (St. Paul: Institute for Learning and Teaching, 1989), and is reprinted with permission.

Educators in other school districts have certainly echoed that strategy, but the situation in East Harlem at the time was especially egregious: in 1973 the district's schools ranked 32d out of 32 districts in reading and mathematics. We had all the problems endemic to inner-city, low-income districts. Less than 16 percent of the students in the district were reading at or above grade level.[1]

District 4 is located in New York City's East Harlem, sometimes called Spanish Harlem or El Barrio. Approximately 65 percent of the population is Hispanic, 34 percent is black, and 1 percent is non-Hispanic white. The district's geographical boundaries extend from 96th Street to 125th Street, and from Fifth Avenue to the East River. The poverty and minority-group isolation of the community are in visible contrast to the affluence of the communities to the south.

East Harlem has the eighth highest rate of welfare recipients in the 26 poorest areas of New York City. Thirty-one percent of the East Harlem population is receiving assistance from the Department of Social Services. This number is double that of both Manhattan and the city as a whole and is nearly three times the New York State median. Twenty-seven percent of the East Harlem households are headed by single parents. This compares with nearly 9 percent in Manhattan and a New York State median of 7 percent. Nearly one-third of the population of East Harlem is adolescent, twice the proportion for New York County.

And yet the severity of the educational and economic problems has proved something of a spur to educational reform in District 4. Meaningful change can take place, in the education of youngsters, under what appears to be the most difficult of situations. I believe in the judo principle, using the force of your opponent or opposition to make headway, turning a negative force into a positive one. A failing system allows for innovation and risk taking that a mildly successful system might not allow. The District 4 leadership in East Harlem chose to take risks and to be innovative in part because it had nowhere to go but upward.

How Choice Evolved

In District 4 we had the opportunity to implement changes and we began slowly. We did not have a long-range plan that has

[1]*School Profiles, 1973–74* (Brooklyn: New York City Board of Education).

158

brought us to where we are today. Rather, the process was an organic development that grew out of the needs, aspirations, energies, and vision of a number of dedicated educators, parents, and community leaders.

In 1974 District 4 started three small alternative-concept schools. One of them was the B.E.T.A. School. B.E.T.A.—Better Education through Alternatives—is the kind of alternative school that is always supported by everyone, even those people who do not support alternative education. Basically it says, "Give us your troubled youngsters and we will take them off your hands." I often thought one could get support for that kind of school if one didn't have a real school but a facade of a school building at the edge of a cliff. Principals in other schools would be happy to send to that type of alternative school their youngsters who are acting out, who take too much of their time, and who are not succeeding.

The B.E.T.A. School was a success from the first day it opened. We were able to provide these acting-out youngsters with a learning environment that accepted them as individuals who had difficulties adjusting to the regular school program. Three years after opening, B.E.T.A. was cited as a model program. It is worth noting that at one time we had 240 students in the B.E.T.A. School. In 1990 District 4 closed the B.E.T.A. School; it had only 35 youngsters.

Whenever possible, I prefer to have more objective commentators write about our schools (to me, self-praise is almost as good as no praise). Accordingly, let us briefly examine what outside observers have said about alternative schools in East Harlem.

In the December 1976 edition of *Encore*, a black biweekly news magazine, reporter Essie Baker had the following to say about the B.E.T.A. School:

> The children are not only enjoying school; they seem to be learning better, too.
>
> This is especially evident at the district B.E.T.A. School where the emphasis is on underachieving students in grades 5–9 who have experienced difficulties in adjusting to a regular school.
>
> John Falco, the school's director, insures that B.E.T.A.'s students get both a sound curriculum and a steady guiding hand. Falco works to provide the students with a sense of self-worth, self-control, and self-discipline, for once a child gains this positive self-image, Falco believes, everything else follows more easily.

159

Everything in the B.E.T.A. School is done to get positive results. . . .

In addition to the basic curriculum, the B.E.T.A. School offers a tutorial program. A reward system is an active part of the school's approach. . . .

Not every rule adhered to in a regular school is followed, but the results may be better—at least the children think so. All who were asked felt it was the best school they ever attended.[2]

At the same time as the B.E.T.A. School was started, we opened both the East Harlem Performing Arts School and Central Park East School. David Bensman, a professor of history at Rutgers University, has described the early days of the latter school:

In the summer of 1974, staff members of what would soon be Central Park East School (CPE) began posting flyers in East Harlem Day Care and Head Start centers to announce the opening of their new elementary school that fall. Their school-to-be had no constituency, no student body, no base of support in the poor, largely Hispanic community where it would be located. Its physical facilities—two floors of a seventy-five year old, run-down elementary school on 103rd Street between Fifth Avenue and Madison—could hardly have been less hospitable to the open classrooms the staff aimed to create.

The school building was already occupied by a school whose principal and staff naturally distrusted the newcomers who would compete for pupils, resources, and playground space.

CPE's way was not smoothed by foundation grants; the school had to make do with the resources available to all the schools in its District. And the school's irregular status was a burden. Its leader lacked a principal's title, prerogatives, and power. Nor was the school exempt from the numerous rules and procedures of the Central Board of Education and United Federation of Teachers.

Most of the educational reformers then active in the District were busy developing a bilingual program; they regarded CPE's efforts with attitudes ranging from indifference to outright hostility. Local educational conservatives,

[2] Essie Baker, "The Schools the Kids Call the Best Around," *Encore*, December 1976.

160

on the other hand, were equally mistrustful of what they saw as the school's "permissiveness" and lack of discipline. What this meant was that every decision the CPE staff made could be challenged; each of its failures could be held up as proof that the venture was misguided, or botched, or perhaps both.

By 1984, as the school celebrated its tenth anniversary, CPE was widely hailed as a success. Well-known educators from across America extolled its innovative practices and its startling successes. At the local level, the school's reputation ensured it had more applicants than it could accommodate, while parents from distant neighborhoods desperately sought admittance for their children.[3]

The third of our original alternative schools, the East Harlem Performing Arts School, is one of our largest alternative schools and is recognized as one of the outstanding performing arts schools in New York City. Students are accepted on the basis of their interest and not on their proficiency in the arts.

By 1976 there were six alternative schools in our school district and I was appointed the first director of the district's alternative schools. My job, as I understood it, was to nourish, support, and protect the existing alternative schools, and to develop new schools that would offer students in District 4 real alternatives to the local junior high schools their geographic location would otherwise fix for them. Having broken the mind-set of one school per geographic location, we were free to design schools as we felt they should be designed, reflecting our own biases and imaginations.

With the support of the district superintendent, I began working with the directors to create a cohesive network of alternative schools. (Directors were teachers who were functioning as heads of the separate alternative schools. They were not licensed and appointed principals.)

How to Develop Good Schools

What makes a good school? Some of my own beliefs follow:

- *Belief no. 1:* I believe strongly in public education; when I speak about choice, it is in regard to public schools. People

[3]David Bensman, "The Story of the Central Park East Schools," in *Quality Education in the Inner City* (New York: Center for Collaborative Education, 1987).

161

attending private schools already are part of a system that offers choices. Choice is meaningful only when quality and diversity are involved. Public education cannot take its constituency for granted. Our responsibility is to provide a variety of high-quality educational opportunities for children. Meaningful change can take place in the most difficult environments.

- *Belief no. 2:* To get somewhere, one has to know where one wants to go. In Lewis Carroll's *Alice's Adventures In Wonderland*, Alice is lost and wandering through the woods. When she comes upon the Cheshire Cat, she asks, "Would you tell me, please, which way I ought to go." It replies, "That depends a good deal on where you want to get to." She states, "I don't much care where." "Then it doesn't matter which way you go," says the Cheshire Cat. My belief: without a dream, vision, or mission for a school, the school will go nowhere. A school is an idea, a vision—not a building.

- *Belief no. 3:* Teaching and learning are so intertwined that it is almost impossible to separate the two. Many years ago, Neil Postman talked about teaching and learning. He cited the following statement: "I taught that, but the children didn't learn it," and then he asked, "Please define 'taught' as it is used in that sentence."[4] I don't think teaching takes place until learning occurs. For example, I would never say that I taught my son to swim, but unfortunately whenever he gets into the water he sinks to the bottom. I may have attempted to teach him, but if he can't swim, I didn't succeed in my teaching. In the alternative schools in District 4, teaching would be understood as inextricably linked to the learning that accompanied it.

- *Belief no. 4:* It is how you treat people that determines how they behave. This idea is illustrated elegantly in George Bernard Shaw's *Pygmalion* when the question is asked about the difference between a lady and a flower girl. It is not how she behaves but how she is treated that makes the difference. When children, parents, and professionals are treated with

[4]Postman said this in a course on language and human behavior at New York University in February 1970.

162

respect and high expectations, they will respond accordingly. On the other hand, when youngsters are treated without respect and with low expectations, you can be sure that they will not disappoint you.

- *Belief no. 5:* Smaller schools are better for children. Youngsters don't get lost easily in small schools. Teachers and students get to know each other in a personal way, and students don't feel alienated.
- *Belief no. 6:* Extending ownership of the schools to students, parents, and professional staff enhances achievement and performance. People treat what they own better than what they don't own.

By encouraging professional staff members to develop innovative programs based on interests, talents, or philosophical beliefs and by giving them the opportunity to realize their dreams and participate in the decisionmaking process, a school district can succeed in maximizing the potential of both staff and students. Ownership is established when students and parents are given a choice in selecting a school that is geared to their interests and abilities. Interestingly enough, in District 4 despite the diversity of personalities and philosophies of the teachers who presented ideas and plans for new programs, their reactions when given the final okay were always the same. They were shocked or surprised and usually asked, "Do you really mean it?" Their expectation of the system was that even when people expressed admiration and support for the new program, the establishment would always find a reason for not being able to do it at this time.

We have 23 alternative schools today, but we built them one by one, expanding earlier schools or adding additional ones when teachers in the district were willing to work together to develop a more exciting place to teach.

In 1987 we opened the Central Park East Secondary School, starting with the seventh grade. Eventually the school will include grades seven through twelve. The school is guided by the principles of the Coalition of Essential Schools, a national organization of public and private high schools directed by Brown University's dean of education, Ted Sizer. These principles include the idea that less is more—that it is better to know some things well than to

163

know many things superficially. High standards are set for all students, with the goal that students be able to demonstrate mastery. Teaching and learning are personalized, so that students are perceived as workers, and teachers function as coaches. Thus, students discover answers and solutions and learn by doing.

This school currently offers a common core curriculum for all students in grades seven through ten. The core curriculum is organized around two major fields: mathematics/science for half the school day, and humanities (art, history, social studies, and literature) for the other half. Every effort is made to integrate academic disciplines, so that students learn to recognize and understand the interrelationships between different subjects of study. The communication skills of writing and public speaking are taught in all subjects by all staff.

The Success of the East Harlem Experiment

By 1982 we had achieved enough of a reputation for our alternative schools—and had enough such schools—to invite all of the students in the district to select a junior high school from a list of offerings whose diversity and quality amounted to a real choice. A *New York Times* editorial praised our move to a districtwide system of parental choice:

> New York's School District No. 4 has done it again. For nearly a decade, the East Harlem community district has been a fount of innovation, offering "alternative" junior high schools that give students unusual choices. Now it will take the further step of allowing seventh-graders to attend whatever district school they like.[5]

The expected benefits of this experiment are most promising. Free choice will require students and their families to consider what they most want in a school. That half the students currently opt for "alternatives" shows they have strong views in the matter. Moreover, the competition for students should invigorate tired teachers and programs.

[5]"Schools That Dare to Compete," *New York Times*, March 25, 1982.

164

The results of our choice program were dramatic. By 1988, 64 percent of our students read at or above grade level (Table 8–1). Furthermore, since 1981 the district has ranked 16th to 18th in reading and 21st in mathematics among the city's 32 school districts. Today, District 4 serves approximately 14,000 students enrolled in prekindergarten to grade nine. The district is noted for its range of high-quality schools. Twenty-one school sites house 16 regular elementary school programs, 9 bilingual schools, 23 alternative schools, and 2 high schools. Each alternative school program has a thematic core, from science to sports, around which curriculum is structured. These high-quality educational option programs have

Table 8–1
SCHOOL DISTRICT NO. 4: PERCENTAGE OF STUDENTS
READING AT OR ABOVE GRADE LEVEL, 1973–88[a]

Year	Percent
1973	15.9
1974	15.3
1975	28.3
1976	27.9
1977	29.7
1978	25.9
1979	25.7
1980	35.6
1981	44.3
1982	48.5
1983	52.3
1984	48.1
1985	53.1
1986	62.2
1987	62.6
1988	64.8

SOURCE: New York City Board of Education, *Pupil Achievement Report,* *1989.*

[a]The citywide testing instrument for the years 1982–85 was the California Achievement Test in Reading. The population reflected in the figures includes grades two through nine. Beginning in the spring of 1986, the citywide testing instrument was changed to the Degrees of Reading Power (DRP); the grades tested with the DRP are grades three through nine.

attracted students from all over the city. The bilingual schools incorporate programs that support the retention of Spanish language and culture while promoting English-language skills and content-area learning. As a result of these educational option programs, District 4 has experienced consistent improvement in student academic achievement in reading and mathematics, and in student placement in academically enriched high school programs in New York City.

A measure that directly reflects junior high school achievement is the rate of admission into New York City's specialized public high schools—the Bronx High School of Science, Stuyvesant High School, Brooklyn Technical High School, and La Guardia High School (the old Music and Art and Performing Arts High School), all of which require an entrance examination. The exam is basically one of reading and mathematics ability. In 1973 only 10 youngsters from our district were accepted into the specialized high schools, whereas in 1988 more than 250 of our youngsters were accepted.

We encountered resistance, of course, but most of it has been overcome by the improvements in mathematics and reading scores and by the enthusiastic support of students and parents in our district. We did not allow anxiety over unforeseen consequences of the change, or the attitude of educational authorities, to dictate the form of adequacy of the schooling we provided.

There are many cop-outs for not doing anything. When I was a young teacher, I taught for nine years in Central Harlem's P.S. 129, an elementary school that was a demonstration school for the City College of New York. I would often go beyond the prescribed curriculum and methodology with my sixth-grade class. Older teachers would say, "You can't do that, the Central Board of Education wouldn't let you." I would ask my colleagues if they could name the members of the Central Board of Education—I knew that they had never met any of its members. Then I would ask, "Why should someone you can't name and have never seen prevent you from doing something you believe to be educationally beneficial for your students?"

In recent years the warning has been, "The union won't allow you to do that." New York City has the strongest teachers' union in the country. We have made many innovative changes, and the union has never been an obstacle. Often, the only obstacle turns out to be our own fear of opposition.

166

Today, we have 23 alternative-concept schools and 2 high schools in District 4. At some time or other, each of these schools has been cited as an exemplary school. The district has received recognition from many diverse segments of the educational and larger world. In 1987, for example, President Ronald Reagan said, "Inner-city schools in poor neighborhoods—like those in East Harlem's District 4 . . . stand among America's best."[6] The House Committee on Labor and Human Resources amended its magnet-school legislation to include monies for parental choice as a direct result of a 1987 "MacNeil/Lehrer Newshour" story about District 4. The U.S. Department of Education cited District 4 in the 1987 edition of *What Works: Educating the Disadvantaged* and presented us with a certificate of merit for outstanding progress toward excellence in compensatory education. On the advice of former secretary of education William J. Bennett, Prime Minister Margaret Thatcher sent her minister of education, Kenneth Baker, to visit District 4's schools.

Choice Is Not a Panacea

Let me offer some cautions and suggestions regarding systems of parental choice. As choice becomes popular, it becomes attractive as a way to solve larger educational problems. However, it's worth remembering that although we are always looking for panaceas, we seldom find them.

Choice has to be approached carefully and slowly, and development has to be organic. In East Harlem, we did not have a grand plan that envisioned 49 different schools in 20 buildings. When I hear about a school district deciding to become a complete choice system in one blow, I worry. It will do no one any good if all that such a system does it allow parents and students to select one inadequate school over another. High quality takes time to develop. It is much better to start with a few schools that are oversubscribed because of the excellent quality and diversity they offer than to have poor choices for everyone. Once those few schools are established and demonstrate that a high-quality educational environment can be provided for all students, it encourages the development of a network of alternative schools that eventually opens choice to all

[6]Ronald Reagan, Remarks to the National Governors Association/Department of Education Conference, Columbia, Missouri, March 26, 1987.

students. In East Harlem, we started with three alternative schools; we were concerned about developing high-quality schools that offered some diversity.

My advice: start in a small way, but make it successful, and determine what kinds of schools have appeal to parents and students. It is easier to start an open education or progressive educational elementary school because there are always parents interested in that philosophical approach and who usually are dissatisfied with the existing traditional schools. On the junior high school level, performing arts schools or schools for science and mathematics are the most attractive.

Our experience in East Harlem has underscored the benefits of starting small, with only one grade. On the junior high school level, it's best to start with two classes of seventh graders. Over the course of the next two years, another two classes of seventh graders can be added. At the end of three years, there will be six classes in the seventh, eighth, and ninth grades. For some reason, administrators like to expand when they have a well-organized and productive school that is able to maintain a family atmosphere and allows staff and students to get to know and care for each other. But I say: avoid the growth trap; if you must, add two more classes and stop.

The question of exceptional leaders is raised whenever the possibility of replication is discussed. I feel that every school district in this country has the potential leaders. In District 4, we created a climate that encouraged teachers to come forward with their dreams, visions, or ideas on how to educate youngsters. Most of our successful schools were developed from a concept by directors and/or principals who had a vision and an opportunity to develop that vision. They were able to communicate that vision to teachers, students, and parents, who then took ownership of the dream.

Our requirement was that a new director had to be successful at what he or she was presently doing and willing to put in extra time, energy, and enthusiasm to make the dream a reality. Once a school director was identified, it was my responsibility as director of alternative schools to provide support in terms of adequate space, funds, and personnel. Any new school needs time, encouragement, and protection for development of its philosophical base. Mistakes will be made whenever risk taking is involved. The district leadership must have confidence in the new school's leadership even when the latter does some foolish things. For example, if the alternative school is sharing space in an existing school, at some point it will infringe upon or slight the principal of the building. It becomes the director of alternative schools' role to somehow soothe the injured party. Nothing is as soothing as some additional funds or educational materials or equipment.

Inherent in the establishment of a new alternative school is autonomy to carry out its vision. All our schools must adhere to the following three guidelines. The mission of the school is to improve instruction and learning. It is the responsibility of principals and directors to provide instructional leadership by ensuring an environmental climate that is conducive to intellectual, emotional, and social development. Our schools have to be good places for youngsters and adults to share experiences and engage each other for their mutual growth and development.

What I have discussed above are the steps in establishing any alternative school for choice. The same steps can be taken when selecting or changing an existing school into a school of choice. In many ways it is better and easier if an established principal and his staff opt for becoming a school of choice. It avoids a great deal of petty maneuvering for territory and power. Of course, the best way to support and develop a school is by having that school provide high-quality education for its students. And high scores on standardized tests never seem to hurt.

Parental support built in at the school's inception goes a long way in protecting the school. Critics say choice cannot work in inner-city schools because parents lack the necessary education to make informed choices. They are wrong. Inner-city minority parents are no less concerned than their middle-class counterparts about having their children educated in stimulating, orderly, vigorous schools, and no less capable of choosing those schools when information is made available to them. Their lack of resources rarely presents them with a choice in education, but their aspirations for their children are no more limited than those of more affluent parents. Schooling often represents their children's only avenue of escape from the debilitating effects of poverty.

When parents are provided information about individual school profiles, student achievement, and school practices and philosophies, they make good choices. Selections are also based on experience, word of mouth, and public information about the schools.

Remember, I believe strongly in the concept of ownership; the more people who feel that they own the school, the better it is for everyone involved. Furthermore, to repeat myself, one of my major biases is the belief that meaningful change in the education of youngsters can take place under what appear to be the most difficult of circumstances.

I would like to close with the story of the Manhattan Center for Science and Mathematics. In District 4, we had demonstrated that elementary and junior high school students in an inner-city district could achieve and compete. Unfortunately, the quality of high school programs offered in New York City is limited. We were graduating fine youngsters from junior high school and we had little to say about which high schools they would attend and even less to say about the educational program they would receive. In our community, the zoned high school was Benjamin Franklin High School. Many years ago, when it opened, it was a good high school. One of its most outstanding graduates is Sen. Daniel Patrick Moynihan (D-N.Y.). Unfortunately, from 1973 to 1982, it was a failing school.

Only 7 percent of Benjamin Franklin's entering freshman class graduated; that left 93 percent as dropouts. Attendance in the morning was 44 percent. District 4 sent only a handful of its students to Benjamin Franklin. The rest went to specialized, option, or choice schools. New York's Central Board of Education finally closed the school in June 1982. However, three months later, District 4, in partnership with the central board, reopened it as the Manhattan Center for Science and Mathematics.

The center is now an educational complex that contains a separate elementary school, junior high school, and senior high school. Each school within the center provides an enriched curriculum in mathematics and the sciences, with computer literacy being a major subject. Our goal here is to prepare youngsters for a technological society and get them to go to college.

We graduated our first class on Sunday, June 29, 1986. Every student was headed for college, including Yale, Amherst, MIT, and Hunter.

Choice Is Working

It has been a long time since I was last disheartened by the inadequate response we had to give to parents who were dissatisfied with the junior high school to which their children were assigned. Today, parents in East Harlem do not have to present a phony address to enroll in a superior junior high school. They receive a simple application after an orientation process that includes classroom lessons in decisionmaking, a decisions booklet that describes all the schools, parent meetings in which school representatives and parents discuss each of the choices available, and school visits by parents and prospective students. This process enables parents to make the best choice for and with their children.

District 4 has received recognition from many sources outside our community. The greatest satisfaction, however, comes from the pride and support we receive from our students, parents, and staff members. The media and educational observers focus on reading and math scores. But it is the spirit of our district and its excitement over the countless student performances, exhibits, and daily experiences that make life for youngsters meaningful.

How do we measure the value of the trip to the Soviet Union that our championship chess team made in 1989? For the 15 minority students from East Harlem, it may have been the most significant experience of their lives.

Now that's a pleasant thought to close on.

9. Choice and Change in Public Schools

Robert S. Peterkin

There's an old song about love and marriage with the line, "You can't have one without the other." The same can easily be said about choice and change in public education.

Everyone agrees that change in our public schools is an agenda that needs desperate pursuit, and everyone agrees that one element of any change panorama must be choice.

But one major problem in discussing educational choice is to define what we mean. One could probably find a dozen definitions in the book, *Public Schools by Choice*, edited by Joe Nathan, in which I have written an article describing the controlled choice experience in Cambridge, Massachusetts.[1] Other options range from a choice program confined to public schools to the establishment of vouchers to pay for students to attend for-profit schools. Regardless of how "choice" is defined, the real issue is how to use choice as a vehicle for positive change, at least for those of us in the public school system.

Despite this laudable goal, if advocates of choice believe that they have a natural constituency in the black community, they are wrong. I make this arguable assertion to give us pause in how we approach the choice issue in urban school systems. The majority of the African-American community leadership in this country looks upon choice as something that will probably continue to rob their children of educational opportunity. So what might seem to be a natural constituency is not, as evidenced by my experience in Cambridge, the current Boston experience, Seattle's current move to a choice plan, and developments in several other jurisdictions. Most black politicians and community leaders are vociferously against choice initiatives. Let me discuss some of their concerns,

---

[1] Joe Nathan, ed., *Public Schools by Choice: Expanding Opportunities for Parents, Students, and Teachers* (St. Paul: Institute for Learning and Teaching, 1989).

because I think that Cambridge serves as a model for overcoming them.

The first issue is equity. Equity has to start at the programmatic level. It has to reinforce the benefits of magnet schools without magnifying their inequities. Magnet schools offer programmatic intensity and thematic cohesion and elicit parental support and student interest. But they also perpetuate certain inequities of access and resources. If there are magnet schools, there are also nonmagnet schools.

In Milwaukee we call magnet schools specialty schools, and so the others are "nonspecialty" schools. Parents whose children don't go to specialty schools call themselves "lottery losers": that's the downside of magnets.

Access—being able to get into a desired program—is very important to the minority community. In large measure, access depends on information, so the task is to get adequate information to those who usually are not well informed about their options in this society. We have to look for nontraditional ways of getting information to those people so that they really have access.

A second major concern is equivalence. A choice program requires schools that are good enough and have offerings that are wide enough and taught in great enough depth. Even then, I want to note, competition will not necessarily close down bad schools, because people find reasons to send their children to bad schools. Maybe those schools are in the neighborhood; in Cambridge there was an ethic in a certain part of town that you wanted to walk your child across the street, and that filled the nearest school even when the school was not doing well. In the ultimate sense, a choice was being exercised, but it certainly was not based on quality education.

A third major concern is empowerment. Districts must allow parents to pursue new options or to withdraw their children from schools if they are dissatisfied. At the same time, we want to empower teachers. We don't talk enough about opportunity for teachers, in a choice system, to get into a school where their teaching style matches the school's theme and the learning styles of the children.

Minorities are also concerned about accountability. The data on student achievement have to be disaggregated. We have to analyze not just how children in general are faring, but the status of children of all races and social classes and both genders. We need that kind of information to judge the beneficial effects of choice on academic outcomes for these discrete subsets of the general population.

Choice makes sense only if it works as a school improvement vehicle in conjunction with other important components of school restructuring—integrated decentralization, curriculum and staff development, collaboration with extended support agencies, shared decisionmaking, and teacher and parental empowerment.

Curriculum reform has to be added to the package. Choice cannot lead to improvement if schools teach the same old material the same old way. In addition to discussing basic skills, and the humanities, we have to get down to the issues of comprehension and cognition. Are our students making connections across subject areas so they can use and generate knowledge? That's complicated; it never makes the news reports. I've been talking about it in Milwaukee for a year and a half, and the reporters walk away saying, "What's he talking about?" I'm talking about what happens in the classroom. And if we do not change what happens in the classrom, choice cannot and will not make any difference.

Finally, we need changes in school organization. Along with public, private, and for-profit models, we need to talk about the structure of the school day. We have to restructure the way we present curriculum, the way we design schools. We have to give teachers enough time to explore subjects. If we just make choice possible, give people the opportunity to go to any school, and ignore substantive reform of the organization of the day, the year, or the school itself, we are going to be in trouble.

Let me illustrate my points with a tale of two cities. Cambridge was, and is still, a reasonably affluent suburb of Boston with 8,000 students. It was not under court order to desegregate. A desegregation suit was never filed, but it was likely that one would have been filed if constructive action had not been taken. There was pressure from the Bureau of Equal Educational Opportunity of the State Department of Education, charged with implementing the Massachusetts Racial Imbalance Act.

Many parents, citizens, and political leaders, having observed the turmoil across the Charles River in Boston for nearly a decade after U.S. District Court Judge W. Arthur Garrity ordered those schools desegregated, were fearful of similar trouble. Despite those

175

fears, most Cambridgians wanted to do what was required, to do it properly, and for the benefit of all the students.

Initially Cambridge sponsored a desegregated plan based on the attractiveness of magnet schools. Magnet schools worked well, and they were integrated. The problem was, once again, that there were nonmagnet schools where student performance was unsatisfactory, and those nonmagnet schools were, predictably, heavily minority. There was some mischief involved in this type of enrollment. Principals tried to select the best students from affluent or "trouble-free" families. That kind of mischief goes on all the time in public schools, and I would argue that it sometimes went on in private and parochial schools when I was a student in New York City. It has to be guarded against.

For the purpose of enhanced and fairer desegregation, Cambridge eventually adopted a controlled-choice plan. Stated simply, the Cambridge plan expands the concept of neighborhood from a small area to the entire city. A parent may request any school, and the child is assigned, on a first-come, first-serve basis, to the chosen school, provided there is space in that school and the assignment has a positive effect on the racial balance of the relevant grade in the school.

The access issue was important. Middle-class students dominated enrollment in magnet schools, while the poor kids went to nonmagnet schools. Under controlled choice every school is a "magnet school." We had a lot of suggestions about what kinds of schools parents wanted. Cambridge was mentally somewhere in the late 1960s; parents were really into alternative schools, so we opened a number of them.

With every school a magnet, parents get to indicate their top three choices, or they can rank all 15 schools in order of preference if they wish. In Cambridge, parents' options are limited only by space available and racial balance. During my tenure some 93 percent of people got one of their first three choices, and approximately 80 percent got their first choice. We maintained a waiting list. If you could not get your first choice, you were put on a list, and lo and behold, three months later, if an opening occurred, we called you and processed the transfer.

We gave a neighborhood preference; all things being equal, if the school was oversubscribed, we did let residents who lived closer to the school attend.

176

We allowed a sibling preference for families to progress through our schools. And finally, there was a hardship appeal directly to the superintendent.

Probably the most critical component of the success of the Cambridge experience is the Parent Information Center, which is staffed by a group of parents who are paid to disseminate information about schools to all parents so that at enrollment time, everyone lines up and has the same chance at the same time for the same number of spaces.

I often tell the story of Bill Walton, the famous basketball player, who came to Boston to play for the Celtics and moved to Cambridge. He came to the Parent Information Center, and he requested that his child be enrolled at Peabody School. The assignment officer called and said, "Walton's here; he wants his child to go to the Peabody School." I answered, "Do we have any spaces?" And the assignment officer said no. I responded, "Tell him what options are available." Bill Walton got the same consideration as the parent from the Jefferson Park housing project, no more, no less. We set up a process with integrity; everyone knew that his child had an equal chance of getting into any one of the elementary schools in Cambridge.

We provided transportation in our little district to get children to the schools they had chosen. We never limited the choice of schools because we couldn't provide transportation. And transportation is extremely costly. A school system can't create a choice plan without extra money for transportation. If you are going to tell people that they will have access to schools, you have to help them get to the schools they choose.

Every year I was in Cambridge, and I was there for four years, the public schools gained a percentage of the school-age population. Cambridge came in the end to have 86 percent of the school-age population—up from 78 percent when we started the program in 1980. That's significant, because that area has some very good private schools. We had a 30 percent increase in students who passed the required state tests and a 5 percent increase in attendance at the elementary level.

Let me turn now to Milwaukee. For 12 years that city underwent a standard desegregation process; essentially, a series of specialty schools was created. They closed schools in black neighborhoods, bused black kids to white schools, and enticed whites into the magnet schools in the city. There were gross inequities in the busing burden. Finally in 1988, the black community went to the state legislature and tried to take its schools out of the Milwaukee public school system. The measure passed in the House and lost in the Senate. It got our attention.

We began working with some seven to eleven private community schools that had had a lot of success with students who were similar to ours. Those schools were very interested in working with our students and creating a partnership with the Milwaukee Public Schools. We now have contracts with six private, nonsectarian community schools at the high school level for approximately 400 of our "at risk" students. We also have contracts with five private day care centers for all-day kindergarten, a program with 500 students. Both programs have Milwaukee teachers on site.

We proposed, with the governor's support, to enter into a partnership with those schools. The Milwaukee Public Schools would pay the tuition at private schools for approximately 1,000 students. The standards for performance would be set by MPS and the private schools, in an attempt to get the schools to deal with the totality of our student population through equal access and admission policies and also to help those schools avoid the draconian standards that our state has set for public education.

That bill did not pass. I was somewhat surprised, because, as a public school superintendent, I was heavily criticized by my colleagues for introducing such a bill.

People simply got cold feet. The state teachers' union, of which the Milwaukee union is not a member, protested, and the bill lost on strictly political grounds. We are reintroducing it this year, and I hope it will lead to a real opportunity for public schools to work with private schools in a partnership designed to meet the needs of all children.

The essential point is that such collaboration will probably bring more progress on the issue of choice than the mandatory perspective that many governors have insisted upon. That perspective has embarrassed many of us who care about public schools. And we, too, have a mindset that often is obstructionist as a result of the last eight years, during which the demands on the public schools have been heavy. It's the buffeting back and forth of demands that really

178

hurts us and our ability to envision a dream. We need to find a different approach—one that emphasizes collaboration between the public and private sectors to meet the needs of all children.

Postscript

In June 1990, the Wisconsin legislature passed the Milwaukee Choice Initiative. This act, introduced by Rep. Annette Williams, was not the legislation proposed by the Milwaukee Public Schools; in fact, it excluded the Milwaukee Public Schools from participation in all areas with the exception of funding.

The program was designed to serve a maximum of 1,000 low-income students, but ended up serving approximately 350. It is a program that has been widely heralded as a successful one, but the program is plagued by inequities of access and the lack of accountability. The Milwaukee Choice Initiative was declared unconstitutional by the Appeals Court of the state of Wisconsin and now awaits final hearing before the Wisconsin Supreme Court.

10. *Perestroika* and the Private Provider

John E. Coons

In this age of cynicism about the capacity of socialism to do anything right, it is a seventh-day wonder to behold a president who still believes in state monopoly of subsidized schooling. Prior to 1989 this side of the chief executive had not been obvious. Mr. Bush had been known to endorse parental responsibility, and some supposed that he might even extend this principle to low-income families. Guests at the White House Conference on Choice in January 1989 could thus be forgiven a fleeting impression that the president-elect was kidding. Why else would a free-enterprise Republican assemble the very people who practice what he had been preaching and then announce that the only producer he will subsidize is the government? Had Bush mistaken us for a meeting of defense contractors? Not likely. Military procurement would be the last function he would entrust to government producers. Education maybe, but war is serious.

And so, it proved, was Bush. He ended all doubt at a later meeting of private school types when he advised parents who want such an education for their children to dig down and pony up for the privilege. The National Education Association might have said it all for the new president; one wondered if it had.

There is something nicely burlesque about George Bush's post-election conversion to state monopoly. I do not refer to the repudiation of campaign promises; after all, what's a platform for? I mean, first, that this new revelation reached the White House precisely at the historical moment chosen by world socialism to declare its own moral and economic bankruptcy. While Mikhail Gorbachev had been secretly consulting Adam Smith, it seems that Bush had been thrown from his horse by a vision of Albert Shanker. Everyone was trading places; one wondered if Eddie Murphy might be Secretary of Education.

This restoration of the school monopoly to official favor was an anachronism in yet other dimensions. For one thing, it followed a decade of pioneering work on private schools that had shown them to be both less-expensive and more-effective places to educate the children of disadvantaged families. James Coleman and his colleagues had let this secret out, and John Chubb and Terry Moe reinforced the message from a fresh direction.[1] As is often the case, the poor seemed already to know by intuition what the academics had to learn the hard way. The long waiting lists for low-budget, low-tuition private schools have underscored the tragedy of poor families—often minorities—being stuck with the government schools that public educators shun for their own children. The testimony of these queues is the more poignant when we perceive that one by one, and sometimes in bunches, these private havens for the poor are perishing; the clientele they serve cannot meet the modest costs of their operation. The frustration of poverty-ridden families is confirmed by a decade of professional polling that consistently reports their aspiration to escape to the private sector.

Bush knew all this, and one could forgive the casual observer a moment of disbelief at the performance of the "education president." The managers of the existing structure, however, were quick to assure us of Bush's statesmanship. He was, after all, following a new line already circulating among vintage public school apologists. Several with records of survival had already selected public school choice as their next foxhole, and Bush had now given that course a respectability that would obviate the need for rational justification. The cosmetics were ideal. The faithful would rally for choice within the old fortress and raise the drawbridge against private producers. No explanations would be offered; let the wisdom of public monopoly be self-evident. Indeed, such a policy may actually work, at least if its objective is educational stasis. For that outcome, Bush has now furnished great hope.

To those interested in material improvement of the life chances for urban children, this new protectionism may seem tragic and

[1]James S. Coleman and Thomas Hoffer, *Public and Private High Schools: The Impact of Communities* (New York: Basic Books, 1987); John E. Chubb and Terry M. Moe, "No School Is an Island: Politics, Markets, and Education," *Brookings Review* (Fall 1986).

irrational. They had long been hoping for someone inside the garrison to open the window, and now the president himself had sealed it. Nor was it only the president and the educartel that were determined to ignore the evidence. Except for a few lonesome scholars such as Coleman, the university community has steadfastly assumed that, if there is to be salvation for city children, it will lie exclusively in the public sector. Reformers who are otherwise intelligent and well-intentioned find the prospect of a private contribution so utterly foreign and painful as to merit no consideration whatsoever. Some of this was to be expected. Other things being equal, academics prefer large systems that they can explain in one parsimonious hypothesis. Still, given the embarrassing new evidence supporting private education, there must be more to this neglect than mere cultural lag among the professors.

Whatever in fact is bothering these critics deserves to be brought into the open. If there is something negative about allowing the poor to use private schools—something to which a fair-minded person would give weight—let us hear about it. So far, their reasons for objecting to the inclusion of the poor remain largely a secret. Occasionally, honest opponents of authentic choice, such as David Kearns, argue that public schools would collapse in the face of fair competition. Such a despairing premise, however, could explain only that public schools *need* monopoly; it cannot begin to suggest that they *deserve* it.

Public School Choice

In a gingerly way, I propose to lift the veil on this issue ever so slightly by posing an intermediate question. Let me simply assume for the moment what I do not believe—that there is sufficient reason to discourage the private option for the poor; that is, tentatively, let us agree that society should maintain those financial barriers to private education that were erected in the 1840s to frustrate immigrant and urban families. On that assumption—that we should, indeed, conscript the poor for government schools—let us pose this question: could an authentic system of choice even be imagined in the public sector?

The answer, which I can only outline here, is, first, that the technical apparatus necessary to an all-public system of choice can be easily described[2] (and I do so below). That such a regime is imaginable will then pose the real question: does it make sense in a pluralistic society to impose such a stunted intellectual order upon the common family, and should a nation that values liberty narrow its interpretation of the good life to those ideas that can be preached from the government pulpit? This deeper question about the wisdom of an exclusively public policy is not so easy to answer. Which government-sponsored messages justify a state monopoly over the schools that may be chosen by ordinary people? Why is this regime superior to the kind of open competition among ideas that would be characteristic of a mixed public/private system?

But first, what are the legal and economic prerequisites of a state monopoly of subsidized choice? What technical apparatus must the hypothetical system include to qualify even as an authentic instrument of choice? My answer assumes without discussion that we have already agreed upon certain protections that are necessary for low-income families; these include fair admission rules, government-subsidized transportation, and the regulation of any additional charges that individual public schools might impose. Given this indispensable tilt toward the poor (a necessary component either with or without private schools), only two structural features would be critical: (1) there must be effective access to (and transfer from) every school within reasonable distance of the child's residence, and (2) there must be no rescue by the state either of unwanted schools or of the jobs of unwanted teachers.

In short, the public system must amount to an open market in which the consumers are subsidized but the producers are not. Each individual public school must rest on its own bottom. It must survive by its capacity to attract and live on the subsidies that are controlled by parents; failing this, the school's assets must be available to its creditors as with any other bankrupt. Employees of schools that go down must be at risk, just as in the private sector. They must expect to seek other gainful attachments—if necessary, in other professions. This change need not entail their forfeiting pension rights, but they cannot be guaranteed employment as teachers.

[2]Stephen Sugarman and I once tried to imagine various criteria of such a system; see John E. Coons and Stephen Sugarman, "Vouchers for Public Schools," in vol. 1 of *Inequality of Education* (Cambridge: Center for Law and Education, 1973).

Why not prop up failing schools and failing teachers? Because that is precisely what has made public school teaching a nonprofession and public schools a national embarrassment. When this country effectively guaranteed employment to teachers, we promptly got what we deserved. The problem is not that schools hire natural-born losers; most of our present teachers could probably become decent performers in a fair system. Rather, the problem in the present regime is that performance remains virtually irrelevant to teacher security and advancement. And it remains so even when teachers become formally subject to the judgment of their peers. As I lack space to prove this point, I will simply assert what experience suggests: peers do not discipline peers until the life of their common enterprise is threatened. Such a threat can come only from the empowerment of customers. Once parents can effectively exit, peer discipline will emerge without artificial stimulation because every person on the staff is put at risk by the failure of an individual teacher or administrator.

May I add that much that now travels under the banner of "choice" has literally nothing in it to justify this claim. The Chicago solution may be an example. That great city is in the process of radically decentralizing its schools. Each school has now chosen a council that is supposed to have real authority—and maybe it will. This arrangement will be grand for the parent group that controls the council and chooses the principal. For the losers, though, it will be simply a more intimate form of the conscription they have always experienced. Until they are free to go elsewhere, they will remain losers. And the people who are planning this system have so far opposed giving parents the chance to move their children to schools that they prefer. Chicago thus has re-created in its own neighborhoods the politics of the rural schools of the 1900s. This is an idea that resurfaces every generation. It may suit Chicago aldermen, as it suited some in New York 20 years ago, but it should not be confused with parental choice. And, until such choice is allowed to have its natural effect, the careers of tenured teachers will not be at risk.

Is a program of authentic risk and incentives the reform that is being suggested in the public-choice plans that you are familiar with? I hope so, but I have not yet heard about them. Certainly my state superintendent in California has nothing of the sort in mind.

He refuses to extend choice beyond a kind of lottery for problematic "space available" in already popular school districts. And, if he is threatening unwanted teachers with termination, this remains a guarded secret. As far as I know, even Minnesota has yet to incorporate such fundamental economic discipline into the various mechanisms it has called "choice."

Magnet schools have also been prominent in the mythology of choice, but here too nobody gets put at risk, except occasionally the students. This is the device most favored by our education president; it is a solution in which all the employees in the system are supposed to win. And I suppose they do. Good teachers get to cluster in the magnets and to enjoy enhanced resources. Marginal teachers get to move to backwaters where they can peacefully anchor. Every genuine success story such as East Harlem thus has a parallel tale in which the less-enthusiastic teachers unobtrusively transfer to other areas of the city and continue to ply their trade. Do not misunderstand. This is not the fault of the handful of creative wave makers who operate these subsidiary units. Within the system, genius has to solve its immediate problem by assembling whatever resources it can muster. East Harlem and its rare counterparts around the country are monuments to their imaginative founders. My only point is that magnetic education tends to be a zero sum game. Every magnet, you will recall, has one negative pole. The only exception to this occurs in Kansas City Missouri, a district that has repealed the laws of physics by making all schools positive magnets.

My need for sarcasm is now satisfied, and it is time to put directly the awful but stimulating reality that will face reformers engaged in any good-faith effort to provide choice. That reality is this: somewhere—someday—administrative and faculty blood will have to be spilled. There can be no painless *perestroika* even for our only socialist institution.

Market Socialism

In thinking about competition taking place inside the old fortress, there may be something to be learned from those desperately unhappy nations that have tried top-down control not only in schools but also in every area of productive life. How are they going about the reform of the production of services? I am woefully ignorant in these matters, but I could not fail to notice one feature of the new socialist spasm. The theoretical model on which much of it is based is as old as Gorbachev. The economists of Eastern Europe are only now retrieving from the dustbin what seems to be the best socialist thinking of the 1930s. This model—whatever you think of it—specifies a role for competition among government producers. The following brief passage is from a work quietly admired by Soviet-bloc economists even in the days of Stalin:

> The state should determine the money income of the citizen; and (2) the citizen should dictate to the state what shall be produced in return for that income. The former provision would insure that the interests of citizens generally would not be sacrificed to the interests of particular individuals; the latter provision would insure that the peculiarities of tastes and needs characteristic of each individual would not be sacrificed to some standard of consumption set up by an all-powerful state[3]

This paragraph is from the presidential address by Fred M. Taylor to the 1928 meeting of the American Economic Association. It was reprinted in 1938, together with a more famous essay by Polish economist Oskar Lange, which gave the book its title: *On the Economic Theory of Socialism*. The passage from Taylor quoted above is a summation of the position that Lange put into more technical terms. Their common hope was to prove that socialism could become as efficient as capitalism in deciding just which goods to produce while avoiding the social injuries that Taylor and Lange both associated with capitalism. After World War II, Lange, then at the University of Chicago, was persuaded by the United States to surrender his U.S. citizenship and to return to his homeland to become the Polish ambassador to Washington. Once in Warsaw, he promptly disappeared; for a half a century, so did his heretical approach. I am told that his work has reemerged in socialist intellectual circles as a plausible framework for a quasi-competitive state economy.

This general idea has an obvious application to our imaginary provision of choice among state schools in the United States. Even

[3]Fred M. Taylor, "The Guidance of Production in a Socialist State," in *On the Economic Theory of Socialism*, 2d ed., ed. B. E. Lippincott (Minneapolis: University of Minnesota Press, 1938), p. 48.

among a set of government providers that has been hermetically sealed from private competition, a form of market struggle could in theory be established. For example, under a set of legislated rules, a headmaster or cadre could be designated by a central authority to manage each individual government school. Every school—the basic unit of production—would be provided with its start-up capital from tax resources. Its potential customers—all families—would receive grants redeemable for education in any one of these government schools. Add whatever particulars you like to this scheme; again, only one is critical: the school must be on its own. If it lacks customers, it must go to the wall; its workers and managers must lose their jobs, and the school's assets must be made available to creditors. Such a natural mechanism for the extermination of failing units is essential. This I take to be the message from the East.

Oskar Lange and George Bush differ on this issue. The proposals supported by Bush show no commitment to put the unproductive workers in our schools to the discipline of the market. To put it plainly, there is no sign that authentic choice is what anyone has in mind—except possibly the Soviets. It is my own expectation that protectionism of this sort will triumph in this country at least as long as the prestige of the presidency is committed to state monopoly. Hence, authentic choice is impossible for the foreseeable future even in the public sector.

For one moment, however, let us assume that the thing actually happens—that there emerges an all-public system of subsidized choice, including open access for students and economic death for unsuccessful firms and practitioners. Let us also assume that these government schools offer whatever range of intellectual variety is constitutionally tolerated in the public sector; they become worthy producers of a certain popular, if intellectually narrow, brand of education. Would this quasi-competitive socialism for the poor be a healthy thing? We will have successfully excluded private schools, but was this a good idea?

Hostility to Private Schools

Straightaway I want to deal with the most extreme position on this question. There are a fair number of well-placed Americans who object to encouragement of private choice whatever the consequences may be for the quality of education. They would continue

188

to conscript the children of the poor even where government schools are bad and private schools are good, available, and cheaper. As this hard-nosed view is not ordinarily trumpeted in scholarly journals, my report of it rests largely on my own experience. If the reader's experience is different, he can correct me. As exhibit A, I offer a recurring vignette taken from personal encounters. For 15 years lawyers who like myself are interested in the plight of disadvantaged minorities have been interested in the possibility of using private schools to relieve de jure racial separation. Typically, the guilty districts are pathetic educational derelicts such as Detroit or Kansas City. Usually there are too few whites to make desegregation meaningful. Suburban public schools may be close by. They have both white children and space, but, for whatever reason, they will not cooperate by accepting voluntary transfers even when accompanied by attractive subsidies. Our proposal for such cases has been simple enough; let the guilty defendants pay for transfers to integrated private schools, if the parents want such a transfer. Inevitably, these private schools are less costly. Hence, the court can get more integration for fewer tax dollars. Nobody loses, except the failing schools that these families are trying to escape.

Throughout the past decade we have tried to peddle this form of judicial intervention to civil rights leaders. Their typical reaction has been to evade the question and to execute a quick getaway. Only with obnoxious persistence can one drag a responsive answer from most of the lawyers who still claim to cherish the values expressed in *Brown* v. *Board of Education*. When driven to the wall, they admit that private schools would be good for particular children. They admit that such transfers would further desegregation. They then conclude roughly as follows: "Don't ask me to do it; it would help private schools. Worse, it would help religious schools. I believe you mean well, but go away." (Sometimes they are not so sure that I mean well.)

This is fascinating. The device we have in mind would serve the apparent end that these reformers have consistently pursued. Nonetheless, it is intolerable to them, even where it is the only available solution. Presumably, then, the provision of choice among private schools would be even more intolerable where an all-public

189

system of choice actually was already educating children and producing integration. There would then be no justification whatsoever for encouraging choice in the private sector. The real objection of such opponents turns out to be something peculiarly negative about private schools as such. These critics would not subsidize parents in their choice of these schools, even if this policy would solve what most of us think of as the educational crisis. Fifteen years ago this attitude could have been cloaked as a superficial reading of Supreme Court opinions interpreting the Establishment Clause. That moment in our legal history has passed.[4] The real objection is now revealed as purely ideological, and, like every other dogmatic commitment, it is difficult to analyze simply in rational terms.

It cannot be that private schools are expensive and inefficient or that children from disadvantaged families cannot learn there. If there were evidence of this, it would have been presented in the journals, in the debates, and in conversations of the sort I have just described. Indeed, the objection to private schools has nothing to do with quality. It is also plainly independent of the issue of class or racial discrimination, and it transcends even the welfare of individual children. The complaint seems to be almost the precise opposite of those heard daily about the public schools. Private education is *too* efficient in teaching what some do not want the young to learn. It succeeds, they say, but it succeeds in being "divisive." It is hard to get a grip on this vague expression, but I will give it a try.

A recent paper on choice by a Stanford University education professor, Henry Levin, provides at least an oblique perspective on this objection. Levin opposes subsidized parental choice. He would not deprive the rich of their right to pay tuition, nor would he withdraw the right of private schools to subsidize the poor from the school's own resources. But he would maintain those legal and political fences erected in the 19th century to keep ordinary and low-income people from taking the educational initiative on behalf of their own children. And he has reasons.

[4]For an objective evaluation of the present law, see Jesse Choper, "The Establishment Clause and Aid to Parochial Schools—An Update," *California Law Review* 75 (1987): 5–14.

Levin believes that there is an inevitable "conflict between the private interests of citizens and the public interest of the commonwealth."[5] Education, he asserts, has a split personality. The family advances the child's best interest by choosing the school but simultaneously undermines the society in which the child must live. Here is a longer quotation:

> Education lies at the intersection of two sets of competing rights. The first is the right of parents to choose the experiences, influences, and values to which they expose their children, the right to rear their children in the manner that they see fit. The second is the right of a democratic society to use the educational system as a means to reproduce its most essential political, economic, and social institutions through a common schooling experience.[6]

For Levin this is a true dilemma between private and public interest. Somehow it all reminds me of the mechanical hand that emerges from the toy box to close its own container. Parents make choices that open the minds of their own children but close the mind of society. Given this inevitable self-canceling mechanism, Levin concludes that the only way to promote cohesion and tolerance in society is to force people into a "common schooling experience," thereby ensuring a worse education for the individual child. For Levin, this is not a hard decision. He prefers the public good to the private good. Hence, he cannot allow society to help send your child to a school where the families share your vision of the good life. That would be socially destructive, even if it were advantageous to your son or daughter.

I must address the substance of this important if paradoxical idea, but first a parenthetical note about its political credentials. People who assert this view bill themselves as "democratic." Levin certainly does so. This claim seems to rest upon two premises: (1) that intellectuals effectively represent the common citizen, and (2) that public schools are efficient teachers of democracy. A brief comment will suggest my assessment of both claims.

[5]Henry Levin, "The Theory of Choice Applied to Education," in *Choice and Control in American Education*, ed. William H. Clune and John F. Witte (Madison: University of Wisconsin Press, forthcoming).
[6]Ibid.

First, I should have thought that any solution to the education problem that claims to be democratic would invite the common citizen to take charge of his own interests and make his own decisions. Democracy supposes even poor citizens to be competent at the normal tasks of life. Second, although academics are certainly welcome to make claims of civic virtue on behalf of the public schools, they cannot expect skeptics to ignore their strikingly anti-democratic history. Some of us find it hard to hear Horace Mann portrayed as an apostle of tolerance. Charles Glenn and others have reminded us how 19th-century elites carefully herded immigrants into state schools to hear the received truth preached only by people who believed the right stuff.[7] In reality, democracy has been one of the consistent casualties of the school system. Lest we forget, it was the judges who had to lead the schools kicking and screaming to racial desegregation. Even in our own time, the Supreme Court has had to order the schools to respect the rights of religious dissenters and to open their doors to the children of illegal aliens. This elitism of "public" institutions has itself been an embarrassing lesson in intolerance for all of us. No one who has witnessed the exclusivity of a New Trier, Grosse Pointe, Piedmont, or Palo Alto could ever suppose that democracy is public education's most important product.

Nonetheless, Levin maintains that it is private schools that make it difficult for Americans to work and live in harmony: "[These schools] must necessarily create a divisive experience rather than one which converges on a common educational experience."[8]

What a dilemma! Either the children from ordinary families will be rounded up and given their education in "common," or necessarily their education will be "divisive." What a piece of luck for our society that the children of the rich are an exception to this rule. Having money apparently ensures that the schools such families choose, whether private or public, will be effectively democratic. It is only the rest of us that must be clustered in schools we have not chosen. State monopoly is nature's way of teaching nonrich Americans the civic virtues.

[7]Charles Glenn, *The Myth of the Common Schools* (Amherst: University of Massachusetts Press, 1988).

[8]Levin.

192

The evidence that private schools produce uncivil and ill-natured citizens is unknown to me. It also appears to be unknown to their detractors, for it is never cited. I do not claim that no such evidence exists or could never be assembled. Doubtless something politically unflattering about the graduates of the private sector could be found. In the meantime I will cite the considerable evidence of their tolerance and civility that I have gathered firsthand. Over the years I have read or written a bit in this area, but my primary experience comes as a parent who was able to afford a choice. My unimpeachable source is 130 semesters equally divided between public and private schools.

For me, it amounts to this: within formal education the major threat to civility has consistently come—and still comes—from the systematic disenfranchisement of the family. The specific forms of tax-supported elitism that I already cited are part of this process. But first and foremost is the coercive structure itself—this leviathan within which the poor are conscripted by bureaucratic strangers for schools the parents do not want. This system could not have been better designed to create hostility in its clientele. Of course, this response includes class and racial hostility, but antecedent to these is the simple despair of the parent of ordinary means who loses authority over a child for the prime hours of the day. The rich can buy out of this social and ideological draft and thereby maintain family sovereignty, but most parents are stuck.

This appropriation of parental authority by the state makes the present regime a cauldron of social discord. It takes no genius to see this; it takes considerable ingenuity to avoid seeing it. The problem is not that poor parents are hostile or indifferent to school itself; like the rest of us, they want education for their children. What they do not want is to lose their children to an alien institution—one that may not represent their own ideals but from which, in any case, there is no escape. Parents do not want schools that are competitors for their authority; they want schools that are an extension and confirmation of that authority. The rich already have this with society's blessing; the poor could easily have it, but society—including the president—will not give it to them. This discrimination and this injury are deeply resented. Here is division, indeed.

The Benefits of Private Schools

That sums up the negative side. Intellectual conscription breeds division. But why would a choice among public schools not be enough to cure this disease? Is the claim here that private schools have a special positive capacity to heal social division? I think the answer is yes. Before I explain this, however, let me stress that government schools would be prominent in any open system. By definition, they would have to be, for the driving principle is choice, and I assume that many—probably most—parents in the United States would want their children in schools operated by the state. That is one good reason that deregulated government schools should flourish in a subsidized competitive market. The private option, however, remains necessary to avoid social division because public schools cannot begin to supply the range of reasonable parental choices. To the extent that social division is a direct function of parental frustration, the responsible civic answer lies in subsidizing the choice of schools whose curricula represent the full range of parental beliefs and values. In the case of some beliefs—religion is but one—the schools will by legal necessity be in private hands. In short, an all-public regime could not satisfy the objective of social cohesion because in such a system the values of many parents simply cannot be served.

The idea, then, is embarrassingly simple. Parental choice claims to be a specific remedy for social conflict because it is the only regime that respects the family's values. Poor and minority families have never been trusted, and their historic reaction to this mistrust has been resentment. A new policy respecting their ideals would help, over time, to heal this pathology. Equally important, it would give such families a critical stake in the educational process. Necessarily, the parents would be transformed from their present state of impotence to one of decisive authority. My claim is that most will prefer such trust and responsibility to their present dependence and impotence. They will cherish and support the society that made it possible for them to extend their authoritative role as parent into the school years of their children. Politically, they will be zealous to protect the system that has respected and protected them.

Family aspirations for children, of course, will be diverse, and sometimes they will be very distinct. For those obsessed with ideological neutrality, that indeed is the rub. Neutralists discover that they are more neutral on some philosophies than on others. Not that they would ever be intolerant. To avoid being misunderstood here, they would rephrase the ultimate question in the following way: Should we encourage schools that individually are market-places of conflicting ideals, or should we encourage a marketplace of schools, each of which individually promotes some consistent ideal? Should each school contain within its walls a neutral smorgasbord of values, or should ideological variety be allowed to flourish also between and among schools that are devoted to particular visions?

This form of the question is fair, as long as the reader first sees the factual assumptions that it entails. Apart from its crucial exclusion of religion from the formal education of the poor, this restatement of the issue presupposes that public schools can achieve two goals that in fact are profoundly elusive. The first goal is the maintenance of a true neutrality even among those values that in fact make their way to the public curriculum; the second goal is the fair representation in that curriculum of the full range of nonreligious values that compete in the larger society. At very close range, I have watched well-intended neutralists consistently fail at both tasks and even remain unconscious of their own powerful bias. This experience seems confirmed by the literature on the question.[9] I can only conclude that we have never achieved even these very limited forms of neutrality, and I see no reason to suppose that we ever could. I find myself in rough agreement with my distinguished colleague Czeslaw Milosz:

> The peculiar traits of American schools provide the young generation with something that can only be called nihilism. The raising of the young without indoctrination is something new—until now there have always been attempts to indoctrinate them with a religion or a socialistic or nationalistic creed, yet American educators themselves have no fundamental creeds from which to operate. According to Herbert Marcuse, it is exactly this lack of any direction which constitutes the insidious preparation for a bestial existence reduced to earning and spending. . . . The quarrel of Marcuse with America is a quarrel with an indefinite opening up to what is called culture, something in which bourgeois Europe specialized on a less gigantic scale. That opening up

[9]For a set of references on this point, I might with diffidence recommend a work of my own: John Coons, "Intellectual Liberty and the Schools," *Journal of Law, Ethics, and Public Policy* 1 (1985): 495. And see generally John Coons and Stephen Sugarman, *Education by Choice* (Berkeley: University of California Press, 1978).

usually resulted in the equal importance and relativity of all ideas, while in practice sonority and range were granted only to ideas shaping attitudes of bitterness, despair, and the sense of man's superfluousness in the universe. The fruit of all this was either the acceptance of earning and spending, or, among bohemians, the worship of Art as the only absolute. Also, in the next phase, a longing for political terror.

The lack of indoctrination today is not only equivalent to an opening up but also to a submission to certain kinds of unplanned propaganda.[10]

This is a bit stronger than I would put it. In their indictment of the schools, Milosz—and certainly Marcuse—missed the power of the implicit and generally idealistic messages that are radiated individually by strong teachers. The idea, for example, that a distinctly religious (or anti-religious) teacher would project none of his or her ideals and beliefs to the students is unrealistic. There are unspoken treaties within the public system that allow precisely for this. These understandings are in-house secrets, and it would be surprising for immigrant observers to catch their significance. Their effect on the individual child, however, is wholly adventitious and even chaotic. Everything depends on the luck of the draw. Taken all in all, Milosz's dark picture is not far from reality.

Still, in the end, the case for tolerance through parental choice ought to be made in more positive terms. Is there anything educationally progressive to be said for the indoctrination of the child in the values of the parent, even in a society in which family values are no longer moderated by a predominant culture or by the church? The case for choice would be strongest if we could see that the very effort to maintain strong and specific parental values—both secular and religious—had a benign effect upon the civic outlook of the child.

I think that it does. My sense is that not always, but typically, the parental choice of a strongly ideological education sensitizes the child to civic values, and I predict that the extension of choice to all families would increase this outcome. The theory is simple enough. Whereas Socratic neutrality in the schoolhouse may be

[10]Czeslaw Milosz, "Biblical Heirs and Modern Evils," in The Immigrant Experience, ed. Thomas C. Wheeler (New York: Penguin Books, 1971), p. 202.

best for some children, in most cases the moral development of the child—the sense of basic duty toward others—is a product of a more pointed experience. To generate a real concern for justice, it is best to connect children to teachers who represent—are a proxy for—the authority of their parents; children prosper by steady mastery of consistent ideas concerning who they are and where they are supposed to be headed. True, in such a regime, different children will learn that they are headed in what appear to be different directions; nevertheless, what most will grasp is the importance to the whole self of individual commitment. The child who learns early and consistently to care about truth and justice in some particular form is the one most likely to be emotionally committed as an adult to truth and justice in every form. One must learn to love something before one can learn to love everything.

If this be heresy, there is one consoling thought for the diehard neutralist. In the end we may be on the same team. Given the reality of the media and the rest of modern life, few children could remain insulated from the "neutral" message of secular society. In its curious way, social and economic evolution has reversed the 19th-century justification for the neutralist dogma. In the isolated villages of a rural and parochial America, the problem was to find a way to broaden the outlook of all these narrow and inward-turning populations. Today, the challenge is to provide the child with a coherent message about the good and about his or her responsibility to fight for it. If ever we had a coherent message as a society, we have it no longer. The capacity of the family to choose a private school represents its plausible source. To me, it will be no paradox if we find that the best hope of the neutralist educator for solidarity among diverse peoples lies in the indoctrination of the child in the values of the parents. There is good reason to believe that respect for parental authority is the path to community and, through community, to effective education. I would add that here also lies the authentic form of neutrality among the conflicting ideals that we hold for our children.

11. How to Help Low-Income Students

James D. Gwartney

Why are our schools failing? Economic analysis indicates that they are failing for the same reasons that the socialist economies of Eastern Europe and the Soviet Union are failing. When production is regulated by politicians (and bureaucrats) rather than by competition for consumers, producers will spend more time catering to political officials and less time satisfying their customers. Since consumers are unable to shift their business to producers who provide them with "value for the price," suppliers have little incentive to produce efficiently, to innovate, or to figure out better ways of doing things. Simultaneously, since producers are operating in a noncompetitive environment, high costs and a poor-quality product (or service) do not lead to the loss of customers. Inefficient suppliers continue to survive and drain the resources of the economy.

Perhaps a thought experiment will help to explain why the current structure of our educational system does not work. Suppose that the government sought to provide us with a "world-class" restaurant system. The following structure was set up to accomplish this goal. A system of local restaurant districts was established. Taxes were levied to finance the cost of the government-operated restaurants in each district. Citizens were not allowed to patronize public restaurants outside their local district. Of course, snobs were free to choose private restaurants as long as they were willing to pay for the cost of the food twice—once as a taxpayer and again as a customer. If a private restaurant were to survive, it would have to figure out how to attract customers from the tax-financed public restaurants that were giving food away to district residents.

It does not take a genius to figure out that this restaurant system would have major problems. Because the managers of the public

A longer version of this article appeared in the *Cato Journal*, vol. 10, no. 1 (Spring/ Summer 1990.)

restaurants would derive their funds from government, predictably they would spend more time trying to satisfy politicians and less time trying to satisfy customers. The incentive to keep costs low would be weak. After all, higher costs and a lower quality of service would merely highlight the need for additional funding of the public-sector restaurants. Since consumers cannot take their funding and go elsewhere, they are in an extremely weak position to discipline the district restaurants that are doing a lousy job. The outcome of this organizational structure is predictable. Compared with the current competitive system, food costs would rise and quality would deteriorate. It would not be long before people would be writing about the "crisis" of America's restaurant system.

Most people recognize that this organizational structure will not work in the restaurant business. Why do we think it will work in education? The structure of the system is flawed. Because public schools do not have to meet the competition of rivals, their costs tend to rise. Lacking freedom of choice, educational consumers are unable to reward producers who supply value at a low cost or to penalize those who do not.

Competition among rival suppliers offering a diversity of products is the foundation of America's prosperity. Producers try harder when they have to compete for consumers. When competition is absent, resources are wasted, costs rise, and quality declines. The provision of education is not an exception to these general propositions.

A Voucher Plan for Low- and Middle-Income Families

Those who are serious about improving the quality of our schools should seek to promote parental choice and competition among schools. An educational voucher system is the easiest method of accomplishing this objective. The concept of an educational voucher system is really quite simple. Instead of providing aid directly to public schools, the government would provide parents with an educational voucher redeemable at any school, either public or private. Empowered with both purchasing power and choice, parents would choose the best school for their children. In some cases, this would be a private school or a public school outside one's current school district.

Under a voucher plan, schools would compete for students, and parents would be free to choose among schools. The best schools—

those providing quality education at an economical cost—would thrive and expand. The demand for outstanding teachers would increase, which would add prestige to the teaching profession and help attract quality people into the profession. Competition among schools would encourage innovative ideas and the discovery of more effective teaching techniques. And perhaps even more important, the lousy schools would either change their ways or be driven from the market.

In the past, two major objections have been raised by the opponents of educational vouchers. First, some have opposed the idea because they believed that high-income families would reap the major benefits from the vouchers, at least initially. After all, those with high incomes are overrepresented among families currently sending their children to private schools. The voucher plan would shift this cost to the taxpayer, perhaps to the detriment of educational funding for students from low- and middle-income families. Second, others have expressed a fear that a voucher plan would increase the racial imbalance among schools.

Overcoming the Objections to Vouchers

A voucher plan directed toward low- and middle-income families would overcome the objections raised against vouchers. Consider the following plan. Suppose that low-income families, say those with annual adjusted gross incomes of less than $15,000, were given vouchers of $4,500 per student (a little below the current level of operating expenses per student in the United States) redeemable at any public or private school.[1] Similarly, suppose middle-income families were given vouchers worth $4,500 per student minus $150 for every $1,000 of family income above $15,000. As Table 11–1 shows, the educational voucher would be worth $3,750 for families with an adjusted gross income of $20,000; $2,250 for those with an income of $30,000; and $750 for those with a family income of $40,000. The value of the educational voucher would be zero for family income levels of $45,000 and above.

---

[1]In the United States, educational policy is a responsibility of the individual states. Since the per-pupil expenditures vary by state, the maximum value of the voucher would differ among states. Thus, the dollar figures suggested here are designed merely to illustrate the concept.

201

Table 11–1
VALUE OF THE PROPOSED VOUCHER AS FAMILY INCOME INCREASES

Adjusted Gross Income	Value of Voucher
$0–15,000	$4,500
20,000	3,750
25,000	3,000
30,000	2,250
35,000	1,500
40,000	750
45,000 and above	0

This voucher plan would enhance the educational opportunities available to children of low- and middle-income families without providing a windfall gain to high-income families who send their children to private schools. In addition, the plan would actually promote racial and economic balance among schools. Since blacks and other minorities are overrepresented among the low-income families receiving the highest valued vouchers, those groups would also be overrepresented among families shifting to private schools (and high-quality public schools outside their district). More generally, the representation of children from families with modest incomes would increase among private and elite public schools.

In essence this plan would make educational choice meaningful for low- and middle-income Americans. Currently, the rich use their purchasing power to choose schools that improve the quality of education available to their children. If given the opportunity, low- and middle-income families will do likewise.

The plan would promote competition among schools—a vital ingredient that is largely absent within the current system. If allowed to compete on something approximating a level playing field, private schools and quality public schools will prosper, expand, and improve the quality of education in the United States.

Some people worry that student learning at schools receiving vouchers would be low either because parents would make poor choices or because the schools would make things easy, to attract students. Administration of standardized basic skills tests (which the state already administers) at several grade levels and publication of the results *by school* would resolve this problem. Publication of test results by school should include not only performance at current grade level, but also the student's prior achievement scores at the previous grade level at which the standardized test was administered. These data would provide parents with information on the *change* in achievement level of students attending specific schools. No doubt, some schools would specialize in the provision of accelerated programs or programs designated for disadvantaged students.

The standardized test results by school should be published in a form that would make it easy for parents to determine (and for schools to communicate) the effectiveness of schools for various groups of students, including both gifted students and those with a *prior* record of low-level performance. The vouchers could be limited to elementary and secondary schools willing to participate in the standardized testing program at three or four grade levels. However, other than publication of average basic skill levels achieved by students, state regulation of schools—including local public schools—should be minimal. Publication of the standardized test results in this form would provide parents with better information concerning the quality of schools than they currently are able to obtain. Armed with this information, parents would have both the incentive and the resources needed to make wise choices.

The voucher plan would also promote diversity and allow a larger number of Americans to choose and receive the type of schooling that they really want. Some parents would choose a highly structured school; others would prefer the open-school concept. Some would select a school that stresses religious values; others would opt for secularism in education. Some would choose a school with a traditional college prep program, while others would prefer schools that provide technical and vocational training. Under a system of parental choice, each of these diverse preferences could be satisfied. In effect, an educational voucher system provides proportional representation; it permits members of each group to vote for and receive their preferred type of education. This characteristic is one of the voucher system's most admirable attributes.

In contrast, the public school curriculum tends toward a homogeneous level that fits only the middle spectrum of students. This homogeneity is a major defect. People are different. There is not one best school, or best automobile, or best television program that fits everybody. Some students will do better in one educational environment, while others will flourish in a very different setting. We do not all choose the same church or civic organizations. Why in the world would anyone think that we would all prefer the same type of school?

How much would this voucher plan cost? Interestingly, it would not add much to current expenditure levels. When children from low-income families shift from public to private schools, the cost of the voucher is offset by lower public-school expenditures resulting from a reduction in the number of students in public schools. When middle-income children shift, the cost of the voucher is less than the savings resulting from lower in-district enrollments in the public schools. For upper middle-income families, the cost of providing the voucher is substantially less than the savings resulting from in-district enrollment reductions. For families with incomes above $15,000, switches to a more preferred school actually reduce public-sector educational expenditures.

Of course, some low- and middle-income families already send their children to private schools. Providing vouchers to these families will increase public-sector expenditures. However, this fact raises an interesting question: do we really want to force these modest-income families to pay for education twice? The current system discriminates against these families. It forces them to pay for education once as a taxpayer and again in the form of a tuition payment—merely because they care deeply about the quality of the school that their child attends. This double payment is an injustice that needs to be corrected. The proposed voucher plan would do so.

It is time to quit protecting the public school's monopoly and to begin allowing private schools to compete for students on a level playing field. Studies indicate that private schools provide their students with a quality education at a fraction of the public-school expenditure levels. In fact, the most comprehensive study in this area, conducted by James Coleman of the University of Chicago, found that the verbal and mathematical skills of high school students in private schools (mostly Catholic) *increased* 50 percent more than the skills of similar students in public schools. According to Coleman, the basic skills of private school students increased three grade equivalents between the tenth and twelfth grades, compared

204

to the two grade equivalents of similar public school students.[2] Coleman believes that the "community environment" and improved relations between parents and school administrators in private schools explain their greater effectiveness relative to the typical public school.

Should parents desiring to send their children to a school operated by a religious institution be eligible for the vouchers? Absolutely. Why would we want to discriminate against a parent and that parent's child because of their religious preferences? The U.S. Constitution protects the free exercise of religion. Surely the free exercise of religion includes the right to choose a school that reinforces the religious values of one's home. The GI Bill's treatment of educational benefits provides an example of nondiscriminatory treatment across schools. Persons attending college at both secular public and private schools *and* religious-affiliated schools were eligible for educational benefits under the GI Bill. The same principle should be applied here. Given choice, some will choose schools with a religious emphasis (including Protestant, Catholic, Jewish, and Moslem schools). Others will choose completely secular schools. Secularism and religious views would be treated equally. One of the marvelous attributes of a free-choice system is that it would allow both the religious and the nonreligious to choose and receive the type of schooling that they prefer.

Voucher Plans and the Status of Educators

Educational administrators and leaders of teachers' unions have often been at the forefront of those opposed to parental choice and educational vouchers. In some respects their opposition is understandable. Parental choice erodes the monopoly power of the public schools and those who administer them. Competition replaces politics as the regulator of educational quality. Compared to the current system, the demand for administrators and teachers who are unable to deliver a quality product will decline.

However, that is only part of the story—the demand for high-quality teachers and administrators will increase. Competition

---

[2]James S. Coleman, "Do Students Learn More in Private Schools than in Public Schools?" *Florida Policy Review* 5 (Summer 1989): 9–14. See also James S. Coleman and Thomas Hoffer, *Public and Private High Schools: The Impact of Communities* (New York: Basic Books, 1987).

among schools also means competition for the services of first-rate teachers and innovative administrators who are capable of attracting students. In contrast to the salaries of low-quality educators, the salaries of outstanding teachers and administrators would rise under a choice system. Similarly, the respect and prestige of professional educators would be enhanced.

It is also important to recognize that the diversity accompanying choice will also expand the opportunities available to teachers. With choice, it will be easier for teachers to obtain employment at a school with an educational program consistent with their own views. Some teachers will prefer teaching in an open-school environment, while others will feel more comfortable in a highly structured setting. Some teachers will consider only secular schools, while others will be attracted to schools with a religious affiliation. Choice will broaden the options available *to teachers*, as well as to students. Thus, it will improve the fit between the availability of positions and the types of jobs preferred by teachers.

Conclusion

President Bush and the nation's governors have outlined a set of goals for a "world-class" education system. While goals are fine, we must not lose sight of the difference between goals and achievement. Our current problem is not the absence of goals; rather it is the absence of a sensible plan to achieve the goals.

The current education effort is yielding a scandalously low return because the organizational structure of our educational system is unsound. Without structural change, the experience of recent decades indicates that additional spending is unlikely to improve the quality of education. More money will not solve the problem. Fundamental reform—providing for parental choice, competition, and greater flexibility—is needed. Let's get on with the job before we ruin another generation of young Americans.

12. Education Enterprise Zones
Pete du Pont

Education in this country is in many cases not just substandard but downright destructive. The public school system is robbing a whole generation of young people of their birthright as Americans—an education good enough to enable them to be productive citizens and to lead fulfilling lives.

There is abundant evidence that the U.S. education system is shortchanging students of every kind—of each sex, of every race, of every ethnic group, in every part of the country, and at every level of ability. For example, the number of seniors scoring above 600 on the verbal part of the Scholastic Aptitude Test (SAT) is 30 percent lower than it was in 1972. The number of seniors scoring above 750 on the SAT—on both the verbal and math sections—is 50 percent lower than it was in 1981. Moreover, the dropout rate in U.S. public schools is almost 25 percent, and nearly 20 percent of the parents in the United States are choosing not to avail themselves of a free product called public education but to spend money to send their children to private schools. In other words, 45 percent of the potential customers of the public school system are saying "No, thank you," either by dropping out or by taking their business elsewhere.

Of course, the reason the public school system is not meeting students' needs is that along with the U.S. Postal Service and the armed forces, it's one of the three great monopolies in America. The failure of socialism is recognized even in Moscow, yet we have based our education system on the socialist model.

One of the preconditions for improving the education system is school choice. Without it, there will not be significant change or competition, each of which is essential for a better education system.

What makes choice such an important tool? It's really very simple—choice produces excellence. It does so by giving people a sense of shared ownership in whatever it is that they have chosen.

But beyond its practical value, choice is American; it embodies the ideals on which the nation was founded. Choice means freedom. We have the right to choose virtually everything that's important in our lives—our churches, our spouses, our jobs, our homes, our leaders. We ought to be able to choose our children's schools, too.

Choice also means fairness. At present, only a few Americans have the opportunity to choose their children's schools. No one would dare to argue that the students in the Chicago, Los Angeles, and New York school systems are being treated fairly. It is obvious that they are being discriminated against by being forced to receive a third-rate education.

Finally, choice means power. The purpose of a democracy is to enable people to improve their lives. What greater power could a parent have than the power to choose the kind of education that best suits his or her child?

My wife, Elise, and I have four children. They're all different, and they all had different educational needs. One is very bright and needed a rigorous academic environment. Another is dyslexic and needed a very special school. Another is scientifically inclined, the other more artistic; they needed schools that would suit them. Fortunately, Elise and I could afford to choose the school best suited to each of our children. All parents should have that opportunity. One cannot treat all children the same way because every child is different. That's why I advocate a school-choice plan to empower parents to match their children to the appropriate school.

In his book *Microcosm*, George Gilder talks about the evolution of computers. You may remember the first computers. In the 1950s there were enormous mainframe computers, each of which was guarded by a man who sat in a little office. When you gave him your stack of punch cards, he would tell you that you could get them back on Wednesday—and he meant a week from Wednesday. All punch cards were treated the same way.

You may also remember the Free Speech Movement, which started in Berkeley during the early 1960s. "I am a human being," said one of the buttons from that era. "Do not fold, spindle, or mutilate." Computers had a bad name in those days because they were folding, spindling, and mutilating people as well as punch cards. Everyone was treated the same way.

Computers don't have a bad name today, and that is because they are small machines that sit on our desks and serve our particular needs. Might our huge school districts be doing something much like what the original computers did—folding, spindling, and mutilating students by treating each one the same way? And might the solution to that problem be a desktop education system in which each child goes to the school that best meets his or her needs?

It is possible to create such an education system in our inner cities or, indeed, anywhere in the nation. Let us consider the policy options that could be adopted by three different segments of society: the private sector, state and local governments, and the federal government.

The chief executive officers of major corporations may be taking the wrong approach by spending corporate money to "adopt" public schools and endow scholarships in various subjects. They're not doing any harm, but they could be doing a lot more good.

For example, a new school in Chicago funded by 60 local corporations is reaching out to the children who need the most help in getting a good education. It's providing free instruction to 50 disadvantaged youngsters from one of the worst neighborhoods in Chicago, and it hopes to enroll 300 students in two years. That enterprise should serve as a model for other corporations. Instead of investing their money in the existing public schools, they could start schools that would really make a difference. Those schools would be free of the problems in the public school system and would give children much more opportunity.

The Sylvan Learning Corporation, a nationwide concern, has established 400 schools that offer remedial education in any subject and have a student/teacher ratio of 3 to 1. The only problem with remedial education is that it is medicine provided after the patient has become sick. Must we wait until students are failing before we put them in an intensive learning environment? The private sector could do much more to help meet that challenge.

In the public sector, most of the new ideas about education are coming from state and local governments, as new ideas usually do. In East Harlem, one of the poorest neighborhoods in the United States, the contrast between what one sees outside a school building and what one sees inside is extraordinary. That's because everyone in an East Harlem school has chosen to be there and the curriculum was developed by the people it affects—teachers, students, and parents. Those conditions foster a sense of ownership in a school. School-choice plans are also being implemented in Minnesota and in Cambridge, Massachusetts. In 1989 the parents of 3,000 children chose to send them to schools other than the ones to which they would have been assigned geographically in Minnesota, as did 60 percent of the parents in Cambridge. Both of those plans, under which parents may choose among public schools only, are drawing students from the private school system back to public education.

In Eugene, Oregon, more than 1,500 students are now attending alternative public schools. Parents or teachers may submit proposals for the establishment of alternative schools.

But the blue ribbon should go to state Rep. Annette (Polly) Williams of Milwaukee, who headed Jesse Jackson's Wisconsin campaign, and to Tommy Thompson, the state's Republican governor. They recently persuaded the legislature to pass a full choice plan—unfortunately available to only about 1,000 Milwaukee students—that gives each of those students a voucher for $2,500 to be used at any nonsectarian school—public or private—in the city and subtracts that money from the public school system's budget. That gives 1,000 of the poorest children in Milwaukee a chance to get a better education—and that's a good start.

The federal government spends only about 10 percent of the money invested in education in the United States, so most of the responsibility for improving the education system lies with the private sector and with state and local governments. But there is something that the federal government could do to maximize the effectiveness of its investment in education: adopt a plan whose central feature is the creation of education enterprise zones.

As a member of Congress, Jack Kemp proposed that the federal government establish economic enterprise zones. I propose to apply the same concept to education. The federal government should identify school districts in which the dropout rate exceeds, say, 40 percent; students are getting low scores on standardized tests; many high school graduates cannot read their diplomas; and drugs and violence have taken over the schools to the extent that a student has a better chance of learning how to become a petty criminal than of learning math or grammar. Then it should designate these 20 or 30 worst school districts as education enterprise zones, thus making them eligible to participate in a five-part federal program.

First, the federal government should create a voucher that parents could use in any school in an education enterprise zone—or, better still, in any school in the country. The $700 in federal assistance that a school receives for each disadvantaged student, under Title I, should instead be made available to such a student in the form of an education voucher. That step would benefit the students who needed the most help in getting a good education.

During the presidential campaign of 1988, I talked with a woman who sorted plastic bottles at the end of a conveyor belt. She spoke English with a heavy Spanish accent. In the course of the conversation, I asked her what her children needed, and she said, "My children need the best education they can get." Looking a little embarrassed, she added, "We don't speak English at home; we speak Spanish. What my children need is to have the best school teach them English, because if you don't speak English in America, you don't succeed."

I asked, "Where's the best school in the city?" She said, "It's across the city, but my children can't go to it because we live on this side of the district line. They have to go to a school where the English instruction isn't nearly as good." Bureaucrats are destroying opportunity for that woman's children by drawing a yellow line down the middle of a map. Replacing her children's Title I assistance with education vouchers would solve that problem instantly.

Second, within those education enterprise zones, the federal government should make space available in public housing projects, at no cost, to any group of parents that wanted to start a school. The government should cover the cost of the space and the utilities.

Third, the federal government should make the same use of its surplus property, which, under the McKinney Act, the homeless have the right to occupy. Surely our children ought to be just as high a priority.

Fourth, the federal government should offer state and local governments—and families—help in overcoming the biggest practical problem in school-choice plans: how to transport children from their homes to the schools their parents choose. It could do so by establishing a matching-grants program that would fund transportation for students who qualified for the school lunch program.

Finally, the federal government should make some Justice Department lawyers available to help school districts overcome legal impediments to school-choice plans. That might be the most important step of all.

The federal government should not impose the provisions of that five-part program on any school district, family, or group of parents that did not wish to participate. Conversely, the receipt of such assistance by those who wanted it should be contingent on only one thing: that a school district agree to give parents the right to choose the public or private schools that their children would attend.

That set of incentives would break up the bureaucratic logjam that has impeded our schools. It would revolutionize education in the worst school districts in the United States, and could then be used to improve education in school districts that weren't in such bad shape. Ultimately, the whole nation would have educational choice.

Three decades ago, when our inner cities were beginning to deteriorate, we as a nation did a terrible thing: we allowed the schools to become part of the cycle of poverty. In doing so, we eliminated the first rung in the ladder of opportunity. Educational choice would put it back. Perhaps we should judge our progress in creating a kinder and gentler America by the quality of the education supplied to disadvantaged students in a kindergarten on the West Side of Chicago. It is a good place to start. It's time we offered those youngsters and their parents some freedom, some fairness, some power, and most of all, genuine opportunity.

Contributors

David Boaz is executive vice president of the Cato Institute.

Bonita Brodt is a reporter and feature writer for the *Chicago Tribune*. She received the 1989 Livingston Award for her series of articles titled "Chicago's Schools: 'Worst in America.' "

John E. Chubb is a senior fellow at the Brookings Institution and coauthor of *Politics, Markets, and America's Schools*.

John E. Coons is a professor of law at the University of California at Berkeley and coauthor of *Education by Choice*.

Pete du Pont is chairman of Ideas for America's Future and a partner in the law firm of Richards, Layton and Finger. He previously served as governor of Delaware and chairman of the Education Commission of the States.

Sy Fliegel is the Gilder Fellow at the Center for Educational Innovation at the Manhattan Institute. He was formerly the director of alternative education for New York City's School District No. 4.

James D. Gwartney is a professor of economics at Florida State University.

Myron Lieberman is president of Educational Employment Services and author of *Privatization and Educational Choice* and *Public School Choice*.

Terry M. Moe is a professor of political science at Stanford University and coauthor of *Politics, Markets, and America's Schools*.

William A. Niskanen is chairman of the Cato Institute and a former member of the Council of Economic Advisers.

Ben Peterson is the pseudonym of a Los Angeles teacher.

Robert S. Peterkin is the superintendent of Milwaukee's public schools and former superintendent of public schools in Cambridge, Massachusetts.

Joan Davis Ratteray is president of the Institute for Independent Education.

Index

Accountability
for educational quality, 91
factors allowing for, 140–41
of independent schools, 46, 101
as monitor for level of autonomy,
139
movement in 1970s for, 120
retention of, 140
Achievement, student
with choice and competition, 147
forces affecting, 63
influences on, 130
international comparisons of, 62
measures in East Harlem of, 166
in other countries, 3–5, 62, 119
relationship to spending of, 4–6, 8,
20–21
research in determinants of, 127
ACT. *See* American College Testing
Program (ACT)
Administrator and Teacher Survey
(ATS), 129
African Americans
arguments against school choice,
34–36, 97, 173–75
experience in magnet schools of,
95–97
independent schools for, 100–103
American Association of Educators in
Private Practice, 44
American College Testing Program
(ACT), 58–59, 67
American Society for Training and
Development, 4
Arizona Business Leadership for
Education, 43
Atkinson, Rick, 29n. 56
Autonomy, school
accountability with, 140
in alternative-concept plan, 169
factors influencing degree of,
135–37, 139
importance of, 22, 134–35
keys to, 140
lessons for reform, 155–56

See also School organization

Bacon, Kenneth H., 3n. 4
Baker, Essie, 159–60
Banas, Casey, 17n. 43
Bennett, William, 66–67, 119nn. 9, 11,
120n. 15, 123nn. 22–23, 124n. 26,
167
Bensman, David, 160–61
B.E.T.A. (Better Education through
Alternatives) school, 159
Bishop, John H., 11
Boaz, David, 32n. 62
Bolick, Clint, 9–10n. 26, 32, 33n. 65,
42n. 76
Boston University, 43
Boyle, Jim, 44
Brigham, Fred, 120n. 16
Brimelow, Peter, 5n. 12
Britannica Learning Centers, 109
Brodt, Bonita, 7
Brown v. *Board of Education,* 189
Buckley, Stephen, 29n. 56
Bush, George, 181, 182, 188
Bush administration, 116
Busing effect, 34–37, 68–69, 178
Butterfield, Fox, 47n. 91

California Business Roundtable, 43
Cambridge (MA) public school choice
plan, 42, 146, 173, 174, 175–77, 210
Campbell, Roald I., 123n. 25
Carlson, Avis, 3
Carnegie Foundation for the
Advancement of Teaching, 7
Carroll, Lewis, 162
Celis, William 3d, 45nn. 86–87
Chelsea (MA) school system, 43
Cheney, Lynne V., 16n. 40
Chicago Panel on Public School Policy
and Finance poll (1985), 41
Chicago public school system
demands for change, 47

215

evidence of failure of, 65–67
experimental reform in, 77, 139, 185
governance in, 43
racial and ethnic representation in,
68–69
Choice, educational
argument for, 24–27, 40, 49
arguments against, 33–40
changing supply of schools with,
143–44, 152
constitutionality of, 31–33
costs of, 150
demand for, 30
in East Harlem, 164–67
effect on public school monopoly of,
205
expectations for system of, 146–47
foundation for concept of, 115–16
information role in, 34, 169–71, 177
as key to school autonomy, 140
objective of, 153
parental, 145–46, 169–70, 205–6,
207–8
role of private schools in, 151–52
supply and demand in system of,
142–43
See also Voucher plan
Choice, school
African-American arguments
against, 97, 173–75
likelihood of competition with
public, 29
limits to effectiveness of, 27–28
public magnet schools in, 28
for public schools, 27–28
reasons for state-level, 24
state and city, 42
tax refund plan in, 26
See also Magnet schools; Schools,
independent; Tax credit plan; Tax
refund plan; Voucher plan
Choper, Jesse, 190n. 4
Chubb, John, 5–6, 12, 17, 22, 39, 46,
48, 52, 116–17n. 1, 182
Cibulka, J., 23n. 54
City Club of Chicago, 43
Clune, William, 191nn. 5–6
Coalition of Essential Schools, 163–64
Coleman, James S., 23–24, 35, 57n. 5,
127n. 33, 154n. 38, 182, 183, 204–5
Coleman Report (1965), 127
Collins, Marva, 23, 40
Community control, Chicago school
system, 77, 139

Competition, school
effectiveness of, 13–14, 141–46
effect of lack of, 6, 19, 22
effect on poor quality school of,
147–50
expectations for system of, 146–47
as key to school autonomy, 140
as means to improve performance,
22–24
methods to promote, 140, 141–42
private schools' role in, 151–52
use of scholarships to promote, 141
Congressional Budget Office (CBO)
studies, 59n. 7, 63, 117nn. 2–3,
118n. 8, 125nn. 27–29, 126
Coons, John E., 184n. 2, 195n. 9
Crane, Edward, 32n. 62

Darling-Hammond, Linda, 135n. 35
Doyle, Denis P., 9n. 26
Dropout rate. See Enrollment systems

East Harlem
Central Park East School, 160–61
Central Park East Secondary School,
163–64
East Harlem Performing Arts School,
160, 161
East Harlem public school choice plan,
42, 146, 158–61, 167, 186, 209–10
Education
examples of poor quality of, 2–4
importance of, 1
importance of good quality, 10–12
Educational choice. See Choice,
educational; Choice, school
Education Alternatives, Inc., 44
Educational Testing Service (ETS)
tests, 20–21, 119
Education enterprise zones, 210–12
Education-related market
college counseling as, 109
music lessons in, 109
summer camps in, 109
Effective Schools Research studies,
128, 132
Elam, Stanley M., 41n. 74
Employment and earnings, post-
school, 57, 60–62
Enrollment systems
changing components of, 118
open, 140, 142

Minnesota public school choice plan, 42, 146, 186, 210
Moe, Terry, 5–6, 12, 22, 39, 48, 52, 116–17n. 1, 182
Montclair (NJ) public school choice plan, 42
Mueller v. *Allen*, 32–33
Murphy, Kevin, 8, 61n. 8

NAEP. *See* National Assessment of Educational Progress (NAEP)
Nathan, Joe, 36n. 71, 157n., 173
National Assessment of Educational Progress (NAEP), 2–3, 20, 62, 117, 118–19
National Center for Educational Information survey, 20
National Commission on Excellence in Education report (1983), 20, 62
National Education Association (NEA), 96–97, 181
National Endowment for the Humanities survey (1989), 3
National Independent Private School Association, 106
NEA. *See* National Education Association (NEA)
Niskanen, William A., 4, 64n. 14
Norris, Michele, 29n. 56, 90n. 1
Norton, Monica, 44n. 85

O'Brien, T., 23n. 54
Ombudsman Educational Services Ltd., 44
Oregon tax credit plan, 47

Parental choice. *See* Choice, educational; Choice, school
Perelman, Lewis, 4n. 7, 6
Perpich, Rudy, 10
Pierce v. *Society of Sisters*, 31–32
Political pressure
    effect of, 22, 139
    regulation of schools by, 11–12, 199
    on school bureaucracy, 17, 22
Postman, Neil, 162
Powell, Lewis, 32
Productivity
    of educational system, 6
    relation to knowledge of, 11

Protheroe, Nancy, 121n. 18, 122nn. 20–21
Purkey, Stewart C., 128n. 34

Ratteray, Joan Davis, 23–24, 101n. 9
Ravitch, Diane, 120n. 13
Raywid, Mary Anne, 145n. 36
Reagan, Ronald, 167
Regulation
    effect of curriculum, 135
    effect on school systems of, 123–24
    effect on teachers and teaching of, 139
    related to school autonomy, 139
Rehnquist, William, 33
Remedial education
    in business firms, 4
    college level, 4, 61
    at elementary school level, 71–74
    federal funds for, 73
    of Sylvan Learning Corporation, 209
Robinson, Glen E., 122nn. 20–21

Sanchez, Rene, 8n. 22, 29n. 57
Scholarships, educational, 140, 141–42
Scholastic Aptitude Test (SAT), 58–59
School completion and advancement rates, 57–58, 61, 118
School councils, Chicago public school system, 77, 139
School environment
    in Douglass High School, 80–87
    effect on student performance of, 63
    in Goudy Elementary School, 65–66, 70–76
    importance of, 52
Schooling
    as part of education, 1
    relationship to learning of, 126
School organization
    autor omy as key to, 139–40
    characteristics of effective, 131–32
    correlation with student achievement of, 128–30
    determinants of effective, 132–34
School performance
    completion and advancement rates as measure of, 57–58, 61, 118
    composite test scores as measure of, 57–59, 61, 62–63, 117–20
    employment and earnings as measure of, 57, 60–62

218

failure of initiative in Oregon for, 47
Tax refund plan, 26
Taylor, Fred M., 187
Teachers
  entrepreneurial services of, 44
  salaries, 16, 53, 121–22
  school choices for children of, 8–9
  starting schools of their own, 144
Teaching as an art, 135
Test scores, composite
  decline in, 2, 124–25
  as measure of school output, 57–59,
    61, 62–63, 117–20
Thompson, Tommy, 45, 210
Tyack, David B., 12n. 35, 123n. 25

Union, teachers'
  effect on school reform of, 123
  influence in Chicago of, 66, 69–70
  perception of opposition from, 111
United Federation of Teachers study, 7
Uzzell, Lawrence A., 2n. 2, 3n. 3

Vander Weele, Maribeth, 48n. 92
Vobejda, Barbara, 7n. 19, 119n. 12

Voboril, Joe, 19–20
Voucher plan
  argument against, 25–26, 30–31, 201
  constitutionality of, 31–33, 205
  for educational choice, 25, 30, 38,
    49, 200–201
  for low-income families, 200–205
  in Milwaukee, 45–47
  to overcome objections, 201–5

Walberg, Herbert J., 8n. 25
Welch, Finis, 61n. 8
Wells, Amy Stuart, 48n. 92
West, E. G., 16n. 41, 25n. 55
West, Peter, 43n. 80
White House Conference on Choice
  (1989), 181
Wilhoit, Gene, 45
Wilkerson, Isabel, 47n. 90
Williams, Annette (Polly), 8, 36–37,
  45–46, 210
Williams, Walter, 18
Witte, John F., 191nn. 5–6
Wolman v. *Walter*, 32

Zewe, D., 23n. 54

Cato Institute

Founded in 1977, the Cato Institute is a public policy research foundation dedicated to broadening the parameters of policy debate to allow consideration of more options that are consistent with the traditional American principles of limited government, individual liberty, and peace. To that end, the Institute strives to achieve greater involvement of the intelligent, concerned lay public in questions of policy and the proper role of government.

The Institute is named for *Cato's Letters*, libertarian pamphlets that were widely read in the American Colonies in the early 18th century and played a major role in laying the philosophical foundation for the American Revolution.

Despite the achievement of the nation's Founders, today virtually no aspect of life is free from government encroachment. A pervasive intolerance for individual rights is shown by government's arbitrary intrusions into private economic transactions and its disregard for civil liberties.

To counter that trend the Cato Institute undertakes an extensive publications program that addresses the complete spectrum of policy issues. Books, monographs, and shorter studies are commissioned to examine the federal budget, Social Security, regulation, military spending, international trade, and myriad other issues. Major policy conferences are held throughout the year, from which papers are published thrice yearly in the *Cato Journal*.

In order to maintain its independence, the Cato Institute accepts no government funding. Contributions are received from foundations, corporations, and individuals, and other revenue is generated from the sale of publications. The Institute is a nonprofit, tax-exempt, educational foundation under Section 501(c)3 of the Internal Revenue Code.

CATO INSTITUTE
224 Second St., S.E.
Washington, D.C. 20003